D0323614

OCEANS, POLES AND AIRMEN

OCEANS, POLES AND AIRMEN

The First Flights over Wide Waters and Desolate Ice

RICHARD MONTAGUE

 Random House · *New York*

ISBN: 0-394-46237-8
Library of Congress Catalog Card Number:72-140720
Manufactured in the United States of America
by The Book Press, Brattleboro, Vermont
9 8 7 6 5 4 3 2
FIRST EDITION

For Doris Parkman

Foreword

And, looking back, we see Romance—that subtle thing that is mirage—that is life . . .

—JOSEPH CONRAD

Perhaps remembered eras inevitably seem more romantic than the present. But to me the years of the twenties and thirties seem far more glamorous and exciting than those of today. I had more illusions then about the future of mankind. Those years represented for me and many others an age of innocence when world-wide depressions, Nazi gas ovens, nuclear bombs, world-wide racial strife, global pollution and seemingly endless Asian wars were unheard of.

Optimism and confidence were in the air. Men and women were individuals, not computer numbers. They could strike out on their own for adventure and fortune and fame. To me the fliers were especially romantic. Brave, headstrong, often reckless, sometimes vain, occasionally slightly mad, they would gladly plunge into deep debt to finance some dubious, dangerous flight or take off into the blue in a rickety plane without bothering to undergo adequate training. Generous to one another, they would lend their money or their skills to rivals. Often they risked—and sometimes lost—their lives in searches for unlucky colleagues.

This book is an effort to keep their memories bright a little longer. It is also an effort to show these fliers as they were, not just as romantic figures but as human beings. A secondary aim is to expose a fraud that has persisted for nearly half a century. It is the only monumental deception I know of that was practiced by the aviators of the period.

As a reporter, I knew many of these people. I talked with them, watched their flights and wrote about them. Since then I have renewed old acquaintances, pored over day-by-day accounts of transatlantic, polar and transpacific flights in newspapers, and studied numerous magazine articles and books concerning the aviation of those times. Most of the old fliers, along with their planes, are gone now. And in time the mirage they were a part of will vanish too.

Contents

x

OCEANS, POLES AND AIRMEN

1

TO THE TOP OF THE WORLD

Years before aviation flared into the fever it became in the mid-twenties, airmen in many lands saw in flying an invisible path to riches and renown. Flying machines, both lighter and heavier than air, had come a long way from the hot-air balloon that lifted two men 3,000 feet above the Bois de Boulogne in 1783 and the small biplane that carried its pilot and co-inventor 120 feet at Kitty Hawk one hundred and twenty years later.

Almost from the time men first took to the air they began thinking about two oceans as promising areas for flying fame. One was the often-stormy Atlantic, plowed by liners, freighters, tankers and tramps. The other was the lonely Arctic, capped by the white ice of the North Pole.

Even before Commander Robert E. Peary reached the Pole, or its vicinity, on foot in April 1909, the apex of the world had fascinated aeronauts. In July 1897, Salomon August Andrée and two other Swedish adventurers tried to reach the Pole in a free balloon, only to disappear in the dazzling wastes above Spitsbergen, that frozen island group above the Arctic Circle. Ten years later Walter Wellman, an American, also tried to reach the Pole from Spitsbergen in a feeble 70-horsepower dirigible with a top speed of 18 miles an hour. Unable to buck a north wind that year, he tried and failed again in 1909 and thereafter abandoned the enterprise.

Sixteen years later—in 1925—the famous Norwegian explorer Roald Amundsen, who was the first man to sail the Northwest Passage and who had pushed to the South Pole in December 1911, led another aerial expedition northward from Spitsbergen. Amundsen, then fifty-two, Lincoln Ellsworth, an American, three Norwegians and one German got into two Dornier-Wal (Whale) duralumin flying boats and headed for the Pole. Their plan was to return to Spitsbergen after they had reached their goal.

For seven hours the clumsy-looking craft flew smoothly beside each other. Then one of the two tandem-mounted Rolls-Royce engines on Amundsen's plane quit, and both machines came down in some open-water channels at latitude 87° 43' north, or 156 miles from the Pole.

The seaplane in which Ellsworth was flying had been damaged on takeoff and had a leaky hull. Aside from a 400-mile trek over the sea ice to Greenland, the party's only hope was the other plane. But the water on which the Dorniers had landed started to freeze over. The men managed to drag Amundsen's machine up on the ice before the floes crushed it. It would be necessary to smooth out a runway and—when the ailing engine was repaired—take off from the ice. These tasks were to keep the six men busy for the next twenty-four days.

They lugged gasoline and food from the disabled machine to the Amundsen plane. They worked on the engine. They cut a passage through fifteen-foot ice hummocks so they could move the craft to a larger floe. Altogether, they estimated they moved 500 tons of ice and snow.

For the last six days they shoveled and tramped snow to make a runway on the big floe. Finally they all crowded into the one plane. Hjalmar Riiser-Larsen, Amundsen's number-one pilot, revved up the 360-horsepower engines. The heavy boat hull bumped along for nearly 1,500 feet. Then, almost at the end of the improvised runway, the plane lumbered into the air.

4

Hour after hour she flew southward, as the fuel-gauge needle sank lower and lower. Off the north shore of Spitsbergen the aileron control jammed. But Riiser-Larsen brought the craft down with half an hour of fuel left. And soon a sealing vessel sighted them and took them aboard.

Before their original takeoff Riiser-Larsen had told them about an Italian dirigible that might be purchased for a polar flight. And they often discussed this aircraft during their stay on the ice. Amundsen and Ellsworth had felt for a year or more that an airship would be better than a plane for a polar-sea flight. Such a craft could carry a much heavier load and could drift with favoring winds with the engines cut off.

After they returned as heroes to Oslo they got in touch with Umberto Nobile, a lieutenant colonel in the Italian Army who had designed two semirigid dirigibles with front frameworks and keels of light steel. They did not have the full-length cylindrical metal skeletons of Zeppelins but were stubbier and more flexible than the German craft. This, some experts thought, would make them more liable to withstand the sudden fury of Arctic gusts.

One of Nobile's airships had already been sold to the United States. There, on a trial run, a stabilizing fin collapsed, sending the ship into a high-tension wire and touching off an explosion of her hydrogen-filled bag that killed thirty-four men. Nobile's other dirigible—348 feet long, with gas cells holding 653,000 cubic feet of hydrogen—had three German Maybach engines of 250 horsepower each, which gave her an economical cruising speed of about 40 miles an hour.

Nobile came up to Oslo, and on behalf of his government, offered to loan this craft to Amundsen for nothing—provided she flew to Alaska under the Italian flag. Amundsen coldly declined the proposal. He had not worked and dreamed for years of crossing the polar sea by air to Alaska while under the aegis of *Fascismo*.

Finally Nobile agreed to sell the craft for about $75,000, plus a

$10,000 pilot's fee for himself, the Italian government to buy her back for $35,000 if she reached Alaska safely. He also agreed to modify the craft for polar flight, including strengthening the nose for mooring-mast hitches, and to provide five mechanics.

Mussolini officially approved the transaction and Ellsworth, who had persuaded his millionaire father to back him, came up with the money. It was decided to fly the dirigible to Spitsbergen with a mixed crew of Italians and Norwegians, rather than try to ship her there. Meanwhile Amundsen would lease land from the Kings Bay Coal Company at Spitsbergen and arrange for the erection of a hangar and mooring mast.

Thus, on the morning of April 29, 1926, some of the Amundsen party were at Kings Bay, West Spitsbergen, the hangar was ready and a prefabricated mooring mast was up. The dirigible, now named the *Norge* (Norway), was in Leningrad after an overland trip from Italy and would arrive at the snow-covered archipelago in eight days.

About ten o'clock that morning a sailor on the *Heimdal*, a Norwegian gunboat acting as Amundsen's supply ship, noticed a smudge on the western horizon. Soon a 3,500-ton steamer could be discerned. She turned out to be the *Chantier*, supply ship of a fifty-man expedition led by Lieutenant Commander Richard Evelyn Byrd, Jr., U.S. Navy, retired.

Byrd was then thirty-eight years old and had the face and figure of a movie hero. He had been technically retired for ten years because of a bad leg but had continued on more or less active service and had learned to fly at the Navy's air station in Pensacola, Florida. He was a brother of Harry Flood Byrd, governor of Virginia and later senator from that state. It was a relationship which in no way hampered him in his lifelong quest for fame.

The previous summer Byrd had gone to Etah, on the northwest coast of Greenland, with the Donald B. MacMillan expedition. This project, which was under the auspices of the National Geographic Society, had three amphibious planes with which Byrd and his detachment were to explore the Ellesmere Island area. But a late start, bad weather and other factors spoiled these plans. Now, with a more powerful plane and with Floyd Bennett—his chief pilot on the Greenland trip—he hoped to fly to the North Pole. Bennett was a former automobile mechanic who had enlisted in the Navy in 1917 and learned to fly at Pensacola, where he met Byrd. He had become a chief machinist mate in aviation, but never having risen to a commissioned officer's rank, he had an ingrained awe of Annapolis graduates. Throughout his association with Byrd, he referred to the handsome Virginian as "The Commander."

For the North Pole effort Byrd again had the National Geographic Society's blessing. He also had the financial support of some wealthy men, including Edsel Ford, John D. Rockefeller, Jr., Vincent Astor, Rodman Wanamaker and Dwight Morrow, a partner in the House of Morgan.

Amundsen had learned from Byrd during a trip to America that he would attempt a polar flight from Spitsbergen that year. But to some members of his party the *Chantier's* arrival came as an unpleasant surprise. They considered Byrd an interloper trying to beat their idol to the Pole, and they bitterly resented his presence at this time on the jump-off site.

Amundsen did not appear to share this resentment. When Byrd asked him where a takeoff runway might be built, the Norwegian suggested a gentle slope near the airship's hangar. And when Byrd told him he was being very generous to "a rival," Amundsen demurred. The two of them, he declared, were colleagues in exploration and their flights would complement each other. Byrd would fly to the Pole and return; the Amundsen group would fly over the Pole to Alaska. It didn't matter who reached the Pole first by air; after all, Peary had already been there on foot.

Amundsen instructed Bernt Balchen, one of his party, to help Byrd in any way he could. Balchen, at twenty-five, was on leave as a lieutenant in the Norwegian Naval Air Force. A specialist in mathematics, he had started his career as an artillery officer but found he liked flying so much that he got himself transferred to the air arm. When Amundsen, Ellsworth and the others were downed north of Spitsbergen the previous year, Balchen had been assigned to look for them. He was just about to take off in a floatplane when the lost ones returned. He was blond, friendly and exuding competence, with a build that had enabled him to win the amateur heavyweight boxing championship of eastern Norway, and with an accent when he spoke English that amused himself as much as those who heard it.

Amundsen tried to make his attitude toward Byrd clear to everybody. He gave a little talk to his crew, repeating his statement that he and Byrd were not rivals. Nevertheless, men in both expeditions, as well as several reporters who were present, continued to look on the affair as a race. Perhaps Commander Byrd did too, for he attempted his first trial flight on May 3, four days before the *Norge* arrived.

The plane for the polar flight was named the *Josephine Ford*, after Edsel's daughter. It was a trimotor machine built in Amsterdam by Anthony Fokker, who had designed many of the most lethal German fighter planes in World War I. It was fitted with Wright Whirlwind J-4B engines. At the time, these engines were probably the best in the world. They looked like rimless wheels with fat spokes, for their nine cylinders stood out from the hub—which contained the crankshaft—like radii of a circle, which is why they were known as radial engines.

The outsides of the Whirlwind's cylinders had cooling fins so that the air from the propeller wash could dissipate the heat of combustion. The engine thus dispensed with the hoses, water jackets, radiator and pump that are needed in liquid-cooled power plants. Its two main disadvantages were the head resistance it offered and its comparatively low horsepower output—from 200 in the J-4B to 220 and 240 in the J-5 models, which were to power the famous planes of 1927. The Whirlwind wasn't the only air-cooled radial, but it was the most reliable airplane engine in existence and was preferred by most polar- and ocean-flight aspirants of the day. Its designer, Charles Lawrance, was not only a great engineer but something of a romantic. When they asked him, after Lindbergh's triumph in 1927, if he didn't think he ought to have some share in the flier's fame, Lawrance said he doubted if anybody knew the name of Paul Revere's horse.

The J-4B's in the *Josephine Ford* gave the plane—when she was fitted with wheels instead of skis—a cruising speed on long flights of about 70 statute miles an hour. With skis, which offered more head resistance than wheels, the speed was several miles an hour less.

On the May 3 trial the Fokker roared down the sloping runway which Byrd's men had tramped out of the snow. But near the end of the patch a ski broke and a landing gear strut was bent. Bennett cut the engines in time to prevent further damage, but Balchen and some of his Norwegians had to work all night in the coal company's machine shop to put things right. After the accident Amundsen and Ellsworth came over to inspect the plane and found that Byrd's survival gear was inadequate. They gave the Americans some snowshoes, a hand-hauled sled and three pairs of grass-filled canvas boots such as the Lapps wear on their winter treks with their reindeer over the snows.

The next day after a new ski had been installed, Balchen noticed that Byrd's supply officer was rubbing wax on it. The Norwegian offered a bit of advice: the crystalline snow acted like sand and would quickly scrape off the wax. Norwegian fliers used a mixture of pine tar and resin burned into the wood with a blowtorch. But Byrd wanted to make another test flight at once, so the advice was disregarded.

Again, with a very light load, the Fokker roared down the slope. Halfway down, one ski stuck in the snow and cracked. No more spare skis were available and there was no spare hardwood on treeless

Spitsbergen. But Balchen had an idea. Why not strengthen the skis with the heavy hardwood oars of the *Chantier*'s lifeboats? This time Byrd accepted the suggestion. Some oars were cut to size, and holes were bored in their shafts, which were bolted to both skis as strong reinforcements.

On May 7 the *Norge* arrived after an overnight flight from Vadsö, near the northern tip of Norway. Several things had to be done before she could start for the Pole. One of the engines was acting badly and would have to be replaced. Water-filled ballast tanks and additional gasoline tanks would have to be installed. Food would have to be put aboard. The whole job would probably take three days.

Nobile, seeing the Byrd plane, wanted to hurry things up so the *Norge* could get away first. Amundsen vetoed the proposal, declaring again that the airship wasn't engaged in a race. He had had disturbing news about the Italian from Riiser-Larsen, the big Norwegian who was second-in-command of the *Norge*. On the flight up from Italy, Nobile had shown himself to be conceited, stubborn and a poor pilot, Riiser-Larsen said. At one point he had asked again that the airship fly under the Italian flag, and when the Norwegian said no the mercurial Nobile threatened to lead the Italians off the ship at the next stop. What would the Norwegians do then? he inquired. "Sir," Riiser-Larsen told him, "I am an airship pilot myself and we will carry on."

Like Nobile, Byrd was anxious to be off. On May 8, at one-thirty in the afternoon, he and Bennett tried again. The Fokker roared down the hill for the third time. But Bennett couldn't make the plane rise. At the end of the runway she bounded over some rough ice hummocks, tipped half over and smashed into a snowbank. This time, however, the reinforced skis did not break.

For a successful takeoff the Fokker would have to be lightened. Three hundred gallons of reserve gas and some 200 pounds of souvenirs, smuggled aboard the plane by Byrd's crewmen, were unloaded and the plane was taxied back uphill to the starting point. Then Balchen made another suggestion. Why not wait until midnight, when the sun would be closer to the horizon and the runway would be frozen and harder?

Again Byrd found the advice good and took it. And on May 9, at thirty-seven minutes past midnight, he and Bennett tried to take off once more. This time they succeeded.

The straight-line distance from Kings Bay to the Pole and back totals about 1,535 statute miles. Without favoring winds, such a journey would have taken the Fokker 21.9 hours at 70 miles an hour or—as seems more likely in view of the plane's capabilities— 23.6 hours at 65 miles an hour. Byrd apparently figured it this way, too. He had enough gas in the tanks to fuel the engines for from twenty to twenty four hours, depending on the wind. And he had told Odd Arneson, aviation editor of the Oslo newspaper *Aftenposten* (Evening Post) that he expected to reach the Pole and return in about twenty hours.

To help him navigate, he had a sextant, an altimeter, two magnetic compasses and a sun compass. The sun compass had been developed by Albert Bumstead, chief cartographer of the National Geographic Society, for use in regions where magnetic compasses are unreliable. It is sometimes likened to a sundial. With a sundial the direction north is known and the shadow of the sun gives the time of day. With the sun compass the time of day is known and the sun's shadow—when it bisects the hand of the spring-driven twenty-four-hour clock—indicates the direction north. To assure accuracy of the readings, Byrd carried two chronometers.

The plane flew northward under the midnight sun lugging a cargo of three tons, including the crew. Its roar faded to a hum, to a murmur, into silence. The long hours at Kings Bay dragged on.

Then, late that afternoon, Arneson radioed *Aftenposten:* BYRD OVER CROSS BAY [near Kings Bay] AFTER 15½ HOURS OF FLYING. TEN MINUTES LATER THE TWO COURAGEOUS FLIERS LANDED IN GOOD CON-

DITION. THE FLIERS THEMSELVES INSIST THEY WERE OVER THE POLE
BUT ON THE BASIS OF THE TIME THEY COULD HARDLY HAVE BEEN
THERE. PROBABLY NO FARTHER NORTH THAN AMUNDSEN. (Arneson
was referring to the 1925 flight in the two Dornier-Wals.)

Both Norwegian and American observers agreed that Byrd had
been gone 15½ hours.

In a follow-up story on the Byrd-Bennett flight the Norwegian
correspondent wrote:

> Most of the people here have difficulty believing that the plane
> coming back is really the right one, since it has been in the air only
> 15½ hours.
>
> The plane cruised over the mining community at 1,500 to 2,000
> meters and people streamed out from the various shacks and build-
> ings. In a great circle the plane came down, the sun playing on the
> wings. In about five minutes [at 4:07 P.M.] the plane landed. Roald
> Amundsen and Lincoln Ellsworth were among the first to greet the
> fliers and welcome them back. They embraced and kissed them.
>
> Byrd and Bennett were now subjected to a cross-fire of questions.
> Had they been to the North Pole? Did they find any new land there,
> etc.?
>
> The fliers, smiling, tired and perspiring, were escorted down to
> the dock near which *Chantier* was anchored. The two men were
> restless, standing first on one foot and then the other. They said
> that on the basis of their observations they believe they were at the
> North Pole. They cruised around it in a circle to be certain that they
> exactly circled it. . . .

Doubts that Byrd and Bennett had reached the Pole also were
aired in Rome and Oslo. In the Italian capital the newspaper *Tribuna*
said that a flight to and from the North Pole in 15½ hours, while technically possible, seemed highly improbable under Arctic conditions.
"We await confirmation," the daily added. "If it comes, as is probable,
we shall salute with joy the Byrd victory, which does not in any way
minimize the flight of the *Norge*."

In Oslo, Ole Skattum, president of the Norwegian Geographical

Society, argued that until Byrd's observations were published, it would be impossible to accept his claim that he had reached the Pole. It must be remembered, Mr. Skattum added, how difficult it had been to establish positions during the Amundsen-Ellsworth flight a year earlier when there were two observers in each plane, compared to the single observer in the Byrd machine. And Captain Johan Fossum, headmaster of the Nautical College, said he did not believe Byrd could fix his positions by sun observations.

It could be—and was—argued that both the Italians and the Norwegians, who had wanted the *Norge* to be the first aircraft over the Pole, were prejudiced against the American naval officer. Certainly no public doubts about the flight were expressed in the dispatches filed by Frederick Ramm, William Bird and Russell Owen to the *New York Times*. These reports said that the crew of the *Chantier* went "wild with joy" when Byrd and Bennett returned. "Many of the crew," one story said, "completely broke down with emotion, and with tears streaming from their eyes embraced the fliers."

The early dispatches, and later accounts of the flight by Byrd himself, stated that during the journey the fliers became alarmed by an oil leak affecting the starboard engine. The oil was running out of a reserve tank which had been installed to hold the extra lubricant that would be needed on the long flight. It was caused, they discovered after their return, by the loss of a rivet which had been jarred loose by vibration. At the time of discovery it seemed much more serious than it actually was.

Byrd wrote in one of his four by-line stories in the *New York Times* that on the way to the Pole the plane averaged about "ninety miles an hour." He had spotted the oil leak when they were an hour away from their objective. Bennett throttled the ailing motor, Byrd said, and found that the two others would keep the plane going at 60 miles an hour. The two men decided to keep on. The starboard engine continued to run. Bennett soon turned it up again, and after a while the leak stopped. This, they learned later, was because enough oil had been used to bring the level in the reserve tank below the rivet hole.

At 9:04 A.M., Byrd said, they reached the North Pole. On the way up he had made six sextant observations. He made four more as they circled the Pole at 3,000 feet for fourteen minutes. This enabled him, he told *Times* correspondent Bird to "verify in every detail" the report made by Peary seventeen years earlier. He did not explain how this was possible in view of the constantly changing ice formations in the landless area, but he added that he took some photographs at the Pole.

On the way back, Byrd said in his fourth by-line story, the wind "began to freshen and change direction" so that it added 10 miles an hour to their speed. He estimated the wind speed at 20 miles an hour, but explained that the wind was not directly behind them.

> The elements were surely smiling on us that day, two insignificant specks of mortality flying there over that great, vast, white area in a small plane, speechless and deaf from the motors, just a dot in the center of 10,000 miles of visible desolation.
>
> We felt no larger than a pin point, as lonely as a tomb, and as remote and detached as a star. Here, in another world, far from the herds of people, the passions and smallnesses of life fell from our shoulders. What wonder that we felt no emotion of achievement or fear of the death that lay stretched beneath us but instead impersonal and disembodied.
>
> On and on we went; it seemed forever onward. Our great speed had the effect of quickening our mental processes so that a minute appeared as many minutes, and I realized fully that time is only a relative thing. One instant can be an age and again an age an instant . . .

After they left the Pole, Byrd's sextant fell off the chart rack. The glass marking the horizon was broken. Thus there were no further observations, and the return trip to Spitsbergen was made, Byrd added, by dead reckoning.

The flight made big headlines in America, and President Calvin Coolidge was not slow to acknowledge the feat. His message read: "The President sends his heartiest congratulations to Commander Byrd on the report that he has flown to the North Pole. It is a matter of great satisfaction that this record has been made by an American."

Arneson, of *Aftenposten*, continued to wonder about the flight. Could Byrd really have reached the Pole and returned in so short a time? The correspondent, an expert on polar conditions and expeditions, kept asking people about the exploit. When he could get Amundsen and Ellsworth to give him a minute from their own flight preparations he asked them, too. Why, certainly! they said. Certainly Byrd had done what he claimed. He must have.

Young Lieutenant Balchen didn't think much about it. He was too busy helping Amundsen. And when the *Norge* flew northward he was too busy worrying about the dirigible to think about the performance of the Fokker. He didn't even think much about the Byrd-Bennett claim when later, on the *Chantier*, Byrd asked him if he was familiar with logarithms, then widely used in making navigational calculations. Balchen was. Byrd asked him to do some computations of different positions along the route from Spitsbergen to the Pole.

"Byrd gave me four or five different problems and I worked them out and gave them to him," Balchen said recently. "I don't know what he did with them. I can't say he put them on his charts. I gave them to him and that's all I know about them.

"I do know something about the two charts he turned in to the Navy and which were later used by the National Geographic Society's committee of experts to 'verify' his flight. The committee said these charts contained ten positions, given hourly and also when sextant observations were made. When I saw the charts on the *Chantier* they contained just a couple of scribbled notes."

On the morning of May 11, with a favorable weather forecast, Amundsen and Ellsworth walked up to the *Norge*'s hangar, a roofless, wood-framed structure 330 feet long, 102 feet wide and 90 feet high, which protected the airship from the wind. Nobile seemed to be in a state of nervous excitement. He announced that he couldn't take the responsibility for ordering the dirigible out of the hangar in the wind that was then blowing. Riiser-Larsen said the breeze wasn't strong enough to be dangerous; Nobile thought it was. Finally he agreed to let the Norwegian take out the airship.

When the *Norge* started northward at ten o'clock that morning it had eight Norwegians aboard, as well as an American, a Swede, six Italians and a fox terrier. The Norwegians were Amundsen, Riiser-Larsen, Oscar Wisting, Oscar Omdahl, Emil Horgen, Birger Gottwald, Storm Johnson and Frederick Ramm. The American was Ellsworth, and the Swede was Finn Malmgren. The Italians were Nobile, Vincenzo Pomella, Attilio Caratti, Ettore Arduino, Natale Cecioni and Renato Alessandrini. The dog was Titina and belonged to Nobile.

Amundsen, whose furrowed face showed the ravages of many expeditions and polar storms, had been over some of the area by boat. Now he scanned the scene below for land, leads, wildlife and other features. Riiser-Larsen, second-in-command, did the navigating. Wisting, who had been one of Amundsen's four companions on the South Pole trip, was at the vertical rudder wheel. Omdahl, who had been down on the ice with Amundsen the previous year, watched one of the engines. Horgen was at the lateral rudder wheel. Gottwald and Johnson worked the radio. Ramm went along as the *New York Times* correspondent. Ellsworth was measuring atmospheric electricity with a machine installed at the request of the Curie Institute of Paris and helping anybody who asked for assistance. Malmgren, from the University of Uppsala, was the *Norge*'s weather forecaster.

Nobile was in overall command of the ship, a post that was to lead to much altercation. Pomella was in the rear-engine gondola as a mechanic. Caratti had a similar job with the port engine, and

Arduino shared with Omdahl the care of its starboard twin. Cecioni was mechanic in chief. And Alessandrini, a rigger, kept running along the catwalk below the gas cells and climbing up in the envelope (the fabric structure enclosing the cells) to see that things were stored properly, that valves were working satisfactorily, that girders hadn't buckled.

The trip north was not uneventful. Later Amundsen disclosed in his book *My Life as an Explorer* that Nobile nearly wrecked the ship three times. The first time was when the Italian asked Wisting to let him take the vertical rudder wheel for a few minutes so he could get the feel of the ship. Thereupon he carelessly turned the wheel several times, causing the *Norge* to slant down toward the ice. In Amundsen's opinion, she surely would have crashed had Riiser-Larsen not thrust Nobile aside and spun the wheel back in time.

Later Nobile did the same thing again, and Riiser-Larsen again averted disaster—this time by yelling at Nobile to whirl the wheel back. On the third nearly ruinous occasion, Amundsen recalled, Nobile steered the dirigible upward to get out of a fog. But he took it so high that gas pressure threatened to burst the cells. Then he wrung his hands and screamed, "Run fast to the bow! Run fast to the bow!" Three Norwegians did, and their weight forced the *Norge*'s nose downward.

Surviving these perils, the airship reached the Pole at 1:25 A.M. on May 12. There in the daylight provided by the midnight sun, Amundsen dropped the Norwegian colors, Ellsworth dropped the Stars and Stripes, and Nobile disposed of an armful of emblems, including the pennants of the city of Rome and the Italian Aero Club. In keeping with Nobile's decree, the flags that Amundsen and Ellsworth had brought were small. The two men were somewhat irritated to see that Nobile's offerings were great banners, including one huge Italian flag that got stuck to an engine gondola and for a while threatened to foul one of the propellers.

Having reached their goal, they flew on, sometimes at 50 miles an hour. Amundsen looked hard for land but saw none. Presently fog drifted around them, condensing into ice as it settled on the bag, on the canvas-walled cabin, on the propellers. Soon heavy thuds announced that the props were hurling it at the ship.

Ice also coated the radio aerial. It snapped. One after another, five more aerials were shoved out. Now there was no contact with the outside world. In warmer lands people worried about the fate of the airship. The last report they had had from her was just beyond the Pole.

Cold seeped in through the cabin's walls. The propellers hurled more ice at the bag. If the bombardment continued it might puncture the gas cells inside the bag. The airship droned on. Finally Amundsen recognized some landmarks that he had seen twenty years earlier from the *Gjöa*, the 72-foot auxiliary sloop in which he had made the first navigation of the Northwest Passage.

The airship started to follow the coastline down past Bering Strait and on to Nome. But more fog swirled around the *Norge* and hid the land below. Winds and mist turned the crew off course. At one time they felt they were close to the Siberian frontier. They still couldn't send out any news of their whereabouts. On May 15 the *New York Times* ran a three-bank banner:

NO WORD FROM NORGE, MISSING TWO DAYS
MAY BE ADRIFT IN POLAR STORM OFF ALASKA
BYRD PREPARES FOR A SEARCH BY AIRPLANE

Now the *Norge* headed eastward by dead reckoning and tried to claw back to Alaska. After several hours the fog dissolved and the coastline appeared. A frozen bay and a cluster of houses came into view. Amundsen asked Nobile how much fuel was left. "Enough for seven hours' flying," was the reply. However, they decided to come down. At that moment the wind died. Villagers rushed out of their houses, seized the lines from the airship and helped pull her in. The flight ended, after 3,290 miles and about seventy-two hours, at Teller, some sixty miles northwest of Nome. There the bag was deflated for shipment to Italy.

The ill feeling between Nobile on the one side and Amundsen and Ellsworth on the other soon boiled up into a scalding row. The Italian began sending out press dispatches on the flight despite an agreement with Amundsen and Ellsworth, who had a contract with the *Times* for exclusive rights to the story. Things got worse when they returned to the United States. There, at the behest of Mussolini, who had promoted Nobile to general and made him an honorary member of the Fascist party, the dirigible designer delivered a series of lectures in cities with large Italian populations. In these talks he gave cheering audiences the impression that he, not Amundsen, had conceived the polar flight. Still later he declared that Mussolini had thought of it first. Meanwhile Italian newspapers, anxious to give *Fascismo* a boost, announced that six Italian crew members had done all the work on the flight while the rest of the complement slept.

Finally Ellsworth, a gentle and long-suffering man, felt it necessary to issue a statement. He pointed out that while Nobile had designed the *Norge,* she had been purchased by the Amundsen-Ellsworth interests, and the Italian had been retained at a salary merely to act as her captain. "At no time during the flight did he act as navigator," Ellsworth added. "In fact, I doubt if he understands navigation . . . I have the greatest respect for his contribution toward our success. But it would be extremely unfair to Riiser-Larsen, who navigated the entire flight across the Polar sea, and to Horgen and Wisting, who operated the lateral and vertical controls, not to give credit for both the navigation and steering where it is due.

"During the entire flight of seventy-two hours I stood without sleep in the navigating cabin. To the best of my knowledge, General

Nobile's only part in the navigation consisted in relieving the wheel man for three short periods during the flight . . ."

When this statement was shown to Nobile he came up with one of his own: "As captain of the airship, every person on board depended on me during the flight. Riiser-Larsen, second in command of the airship, was appointed navigator by me . . .

"During the entire flight of seventy-one hours I acted all the time as captain of the airship, giving orders to everybody, controlling what everybody was doing. It is obvious that the captain of an airship does not actually handle the controls of the airship himself. My duty was directing and watching. Notwithstanding, for several hours during the most dangerous moments I felt it my duty to personally control the elevator and other controls, when it would have been much too dangerous to leave them to those not so familiar with the manoeuvers of the airship.

"All preparations for the flight were made under my initiative and direction, and for this I worked, with the other Italian people, about nine months, while Mr. Ellsworth was in America without knowing or asking about the expedition.

"Mr. Ellsworth has given $120,000 for the expedition, and that was indeed a sacrifice, but nothing else. But the Italian Government for this expedition has expended more than $200,000, and I, for my own part, have given all my activity and all my heart for the success of the flight.

"We could have been successful also without the contribution of Mr. Ellsworth. But without me the expedition would not have taken place and would not have been a success.

"I tried always to be nice to Mr. Ellsworth, but now I cannot but tell what is known by everybody, that Mr. Ellsworth on our expedition was just a passenger whom I took on board at Spitsbergen and left at Teller."

Nobile did not meet Ellsworth or Amundsen again for years. He went back to Rome on the flag-decked liner *Conte Biancamano* to receive a hero's welcome. Italy gave him her highest decoration, the Military Order of Savoy. France made him a member of the Legion of Honor. And twenty-four cities, including New York and Rome, made him an honorary citizen.

2

DEATH AND DECEPTION

To early aeronauts and aviators a flight over the Arctic Ocean to the top of the world seemed to be a more possible achievement than one across the North Atlantic. From Spitsbergen a trip to the North Pole and back adds up to about 1,500 miles, and in the early twentieth century it was believed there might be land on which to alight in an emergency, as well as ice on which to come down if necessary, with a good chance of survival. In contrast, a flight from Newfoundland to Ireland involved a one-way trip of some 1,900 miles—all of it over water. Nevertheless, the thought of an Atlantic flight had been intriguing adventurous men since early in the century.

Like the ventures in the Arctic, the first efforts over the wider ocean were made in craft that were lighter than air. In 1910 Walter Wellman, who had previously tried to reach the Pole, was ready for the initial attempt. He had another dirigible which embodied some of the parts in the craft that had failed at Spitsbergen in 1907 and 1909. Designed by his engineer, Melvin Vaniman, it was 228 feet long—45 feet longer than its predecessor—and had two 80-horsepower engines. This still wasn't enough to buck strong adverse winds, for the airship's top speed was only 26 miles an hour.

It had one other serious fault. Like the earlier model, it dragged a long tail made up of full gasoline cans. This serpentine appendage was called an "equilibrator" and had two main functions. The line of floating cans was supposed to keep the dirigible stable and at a low altitude. And the floating fuel would relieve the ship of weight. The theory was that the equilibrator would gradually be hauled up into the ship as the motors burned the gasoline in flight—the lifting power to be provided by a donkey engine. But the equilibrator used on the second flight from Spitsbergen had broken, causing the ship to rise so rapidly that hydrogen had to be valved. Too much escaped and the 1909 flight had ended quickly.

In October 1910 Wellman started from Atlantic City, New Jersey, with three companions. In two days he worked the ship out beyond Cape Cod for a distance of 660 miles from New Jersey. But the equilibrator, consisting of twenty-nine cans of gasoline, jerked the dirigible violently as its lower end leaped from wave to wave. And beyond the Cape a northeast wind blew the ship back toward the coast. After seventy-one hours it came down in the sea 400 miles east of Hatteras. The four men were rescued by a British steamer.

Two years later Vaniman, who had been in on Wellman's two polar tries, had a dirigible of his own—thanks to the backing of the president of the Goodyear Tire & Rubber Company. This craft was 268 feet long and had two 105-horsepower engines. Vaniman took it up for a trial flight from Atlantic City on July 2. With him were his brother and three other crewmen.

At a height of 2,000 feet the cigar-shaped bag suddenly burst. The car dropped away, and with the engines racing, plunged toward the water. All five men died, two of them in view of their wives. Apparently the hot sun had expanded the hydrogen in the bag and a gas escape valve had jammed. The resulting pressure had done the rest.

Seven years went by before any airmen crossed the Atlantic, and even then the feat hardly heralded regular passenger service.

In May 1919 a Navy Curtiss seaplane—with five battleships and more than sixty destroyers, cruisers and auxiliary craft deployed along its route—flew from Newfoundland to Lisbon with a stop at the Azores. This first crossing of the North Atlantic by air wasn't a complete success. Despite the fact that the ships, positioned at fifty-mile intervals, gave out with heavy black smoke by day, flares and star shells at night and weather information all the time, two other Navy planes in the group effort got lost in the ocean fog. Both were damaged in heavy seas and one later sank, while the other taxied into Ponta Delgada after riding out a gale. Only the NC-4 reached its destination intact. Moreover, the four 400-horsepower Liberty engines (with which each seaplane was fitted) were barely able to get the heavy aircraft with six crewmen off the water. No passengers were carried.

That same May two British fliers—Harry Hawker and Mackenzie Grieve—also took off from Newfoundland, in a Sopwith biplane bound for Ireland. After a successful start Hawker dropped the undercarriage to reduce head resistance and weight—in those days, landing gears were not retractable—proposing to make a belly-landing in Europe. About a thousand miles out, a clogged filter in the cooling system caused the water in their 275-horsepower Rolls-Royce engine to boil. Fortunately they sighted the small Danish ship *Mary* and came down beside her to be rescued. But the vessel had no wireless and the voluble Hawker was incommunicado for six days. On his arrival in London he made up for it with some cracks about that string of American warships— remarks which his compatriots considered definitely unsporting.

The next month two other Britons put on a performance that eclipsed both the U.S. Navy and the Hawker-Grieve flights. Captain John Alcock and Lieutenant Arthur Brown took off from Newfoundland in a converted Vickers-Vimy bomber fitted with two Rolls-Royces of 350 horsepower each. Although the fliers encountered fog nearly all the way, they made it without a stop to

Clifden, Ireland, where they had to land in a bog. Because of the soft ground the biplane nosed partway over, but neither man was hurt. They had been in the air for 16 hours and 28 minutes, and had flown 1,890 miles. Their feat won them the £10,000 prize that had been offered by Lord Northcliffe, proprietor of the London *Daily Mail*, for a nonstop flight from North America to the British Isles.

A month later the British dirigible *R-34* flew from England to Long Island with thirty-one men, including a stowaway, and a tortoise-shell cat. The airship nearly ran out of gas on the way over because of strong headwinds. But the flight was hailed as an augury of greater things to come, and so was the successful voyage back. Five years later the *ZR-3*, another rigid dirigible (which became the *Los Angeles*) flew from Germany to New Jersey as one of the few reparations the United States ever got out of World War I. She carried fifteen German officers and men, along with four American observers, and was commanded by Dr. Hugo Eckener, who later piloted several other dirigibles on South and North Atlantic journeys.

Several ocean flights had been successful in the early twenties. So why were so many more attempted toward the end of that decade? One reason was the improvement in planes and engines made during World War I. Numerous flights over land masses had convinced many aviators that ocean voyages were feasible, if not entirely safe. Another reason was an impatience among the comparatively new breed of pilots to do something more interesting than lugging the mail for practically nothing or scratching a living from stunts at county fairs. But perhaps the most potent reason for trying to fly the Atlantic was the lure of substantial cash prizes.

The first of many such prizes attainable after Alcock and Brown had taken the Northcliffe award was that offered by Raymond Orteig, owner of the charming Brevoort and Lafayette hotels in New York City. Mr. Orteig said he would pay $25,000 to the man or men who made the first nonstop flight between New York and Paris. He believed such a feat would foster good relations between America and his beloved native France.

The flight would be 1,700 miles longer than one from Newfoundland to Ireland. Indeed, the distance was far beyond the range of the planes of 1919, the year the Orteig prize was first announced. But Mr. Orteig renewed his offer every few years and in the mid-twenties it was still to be won.

After Byrd returned to Spitsbergen following his 1926 flight, he asked Balchen to come to America with him to help with other expeditions. And when Balchen heard about the *Norge's* safe landing in Alaska he agreed to apply for additional leave from the Norwegian Naval Air Force and to accept the offer. Permission was granted, and the young lieutenant was aboard the *Chantier* when it headed out of Kings Bay and started southwestward. The old vessel crossed the ocean ahead of schedule and arrived off Sandy Hook at the entrance to New York Bay before the Mayor's Committee for the Reception of Distinguished Guests was ready to stage an appropriate welcome. As a result, the ship had to stand off for two days while preparations for the parade and celebration were completed. When everything was in order, Balchen, who was acting as quartermaster, steered the *Chantier* up the Narrows and into the harbor, under the direction of a Sandy Hook pilot. The appearance of the supply ship caused a flurry of excitement. Tugs and small craft whistled and honked, fireboats pumped arching streams of water, outgoing liners sounded deep notes of salute, spectators crowded Battery Park.

Balchen didn't have a role in the triumphal ticker-tape parade on June 23. Byrd had made clear to him that he was not a member of the Arctic expedition and therefore could not share in its welcome. So Balchen stayed on the *Chantier* and didn't see Broadway, City Hall, the Woolworth Building and other sights until Grover Whalen—head of the reception committee—came aboard next day and took him on a private tour of the city. Whalen explained that Bennett had told him about the lonely Norwegian on the boat.

After the parade Byrd and Bennett went to Washington. President Coolidge had already raised the handsome officer from the rank of lieutenant commander to full commander, but greater honors were to come. In the Washington Auditorium the Chief Executive presented both men with the Hubbard medal of the National Geographic Society, which had sponsored the polar expedition. The audience, an enthusiastic one, totaled six thousand people. They included Justices of the United States Supreme Court, members of Congress and the diplomatic corps, industrialists, scientists and other distinguished guests. All felt that it was an auspicious occasion indeed, for up to that time the Hubbard medal had been awarded to only six men. They were explorers Robert Peary, Roald Amundsen, Bob Bartlett, Sir Ernest Shackleton and Vilhjalmur Stefansson, and Grove Karl Gilbert, a noted nineteenth-century geologist and explorer.

"We cannot but admire the superb courage of the man willing to set forth on such a great adventure in the unexplored realms of the air," said Mr. Coolidge as he gave the coveted medal to Byrd. "But we must not forget, nor fail to appreciate, the vision and persistence that led him ultimately to achieve the dream of his Naval Academy days. He never ceased to prepare himself mentally, scientifically and physically to meet the supreme test. His deed will be but the beginning of scientific exploration considered difficult of achievement before he proved the possibilities of the airplane."

Byrd, attired in his natty white uniform and accompanied by his wife, replied with engaging modesty. He gave credit to the others in the expedition, especially to Bennett, who "did more to bring success than any of us." Of the future, he said, "Admiral Peary was the last man to go to the North Pole by dog sled. The dog sled must give way to the airplane. America must not rest until the three million [actually more than 10,000,000] square miles of the Arctic and Antarctic are further explored." And then, as if to give the National Geographic Society something new to think about, he added, "The United States must plant her flag at the South Pole."

The gold medals were appropriate to the occasion. The one given to Byrd said: "Awarded by the National Geographic Society to Comander Richard Evelyn Byrd, Jr., U.S.N. for his special achievement in first reaching the North Pole by airplane, 9th May, 1926." Beneath the inscription were the Navy symbols, an anchor between two stars. The medal to Bennett said it had been awarded "for his distinguished service in flying to the North Pole with Commander Richard Evelyn Byrd, Jr."

Six days later the National Geographic Society announced that a careful examination by a special committee of the data Byrd had turned in had "substantiated in every particular" Byrd's claim to have reached the Pole, and made public the report. The committee consisted of Gilbert Grosvenor, president of the National Geographic Society; Frederick V. Coville, botanist of the U.S. Department of Agriculture; and E. Lester Jones, director of the U.S. Coast and Geodetic Survey. The experts, who had checked Byrd's data for five days, were Hugh G. Mitchell, senior mathematician of the U.S. Coast and Geodetic Survey; Henry G. Avers, the Survey's chief mathematician of geodesy; and Albert Bumstead, the Geographic Society's chief cartographer and inventor of the sun compass which Byrd had carried.

In their report, the experts stated that they had examined the two charts used by Commander Byrd, as well as his sextant and sun compass. The report continued:

> ...At 8 hours 58 minutes 55 seconds an observation of the altitude of the sun gave a latitude of 89 degrees 55.3 minutes on the meridian of flight. This point is 4.7 miles from the Pole. Continuing his flight on the same course and at the speed of 74 miles an hour, which he had averaged since 8 hours 18 minutes, would bring Commander

29

Byrd close to the Pole in 3 minutes 49 seconds, making the probable
time of his arrival at the Pole 9 hours 3 minutes Greenwich Civil
Time . . .

At the moment when the sun would be crossing the fifteenth
meridian, along which he had laid his course, he had the plane
steadied, pointing directly toward the sun and observed at the same
instant that the shadow on the sun compass was down the middle
of the hand, thus verifying his position as being on that meridian.
This had an even more satisfactory verification when at about 14
hours 30 minutes GCT he sighted land ahead and soon identified
Gray Point (Grey Hook), Spitsbergen, just west of the fifteenth
meridian. . . .

Grey Hook is about seventy statute miles north of Kings Bay.
If Byrd had sighted it twenty miles away and the *Josephine Ford*
was traveling about 74 nautical miles an hour, she would have
reached her starting point even earlier than 4:07 P.M.—the time
agreed on by competent observers there—and would thus have been
in the air even less than the 15½ hours reported by Arneson, the
New York Times men, and others. Byrd did not state the exact time
of his arrival and apparently the experts did not consider his total
time in the air in reaching their conclusion that his claim was
justified.

The part of the experts' report that struck Balchen was the
statement that Byrd's records were contained on the two charts and
that these included an observation made at 89 degrees 55.3 minutes
north latitude. He remembered those charts. When he had examined them on the *Chantier* they contained only a couple of scribbled notes. And if Byrd hadn't recorded any observations during
the flight, when had he recorded them?

Balchen also pondered another part of the report. It called
for a conclusion which the precise Norwegian was unable to make.

It is unfortunate that no sextant observations could be made on
the return trip. But the successful landfall at Grey Hook demonstrates
Commander Byrd's skill in navigating along a predetermined course

and in our opinion is one of the strongest evidences that he was equally successful in his flight northward. The feat of flying a plane 600 miles from land and returning to the point aimed for is a remarkable exhibition of skilful navigation and shows, beyond reasonable doubt, that he knew where he was at all times during the flight.

(The experts obviously meant "600 nautical miles," for the chart run in the *National Geographic Magazine* with one of Byrd's articles is calibrated in this measure. This over-water and over-ice distance equals 1,380 statute miles for the round trip. To this would be added the approximate overland distance of 140 statute miles from Kings Bay to the north coast of Spitsbergen and return, making a total of 1,520 miles, or 15 less than the usually accepted distance—which often varies slightly in different estimates.)

Among fliers that summer of 1926 there was much talk about the Orteig prize and the best way to win it. But one famous aviator seemed to have the inside track. This was the Frenchman René Fonck, the top ace of World War I, who had a verified score of 75 of the enemy's planes shot down and an unofficial tally of 126. Fonck, a short, stocky man, had a plane already built—a biplane designed by Igor Sikorsky, a Russian-born American. It was fitted with three 425-horsepower Gnome Rhone Jupiter radial engines which the flier had borrowed from the French government. He proposed to fly from Roosevelt Field, near Mineola, Long Island, with a crew of four. The last few months of preparations were filled with acrimony. Would there be a co-pilot or a navigator? Who, beside Fonck, would be chosen? Would the big plane carry any passengers?

Among those who wanted to be passengers was a man who would become one of the most controversial figures of Lindbergh-era aviation. Charles A. Levine was a millionaire. A one-time used-car salesman, he had learned after the war that the federal government was going to dismantle a number of ammunition plants, and dump a large quantity of surplus ammunition and shell casings into the ocean. He had borrowed money, formed companies which dismantled the plants, bought the ammunition and casings. Later he sold the hardware back to the government at a huge profit.

When he heard about the Fonck project he offered Sikorsky $25,000 to let him go along as dead weight. It was the first of many such offers people made to designers and fliers in those years —and several of these proposals were accepted. But this one was turned down and Levine had to wait until the following year to achieve the renown he craved.

It seemed to many of the veteran pilots at Curtiss and Roosevelt fields that the Fonck plane already was carrying unnecessary weight without the addition of Levine. The cabin, prettied up by an interior decorator, sported red leather upholstery, a couch which could be converted into a comfortable bed, and other luxurious items. These appointments were needed, it appeared, because the cabin was to be the scene of a triumphant dinner when the biplane arrived in Paris. And just in case the airmen couldn't find anything fit to eat in the French capital, the dinner was to be carried on the flight, surrounded by heat-conserving insulation. The menu was to include Manhattan clam chowder, Baltimore terrapin, roast Long Island duck and roast Vermont turkey.

Fonck finally settled on U.S. Navy Lieutenant Lawrence Curtin as his navigator; Russian-born Jacob Islamoff, mechanic; and French-born Charles Clavier, radio operator. On September 21, 1926, he was ready to take off. At the last minute somebody stepped up and handed him a box of croissants—a present from Mr. Orteig. Fonck put it in the cabin near the already installed hot dinner.

The plane was heavily overloaded. She was called on to lift a total weight—including her own—exceeding 28,000 pounds. Sikorsky tinkered with the ship all night before the start to be certain she would be in good condition. He could only hope that her burden of gas and luxury items wasn't too heavy.

Shortly after daybreak Fonck revved up his engines and started westward across Roosevelt Field. Once in the air he would bank around to the east and head for Paris and that $25,000, some 3,600 miles away. What happened in the next few seconds was in dispute for weeks afterward. The Sikorsky had taken off without trouble in earlier tests. Now the three engines roared and strained but their total of 1,275 horsepower couldn't pull the machine up to a flying speed of 80 miles an hour.

She scudded along the ground for 3,200 feet as veteran pilots, scenting disaster, started to sprint toward the spot for which she was heading. This was the part of the dusty tract that dropped sharply into Curtiss Field, a dangerous little slope that should have been graded.

When the overloaded biplane reached the slope she dropped sharply. Then she crashed and burst into flames.

Fonck and Curtin escaped from the cockpit. Islamoff and Clavier, farther back in the fuselage, were trapped in the buckled airframe and died in the fierce fire. By the time men with extinguishers and, later, fire engines reached the wreck, there was no hope of saving either the mechanic or the radio operator. Islamoff, some of his friends recalled, had been overjoyed at being selected and had written a happy letter to his wife asking her to meet him at Le Bourget.

A coroner's inquest shed a little additional light on the tragedy. It came out that because of the Sikorsky's heavy weight, auxiliary wheels had been fitted so that they could be dumped after takeoff. One of these wheels tore loose during the run and the plane began to swerve, whereupon Islamoff released the whole auxiliary gear. A piece of this ricocheted and damaged the rudder. Fonck, under criticism for not cutting his engines when the plane failed to rise, said Islamoff shouldn't have released the gear. Islamoff could not defend his action.

The disaster to the Fonck plane didn't discourage other ambitious fliers. Indeed, Lindbergh reveals in his book *The Spirit of St. Louis* that it merely strengthened his belief in single-engined as opposed to multi-engined planes for projects of this sort. On Floyd Bennett and Bernt Balchen it had the opposite effect. These fliers felt that a multi-engined plane, properly loaded and handled, had a good chance of making the ocean journey without trouble.

The two men were now close friends. Moreover, in October they had begun to tour the country in the *Josephine Ford* under the auspices of the Guggenheim Foundation, which had been set up to promote progress and interest in aviation. The tour covered 8,000 miles and took them to forty-five cities. Balchen, who at this time was working for Tony Fokker—who had started a factory at Hasbrouck Heights, New Jersey—kept a careful record of the plane's time in the air, speed, and other phases of performance. His voluminous data included the fact that the average speed for all forty-five hops was 67 miles an hour.

They hadn't been pushing the plane, but even if they had, they could not—on a long flight—have averaged more than an economical 75 miles an hour. Balchen had been thinking about Byrd's northward flight from Spitsbergen. If the Fokker normally cruised at no more than 75 miles an hour it would have covered in 15½ hours— minus the fourteen minutes Byrd said he spent near the Pole—only 1,145 miles. This was 390 less than the distance from Kings Bay and return.

Moreover, the *Josephine Ford* was now fitted with wheels. Burdened with the skis she had worn on the flight from Spitsbergen, she would have been slower than she was now. At least three and perhaps five miles an hour slower.

Balchen puzzled over it. One day he said to his friend, "You couldn't have got to the North Pole and back in fifteen and a half hours."

"No," Bennett replied. "We didn't."

Balchen waited for an explanation. It didn't come. The two men continued to fly the plane. And Balchen soon discovered that Bennett didn't know how to navigate. He liked to follow rivers and railroads to his destination. He was surprised and pleased that his friend could lay out a compass course that would bring them in.

The two men completed the tour with the *Josephine Ford* in a couple of months. Toward the end of it they began to talk about installing the new J-5 Whirlwinds in the plane and taking off in her together for Paris to win the Orteig prize. All they needed was a little money. Perhaps their friend Harry Bruno, the Wright public relations man, could raise it for them. But Byrd gave the plane to the Henry Ford Museum at Dearborn for a permanent exhibit. The commander already had received financial help from Edsel Ford and was going to get more for an Antarctic expedition in 1928.

In December 1926 Congress approved the award of a Medal of Honor to Byrd and another to Bennett, who was described as the naval officer's "mechanic." The decoration was to be awarded in February 1927. And when Balchen next saw Bennett his friend spoke to him briefly about it. "I don't want to go down to Washington and get another medal for that North Pole thing," he said. Balchen asked him why, but Bennett didn't explain. Again Balchen felt that his friend wanted to tell him something but couldn't bring himself to do it.

The award of the second medal was much less ceremonious than that of the first. President Coolidge made the presentation in the White House. The citation said Byrd received it "for distinguishing himself conspicuously by courage and intrepidity at the risk of his life in demonstrating that it was possible for aircraft to travel in continuous flight from a now inhabited portion of the earth over the North Pole and return."

The race to win the Orteig prize was still on. In March 1927 Fonck announced that Sikorsky was building another plane for him. This one would have two engines instead of three, and because of the weight saving, be more efficient. There were some who didn't follow this logic.

Balchen knew that Fokker was at work on another three-engined monoplane for Byrd, who was planning a transatlantic flight that spring. She would be fitted with the new and more powerful Whirlwinds, which would increase her speed. And Lieutenant Commander Noel Davis of the Massachusetts Naval Reserve revealed that he would make a try for the prize in a Keystone biplane, also powered with three Whirlwinds.

Byrd's financial backer this time was again Rodman Wanamaker, proprietor of the famous New York department store and president of the America Trans-Oceanic Company, a concern whose immediate objective was to get the Fokker from New York to Paris. Vice president of the company was Grover Whalen, manager of the Wanamaker store and chairman of Mayor Walker's welcoming committee. In the latter capacity Whalen was to have much to do receiving Byrd's rivals.

Wanamaker, as well as Byrd, was reputed to be a man of lofty principles. And both men let it be known at the outset that the Fokker monoplane's voyage would have no crass commercial aspects. It wouldn't even compete for the Orteig prize. It would make its serene ocean journey solely in the interests of science and to promote friendship between great nations. The successful flight to Paris would demonstrate the tremendous part that aviation was going to play in strengthening international good will by enabling people (presumably those of good will) to make safe ocean flights every day.

Meanwhile Levine (who eventually, like Byrd, would attempt the Atlantic crossing) had bought the Bellanca plane from the Wright Aeronautical Corporation—a model Wright had originally intended to manufacture in some quantity and fit with the Whirlwind engine. Levine thought he could get a profitable government contract to carry mail between New York and Chicago, and believed that the Bellanca plane was the best in the country.

Both Giuseppe Bellanca, the plane's designer, and Clarence Chamberlin, who was later to fly it across the Atlantic, were at this time working for Wright. When the corporation abandoned its plan to employ Bellanca to build additional machines, the designer was out of a job. So he agreed to team up with Levine, in the Columbia Aircraft Corporation, in order to continue to do the work he loved.

It was an ill-fated association from the start. Bellanca's new partner was a short, chunky man who seemed to regard everybody with suspicion. His less than charming attributes were to be amply demonstrated in the months to come. He was hardly the person to run a successful business enterprise with the generous, open-hearted and modest little Italian aeronautical engineer.

Bellanca had become interested in flying as soon as he began to think about birds. He spent long boyhood hours watching them soar and dip over the hills of his native Sicily. In his teens he showed a proficiency in mathematics that led him to the Royal Institute of Milan, from which he graduated with honors, and then into airplane design. In 1910 he came to America, settled in Brooklyn and began to teach himself to fly with a plane he had built largely in the cellar of his home. It was a parasol monoplane, with a pilot's perch below the wing just behind a three-cylinder engine with a tendency to spray hot oil. He kept the contraption at Curtiss Field on Long Island. "The experts gave me fifteen days to live," Bellanca recalled later. "That was hopeful because it gave the impression that they thought the machine would at least get off the ground."

In three months Bellanca was not only alive but flying, having taught himself by taxiing over the field until he familiarized himself with the controls and then taking short hops. He opened a flying school and for four years taught hundreds of people to fly by the same method—adjusting the throttle so they couldn't take off before they knew how to manage the machine. Among his pupils was Representative Fiorello LaGuardia of New York, later to become a pilot in World War I and still later acquire fame as the best mayor America's largest city ever had.

During the war Bellanca had designed planes for both the British and American governments which were more efficient than anything rival engineers could produce. But as Chamberlin says in his book, *Record Flights*, Bellanca got the runaround from the War Department and never could find substantial backing until the Wright company took an interest in him, only to sell his latest creation to Levine.

The *Columbia*, as this machine came to be called, was more efficient than her rivals because the wing struts as well as the fuselage were designed to augment the lift afforded by the wings. For those who don't understand why a plane rises in the air, it may be pointed out that the front, or leading, edge of the wing is thicker than the rear, or trailing, edge, and the top of the wing is convex while the bottom is flat or nearly so. As a result, when the plane moves forward, the air pressure on the top of the wing is slightly less than that flowing across the bottom surface. This difference in air pressure lifts the wing. There are other factors involved in lift, but the shape of the wing provides most of it.

The struts on the *Columbia*, which extended from the bottom of the fuselage out to the wing, acted not only as braces. Each of them—there were two on either side—exerted a lift, for they were formed like airfoils. That is, they were like little wings which still exerted a lift, even though they were not horizontal like the wings but slanted up to them. The struts also tended to stabilize the plane, for when the machine canted over, the struts on the downward side were closer to the horizontal than those on the upward side, and thus exerted more lift than the others.

Additional lift was provided by the *Columbia*'s fuselage, whose top side curved down behind the cabin a bit more sharply than the fuselages of other planes. Thus, because of the strut and fuselage design, as well as masterly wing contours, the *Columbia* had more lift per unit of horsepower than other contemporary aircraft. And since most of the single-engined long-distance planes were about the same size and were using the same Whirlwind J-5 power plant, Bellanca's machine could outperform them all.

Lindbergh knew the Bellanca was a great machine and had been trying to buy it since November the previous year. But the Wright company wouldn't sell it for a transatlantic flight, even though Bellanca wanted Lindbergh to have it. After Levine became Bellanca's partner, the designer thought things were looking up. He telegraphed Lindbergh suggesting that he come to New York to talk over what Bellanca described as an "attractive proposition."

Lindbergh came east from St. Louis to find Levine in charge. The former used-car salesman asked about the mail flier's backers, showing some suspicion, but appeared satisfied when Lindbergh described them. Then (as Lindbergh relates in his book), Levine offered to sell the plane for $15,000, seemingly with no strings attached. Lindbergh went back to St. Louis, consulted his backers and got a cashier's check for the required amount. His troubles about getting a good ocean plane seemed to be over. Indeed, he was convinced he had the best machine of the day.

The young National Guard captain didn't know much then about Levine. When he returned to New York he found that while the offer to buy the plane was still open, Levine reserved the right to name the crew that would fly her. Presumably one of the crew would be Chamberlin, test pilot for Wright and a former stunt flier from Iowa. But there was no indication that Lindbergh would be allowed in the cabin.

When Lindbergh declined this proposition, which now appeared attractive only to Levine, he was asked to think it over and call back in the morning. Lindbergh did so and then was asked, "Well, have you changed your mind?" He hung up, he said later, without answering.

Early in 1927 Lindbergh and his St. Louis friends closed with the Ryan Company of San Diego, California, whose employees began working day and night to build him a plane in two months. It was about the size of the Bellanca, with a wingspread of forty-six feet, but without the latter's wing-strut and fuselage features. And its cabin was amidships, behind the big gas tank. This meant that Lindbergh couldn't see where the plane was going without thrusting his head out of the fuselage window or pushing out a little horizontal periscope. But Lindbergh wanted it that way. In case of a crash he wouldn't be hit from behind with a big load of gasoline and crushed between it and the engine.

It was fairly easy to get financial backing for ocean flights in 1926, 1927 and 1928. Business was booming and the bust was still to come. In April 1927 the newspapers reported that 208 Americans had paid taxes on incomes of $1,000,000 or more—an increase of 182 in a year—while 82 percent of the population was still untaxed. On April 5 Sir Thomas Lipton announced that he had spent $10,000,000 in his four attempts to lift the America's Cup but that he would try again in 1929. On a smaller scale, Babe Ruth signed a three-year contract with the Yankees under which he would receive a total of $210,000.

Aside from yachting and baseball, there was much other colorful news to interest, titillate or worry the American people. Ruth Snyder and Judd Gray, a corset designer and a salesman, went on trial for the murder of Ruth's husband, Albert Snyder, art editor of the magazine *Motor Boating*. Chicago, already notorious for its gangsters, was drawing more unfavorable attention to itself by re-electing Big Bill Thompson for a third term as mayor. Mae West, sentenced to ten days in the workhouse after her play *Sex* was adjudged obscene, was complaining that prison clothes in New York City were uncomfortable. Nicola Sacco and Bartolomeo Vanzetti, convicted on circumstantial evidence of a double killing in a trial which ranged liberals against conservatives all over the world, attempted and failed to get another hearing. Boston banned the sale of Sinclair Lewis' *Elmer Gantry.* And Mme. Frieda Hempel, forty-one, former Metropolitan Opera Company soprano, sued August Heckscher, seventy-eight, millionaire philanthropist and realty operator, for breach of a contract under which he undertook, she claimed, to pay her $48,000 yearly in return for what was described as "a valuable consideration."

On the international scene, Chiang Kai-shek was fighting Communists in Shanghai and presently executed one hundred of their alleged leaders. The United States landed Marines and Great Britain landed infantry in the embattled city to protect their citizens there. Unlike the United States, Britain wasn't doing very well financially. Indeed, it was ASHIVER, one headline said, over HUGE DEFICIT.

On the transatlantic front, the April air was full of statements. Although the Fokker was still in the factory at Hasbrouck Heights, Byrd announced on the twelfth that its radio would begin cranking out call signals soon after takeoff and that the monoplane would thus be linked with various surface ships throughout the flight. The same day a dispatch from Paris said that Commander Fitzhugh Green was there to make tentative arrangements for the Byrd arrival. And on the fourteenth Byrd inflated one of the two rubber boats he planned to take along on the transatlantic trip and was photographed in it, along with Navy Lieutenant George Noville, radio operator, and Floyd Bennett, pilot, as he paddled around off the Battery at the end of Manhattan, where the trio were nearly run down by a couple of tugs.

Meanwhile Lieutenant Commander Davis announced that he also would use a radio and that he and Lieutenant Stanton Wooster might take off for Paris during the week of the eleventh. They didn't, but Clarence Chamberlin and Bert Acosta, another noted flier, took the *Columbia* up for a try at the endurance record set nearly two years earlier by a couple of French aviators. This project, endorsed by both Levine and Bellanca, was designed to publicize the plane's capabilities and create a demand for more machines like it, which the new Columbia company would then turn out.

Acosta was a daredevil who specialized in such stunts as flying upside down a few feet above county fair grounds, picking up a handkerchief with a wing tip, and rolling a wheel on a hangar roof as he came in for a landing. He refrained from these inclinations on the endurance run, however, and the little plane droned over Long Island for 51 hours, 11 minutes and 25 seconds, to beat the old record by nearly six hours.

After that, Bellanca said they could start for Paris in three days. And if he had had his way they probably would have. After all, Davis had completed several tests, and the Lindbergh and Byrd planes were a-building. And so, perhaps, were several other machines.

One of those publicized at this time was to be flown by Second Lieutenant Winston W. Ehrgott, a West Pointer then attached to the 71st Infantry, New York National Guard. The publicist was John Stelling, president of what he called the Aircraft Company of America, who said he was constructing a two-engined amphibian at the College Point (N.Y.) plant of the Sikorsky Corporation. Ehrgott, twenty-three years old, proposed that all other projected transatlantic flights be postponed until summer, when his plane would be ready. Then all could race to Paris under a handicap system. The Sikorsky offices said they knew nothing of arrangements whereby Stelling would build a plane at the College Point plant. And newspapers reported that other fliers showed little enthusiasm for the postponement plan.

Another mystery machine was that of Lieutenant Leigh Wade, who in 1924 had flown part of the way around the northern part of the world with a four-plane Army expedition whose Liberty-powered Douglas biplanes made the distance in a series of short hops which took nearly six months. Wade said he would start for Paris in six weeks if a company to back him could be found in time. He added that he didn't want to compete with the other fliers in an effort to be the first to take off.

Levine had no such compunctions. "We intend to be the first across," he said. "That means that if any other flier should start and our plane is ready we would be able to go after him with as much as a three-hour handicap and beat him across. Our plane is the fastest of those now heading for Paris." The last statement was undoubtedly true. The only other plane known to be anywhere near ready to head for the French capital was the relatively slow Keystone biplane (a converted bomber) of Noel Davis. In France, Captains Charles Nungesser and François Coli were testing a Levasseur biplane for still another effort to win the Orteig prize. But they were planning to fly from Paris to New York.

In mid-April the Byrd plane crashed. Fokker wanted to test it after its completion at his New Jersey factory. A self-taught but competent pilot, the Dutch designer had planned to take the three-engined craft up alone. But Bennett wanted to go along too, and then Byrd and Noville climbed in. Against his better judgment, Fokker let them come along. So four men crowded into a cockpit that was built for two.

When Fokker tried to land the plane at Teterboro Airport, he discovered she was nose-heavy. There was no ballast in the rear of the machine to compensate for the weight of two extra men up front, and no passageway through which they could crawl toward the tail. The Flying Dutchman, as he later called himself in an autobiography, gunned the big plane and took her aloft again. But with fuel running low, he had to make another try at landing. Thereupon the monoplane nosed over and smacked down on her back. Bennett's right thigh was broken and a propeller fragment pierced a lung, Byrd suffered a broken wrist and Noville was badly shaken up. Fokker escaped with scratches, but the plane would be out of commission for three weeks and Bennett would be out for months, and unable to fly with Byrd to Europe.

Levine kept everybody guessing, and himself in the news, with a new series of intriguing statements. As a starter he announced that Lloyd Bertaud, a mail flier on the Cleveland–New Jersey run, would be navigator of the *Columbia* on the Paris flight and that Chamberlin and Acosta would draw lots for the other seat. Levine explained that he would keep the two pilots on their toes by postponing the drawing until the very last minute. "On the day of the flight," he said, "Chamberlin and Acosta will appear on the field in flying togs. Their names will be written separately on slips of paper. One slip will be drawn. The name on it will decide the flier."

In a backhand swipe at Byrd and Davis, both of them military men, he declared that the selection of Bertaud as navigator was in line with his policy of making the flight exclusively civilian. By doing without the assistance of the Army or Navy, he said, he would show that commercial aviation in America "can stand on its own legs." His real reason for choosing Bertaud was his belief that the mail flier could help him get that government contract to fly letters and packages between Chicago and New York.

Soon Levine persuaded the Brooklyn Chamber of Commerce to put up $15,000 as an additional prize for the fliers if they reached Paris. He also got himself elected chairman of the Chamber's Paris Flight Committee. There was even some talk of the Chamber's taking over the expenses of the flight, though this emanated mostly from Levine. However, Ralph Jonas, president of the trade organization, said that the plane would carry letters from him to President Gaston Doumergue, Ambassador Myron Herrick and the president of the U.S. Chamber of Commerce in Paris, thus inaugurating a transatlantic mail service.

The next day the *New York Times* front-paged a story that

whipped up more public excitement over the Bellanca plane and the ocean contest it was expected to win. This was an account of the christening of the plane by Eloyse, Levine's daughter, and what happened immediately afterward.

Eloyse, nine years old, broke a bottle of ginger ale over the propeller hub, and the Bellanca was officially named *Columbia.* Present at the ceremony on Curtiss Field were Mr. and Mrs. Levine, Ralph Jonas and his fifteen-year-old daughter Grace, Chamberlin, Bellanca and several hundred spectators. After the ceremony the two girls asked Chamberlin to take them up for a ride. John Carisi, Bellanca's head mechanic, went with them.

It was a good human-interest tale. The hero was Chamberlin, the heroines the two little girls, the villain a sheared-off pin in the left shock-absorber journal. As the Bellanca climbed into the air, with the two girls as passengers, the left front landing strut was seen to be out of position, with the wheel sagging under the body and useless for landing.

Levine, who observed the takeoff, didn't notice anything wrong. Neither did the Brooklyn Chamber of Commerce president. But several other people did and a couple of fliers grabbed a tire, got into a plane and flew alongside Chamberlin. They held up the tire, pointing at the same time to the Ballanca's undercarriage. Their frantic waving made him look down and discover the sagging wheel.

The plane was carrying 350 pounds of sand in bags, stored well aft to simulate a load of gasoline in the big tank behind the pilots and keep the plane from nosing over when it landed light. Chamberlin asked Carisi to hand him the bags, one by one, then headed for Roosevelt Field, where there wasn't any crowd. Circling the field, he dropped the bags one after another.

An alert motorcycle cop thought the flier was dropping messages and began to dash from bag to bag. He finally found one with a manufacturer's "O.K." mark lettered on it and roared back to Curtiss Field to assure the Levines and Jonas that everything was all right. But an ambulance from nearby Mitchel Field and the emergency wagon from Curtiss, filled with fire extinguishers, axes and other ominous accouterments, had rushed out on the field ahead of him, and Mrs. Levine was crying.

Carisi tried to hang out a window and adjust the strut while Chamberlin held him by one leg. But he couldn't make it and the Bellanca continued to circle. Another plane came alongside with LAND AT MITCHEL marked on its side. Chamberlin nodded. The Army field, a mile or so away, was less crowded than either civilian field; and military guards there could control spectators more easily.

So Chamberlin headed for Mitchel while hundreds of spectators at Curtiss jumped into their cars and set out for the same objective. The plane circled the field until the ambulance could return and the Curtiss emergency wagon arrive. By this time both Carisi and Grace Jonas were airsick from the numerous rotations.

Chamberlin told Grace, who was beside him, to take his seat pad and hold it against her face while they landed. And he told Carisi and Eloyse to stand behind the big gas tank. Then he loosened all the windows in the front of the cabin so that if the plane crashed they might be thrown clear. After that he headed into the wind for the critical landing.

As they came in he banked the plane over to the right and made an unorthodox three-point landing: right wheel, tail skid and right wing tip. The dragging wing turned the plane slightly to the right. Then she lost speed and settled on the unsupported left wheel, which came up and cracked the forward wing strut. But the damage wasn't excessive and the plane skidded to a stop without anybody being hurt.

"Chamberlin jumped out, his face wreathed in smiles," the *Times* reported. "And the girls dropped down into his arms and to the ground. 'Thank you very much, Mr. Chamberlin, for the nice ride,' they said to him, holding their hands out. Chamberlin took them and laughed. 'Glad you liked it,' he said. 'Oh, we did and we would like to go again with you some time.'"

The next day a reporter who was interviewing Levine said he supposed that Chamberlin's performance had won him the pilot's seat on the transatlantic flight. "Why should it?" Levine inquired.

Two days after the *Columbia*'s one-wheel landing, Davis and Wooster's biplane crashed. It was on its last test before the planned ocean flight. The Keystone, named the *American Legion* for the organization that was helping to finance the project, took off from Langley Field at Hampton, Virginia. But it couldn't maintain altitude and sank down nose first in a swamp. The two fliers, trapped in the cockpit, were suffocated by fumes and mud.

Like the Fonck machine, the Keystone was overburdened. Fonck couldn't get his 28,000-pound total load into the air. Davis, with about half as much power, got his biplane off the ground but couldn't keep it up. An acquaintance said later that at 17,000 pounds the Keystone's total load was 1,150 pounds too heavy.

The Davis-Wooster tragedy eliminated the last American plane that was capable of taking off for Paris ahead of the *Columbia*. At the beginning of May—which was destined to become one of the most notable months in aviation history—only the French Levasseur biplane of Nungesser and Coli loomed as a rival for the Orteig prize and the glory that would attend a successful nonstop flight across the North Atlantic.

At about this time Floyd Bennett told Balchen more about that northward flight with Byrd the year before.

Balchen was now chief test pilot for Fokker, and also his performance engineer. The Dutchman was turning out scores of planes, and Balchen delivered as well as tested them. After Bennett emerged from the hospital following the Teterboro crash, he wanted to get the feel of airplane controls again. So Balchen engaged him to help fly the machines to their new owners. One delivery took the two men to Chicago.

In the Congress Hotel one night Bennett brought up the North Pole theme himself. "I want to tell you something that has been on

47

my mind a long time," he said. "You know that Byrd and I never got to the North Pole, because you kept track of the plane's performance during the *Josephine Ford* tour. But I'm going to tell you just how far we did get. We were just north of Spitsbergen when the commander discovered that oil leak. He became quite concerned about it and ordered me to fly back to the north coast of Spitsbergen— fifteen or twenty miles away. We flew back and forth for a while and the leak stopped. We discussed the possibility of flying over to East Greenland [which Byrd had said earlier they might do during the northward flight] but he finally ordered me to fly back and forth and this is what we did till he told me to return to Kings Bay. We flew back and forth for fourteen hours."

Bennett didn't volunteer any further information about the flight from Kings Bay. He didn't say Byrd told him to keep quiet about it. He didn't say Byrd told him to support the claim that they had reached the North Pole. He didn't say anything more at all.

3

THE *WHITE BIRD* OF FRANCE

"All Le Bourget will be on hand to greet you. They will give you a great reception, you may be sure." Thus René Fonck to Lloyd Bertaud, presumed co-pilot and navigator of the *Columbia* at the start of the month of May. Fonck's new Sikorsky was nearing completion but it wouldn't be ready before June.

Even though Nungesser and Coli were said to be running through the last of their tests, the *Columbia* was a heavy favorite to win the prize money. She would have favoring winds instead of the headwinds that would hamper the Frenchmen. Only dirigibles had ever attempted to cross the Atlantic nonstop from east to west against the prevailing air streams. And one of them—the *R-34*—had barely made it.

Things like possible engine or airframe failure were forgotten as far as the *Columbia* was concerned. After all, hadn't the plane stayed in the air for more than fifty-one hours? This, at an average speed of 100 miles an hour, would amount to 5,100 miles. And Le Bourget was only 3,600 miles from New York. Why, Chamberlin and Bertaud could touch down at Paris and then go on to Rome, or maybe even Constantinople, without refueling!

So confident were the experts that the Bellanca would reach the goal first that the president of the International League of Aviators planned to meet the machine in mid-ocean. Clifford B. Harmon of New York, who happened to be in Paris, told a reporter for that city's Chicago *Tribune* edition that he would fly westward over the Atlantic, make contact with the *Columbia* and escort her to her destination. On this project, he said, he would use "a fast plane."

"Every American in Paris is planning to be at Le Bourget in anticipation of the successful termination of the Bertaud-Chamberlin attempt," said a dispatch to the *New York Times*. "An hourly and if possible half-hourly bulletin of their progress will be maintained by American newspapers published here so that the American colony and many thousands of tourists will have ample time to reach the Paris airport."

By this time it was assumed that Chamberlin would be one of the pilots, for Acosta had turned his back on the Levine suzerainty. The dramatic drawing at the last minute was not going to be held, after all. It was reported that Acosta had quit because he felt his 210 pounds would add too much weight on an ocean flight. But since he had weighed the same on the endurance test, the explanation seemed inadequate.

Then Levine refused to finance $50,000 life insurance policies for Chamberlin and Bertaud in case they came down in the Atlantic. The two fliers felt that their wives were entitled to protection, but Levine didn't share this view. Numerous nightly conferences were held at the Garden City Hotel, where the ocean fliers were staying, to resolve the situation. These conclaves followed long days at Curtiss Field, where Chamberlin and Bertaud were trying to resolve two other problems—whether to install a radio and whether to drop the landing gear after takeoff.

Both Levine and Bertaud wanted a radio. Each, without the other's knowledge, was trying to sell the story of the flight, and bulletins from the plane would make the account more dramatic. Levine also had another reason. He felt he would be criticized if the two men—unable to call for help—were lost at sea.

The equipment that seemed best for the job could be heard from 125 to 150 miles away. The set weighed ten pounds, and its generator twenty. The generator was powered by a single blade whirling in the stream of air which rushed past the plane in flight. The best place to mount the device seemed to be on one of the Bellanca's wing struts. But when clamped on, it cut three miles an hour from the plane's speed. Worse, it caused the whole strut to vibrate.

Giuseppe Bellanca was frantic. One of his beautiful struts— which braced the wing and added to its lift—was quivering in mortal agony. What's more, the set affected the compasses. And it might develop short circuits, throwing out sparks which could explode gasoline fumes.

Chamberlin didn't want the radio, either. In addition to the weight and other disadvantages, it had a range which would be too short unless they followed the shipping lanes. And Chamberlin proposed to follow the shorter great-circle route, which would take them over Newfoundland and far north of the lanes used by the liners.

The course was another cause of dispute between Chamberlin and Bertaud. The mail flier was holding out for the more southerly route. He conferred with Giles Stedman, navigating officer of the liner *Leviathan,* and with him worked out a route which would take the *Columbia* due east from New York for the first 1,200 miles. This would probably eliminate the risk of wing icing. It would also enable liners to pick up distress calls or relay radio bulletins from the plane. In order for Bertaud to make observations that would keep the *Columbia* on a southerly course, mechanics cut a hole in the top of the fuselage, aft of the main gas tank.

While arguments about the radio raged, mechanics mounted and dismounted the generator several times. Each new mounting made it necessary to compensate for the effect on the compasses, an operation which cost $75. In the end, Bellanca and Chamberlin prevailed and the only radio taken along was a small battery-powered set capable of sending distress calls only twenty-five miles.

Presently Levine, who had been negotiating with the North American Newspaper Alliance for his own and Chamberlin's story, learned that Bertaud was trying to sell his own version of the flight. The navigator had agreed to collaborate with a free-lance writer who unwittingly approached the same news syndicate with which Levine was dickering. A noisy row followed and Levine ordered Bertaud to drop his project.

The tests with the radio wasted several days. Less time-consuming but equally intriguing was what to do about the landing gear. The one on the *Columbia*, somebody figured, slowed the plane by 15 miles an hour. If the fliers could drop it—as Hawker and Grieve had dropped theirs eight years earlier—they might make a successful belly-landing in Europe, for the plane was sturdy and could probably withstand the shock. The idea was to hacksaw through the steel wheel struts near the fuselage and join the pieces together with eyes and cotter pins. Then wires could be led from the pins into the cabin, and when the plane was in the air the pins could be pulled out. With the landing gear in the Atlantic, the *Columbia* would speed along appreciably faster.

Bertaud and Chamberlin had been running numerous tests and figured that this speed might exceed 140 miles an hour. With a new engine, installed after the endurance effort, and a new brand of gasoline, they had attained a top speed of 127 miles an hour with the undercarriage still affixed to the fuselage. They discussed the matter for several days. Finally they decided to drop the plan to jettison the gear.

Levine dashed up to the hangar almost every morning in one of his three expensive cars. Often he was accompanied by Mabel Boll, a mysterious brunette who added a piquant note to the situation. Mabel's status was somewhat anomalous. She was said to be a

Rochester heiress who wanted to be carried across the Atlantic. Stylishly dressed, she appeared morning after morning, sporting enormous specimens of the gem that later came to be known as a girl's best friend. Some reporters doubted the authenticity of these sparklers. They seemed to be larger than the Kohinoor. Nevertheless, the press labeled Mabel "the Queen of Diamonds."

It seemed to some reporters who were watching the *Columbia* hangar in those days that a dispatch from Moscow provided an appropriate commentary on the whole undertaking. This news item, which appeared in early May, concerned Ivan Federov, a mechanic who belonged to the "All Inventors' Vegetarian Club of Interplanetary Cosmopolitans," an organization of several thousand members who were using a new language based on five vowels and five mathematical signs. Federov had told correspondents that he would fly to the moon in September in a rocket thirty meters long, a vehicle he described as half airplane and half giant projectile. He would be accompanied by Max Vallier, who was depicted as a "German moon fan," and the three most suitable of seventy-five persons who had volunteered for the flight.

Federov estimated that the voyage to the moon would take fifteen hours. On the first trip the men would use respirators and stay on the moon for two days. On the second trip they would take along an apparatus that would process gases obtained from the bottom of lunar craters to make them breathable. The visitors also would build a terminal for a future line of aerobuses to shuttle between the earth and its satellite. At a time when flying the Atlantic was just barely possible, a scheme to put men on the moon seemed harebrained, but not much more so than some of the goings-on around that superb Bellanca plane, which could have flown to Europe months before it did.

While Federov dreamed of the moon, Nungesser and Coli went methodically ahead with their preparations for a westward flight. Soon they had completed all the necessary tests. Early in May reports from Paris said they were waiting only because of the weather, which continued to be unfavorable.

Nungesser, who had shot down forty-five German planes in World War I, became increasingly impatient. He appeared to be nervous and irritated when interviewed between trial flights with a newly installed engine. "Every place I go all I hear is 'Are you ready?' 'Are you going?' 'Will you make it?' " he complained to a *New York Times* correspondent. "I really don't know when I shall leave but what I do know is that all this talk has created an atmosphere of nervousness which is not at all helpful. Now, one does not fly across the Atlantic in the same manner in which these countless questions are asked.

"I am aware," the French ace continued, "that each night in well-known Paris bars numerous aviators successfully cross the Atlantic between cocktails. But so far as I am concerned I have been carefully preparing for three years and do not intend to take off until I am certain of my plane and as certain of the weather as it is physically possible to be."

The *White Bird*, as the French plane was called, seemed well designed for her task. Her total weight of 10,000 pounds was little more than half that of the biplane of Davis and Wooster, but the 450-horsepower Lorraine-Dietrich engine had two thirds of the energy the ill-fated Keystone's three Whirlwinds had churned out. The gas tanks were ahead of the two open cockpits and wouldn't crush the fliers in the event of a crack-up. And when the tanks were nearly empty—as they would be near the American coast—the *White Bird* would float if forced down at sea by engine failure and be able to alight gently. There would be no cause to worry, Nungesser told his friends, if they were not heard from for three days, for they'd probable be drifting in the ocean. They wouldn't be able to communicate with anybody because they wouldn't have a radio. It would add too much weight, and anyway, it probably wouldn't be needed.

Shortly after leaving Paris, the *White Bird* would drop her landing gear to reduce head resistance and increase her speed. Nungesser proposed to end the flight in the water off the Battery. Grover Whalen and his reception committee for distinguished guests made arrangements to dress up their official welcome boat, the *Macom,* and assigned mooring places for yachts and other craft along a line extending south from the Statue of Liberty. Several fast motorboats would stand ready to speed to the floating *White Bird,* pick up her crew and bear them away to a triumphal dinner. They probably would be hungry, for their diet on the flight would consist largely of bananas, caviar and a French food product called Kola, which was said to be noted for its stimulating and sustaining qualities.

The romantic aura around the French project was enhanced by the presence of none other than Cupid on the wings of the *White Bird.* It seemed that the successful completion of the flight would reunite Nungesser and his former wife. A dispatch from Paris revealed that in 1923 Nungesser had married Miss Consuelo Hatmaker of New York, but that her parents objected to his plan to fly the Atlantic and had insisted on a divorce. However, his ex-wife still loved him and had been his "constant companion" on the flying field when he was testing the *White Bird.* "It is believed by their intimate friends," said the dispatch, "that a reconciliation will be effected." All that had to be done was for Nungesser to make the trip safely.

The seeming imminence of the French effort did not appear to alarm the *Columbia* crew members, who continued to putter around their plane. Both Chamberlin and Bertaud declared they would not allow undue haste to abridge their preparations, and their disputes with each other and with Levine continued. On May 8 they received a shock. Shortly after five o'clock that morning, Nungesser and Coli had taken off. The French meteorological service had assured them that the outlook was fair for the first 1,200 miles, though the lack of late reports from Greenland made it impossible to provide forecasts for the western Atlantic.

Weather Bureau officials in New York were astounded that the Frenchmen had started. Off Newfoundland, they said, there were strong headwinds and storms. But soon after takeoff the *White Bird* was reported over Ireland and New York made ready for a boisterous welcome. The *Macom* was decked out in bright varicolored flags, and the French line arranged for a tug to take officials, reporters and photographers down the bay. At Mitchel Field it was announced that five Army observation planes would roar out to greet the Frenchmen. And Richard Sinclair, a wealthy real estate operator, hired the grand ballroom of the Hotel Astor for a great reception on the following Friday, four days after the fliers were scheduled to splash down off the Battery.

Before the French plane could possibly have neared Newfoundland, reports of sightings began to flash in, both from ships and from people on shore. Inexperienced correspondents of news agencies sent all the rumors along without bothering to check them. And they multiplied like noxious microbes.

There were several other planes on routine flights along the coast that Monday and seemingly all of them were mistaken for the *White Bird*. Some of them undoubtedly were privately owned machines which, as the reports came in from farther north, took off from Portland, Boston and other cities to escort the Frenchmen to New York. That is, they took off until thick weather curtailed most flying.

At Curtiss Field that afternoon the successive reports from coastal cities made it seem certain that the French plane would soon roar over New York. Bellanca, always generous, said that the Frenchmen's triumph meant that the *Columbia*'s flight would be canceled. "I am glad and proud they have succeeded," he added. "Of course I would have liked to have had our plane to be the first, but they deserve to win and I'm glad they did."

Chamberlin also expressed admiration for his two rivals. "I'm glad they're safe," he said. And Bertaud, whose forebears came from

France, exclaimed, "You've got to hand it to those Frenchmen. They're real men and fliers."

In New York harbor the gaily beflagged *Macom* steamed around in circles with Mr. Whalen and members of his committee. The French Line tug took officials and newsmen down the bay. Off the Statue of Liberty numerous yachts, also beflagged for the happy occasion, swung at their moorings while owners and guests scanned the skies with binoculars and gingerly sipped bootleg booze.

But the *White Bird* didn't appear. And the Weather Bureau atop the Whitehall Building reported that if Nungesser and Coli had reached the vicinity of Newfoundland they would have encountered rain squalls and light snow. The next morning the New York papers said that after a day of watching and rumors, the fate of the French fliers remained unknown.

In the meantime Paris went wild with joy. The Monday evening papers had taken the early reports at face value and told in big black headlines of the fliers' safe arrival. A special evening edition of one journal featured a detailed description of the New York celebration. All the ships in the harbor, it declared, had sounded their whistles or sirens, and French and American flags had appeared on all the city's buildings.

Nungesser had set the *White Bird* gently down on the water, said this enterprising daily, without the slightest difficulty. The two airmen had hugged each other and then stepped into a fast motorboat which heaved alongside and took them ashore to wildly cheering crowds. The paper even quoted the well-chosen words which Nungesser had spoken to the Americans. It was an exciting tale, and and so were other fakes that sold French newspapers on that historic day.

The same papers carried the words of the fliers' mothers when they learned the good news. "Luck has always been with my son," Mme. Nungesser said happily. And Mme. Coli, in Marseilles, told newsmen, "I knew my son would make it because he told me he would. He's been in many tight spots in his career and always he has come out safely."

In theaters and movie houses photographs of the fliers were flashed on the screens. Audiences stood up and cheered and wept. And because neither the announcements nor the successive editions could get the great news out fast enough, crowds gathered outside the newspaper offices, avidly reading bulletin after bulletin on Nungesser and Coli.

A crowd also swirled around the building containing the offices of the Paris edition of the New York *Herald Tribune,* demanding to know why that paper was not reporting the wonderful event. Angry voices accused the Americans of deliberately withholding the news merely to belittle a great French achievement. It looked for a while as though the mob would rush the place. Finally Albert Jaurette, the distinguished-looking advertising manager of the paper, addressed the crowd from an upper story. Speaking in French and shaking an admonitory white-thatched head, he managed to persuade his compatriots to disperse peacefully.

Eventually the French press had to admit that confirmation of the brilliant feat was lacking. Then some Frenchmen damned the Americans again—this time for sending false reports of the safe arrival. Others charged that the United States Weather Bureau had lured the two fliers to their deaths by announcing that the weather in the western Atlantic was good, whereas in reality it was bad. The immediate result of the Nungesser-Coli flight was hardly the international good will which aviation was supposed to promote.

The French were somewhat mollified by the energetic search which Americans made for the lost ones. The government alerted all ships approaching the coast to be on watch for the *White Bird* and dispatched three Coast Guard destroyers, four cutters, two tugs and the dirigible *Los Angeles*—the former ZR-3 from Germany— to search the sea north of Boston. Several fliers took off in private planes to look for the men, and Rodman Wanamaker offered a $25,000 reward for their discovery. It was the same amount of money they had been trying to win when they headed out across the Atlantic.

Hope for the men died hard, for reports that the *White Bird* had been seen or heard continued to pour in. In Newfoundland three people swore they had seen the plane pass overhead on Monday, May 9. Several Labrador trappers said they had heard a crash in the woods as if a plane had fallen. In Lynn, Massachusetts, the skipper of a rum runner which had been waiting for a shipment south of Nova Scotia on the critical Monday said he had seen a large plane. The reporter who sent this message tactfully withheld the names of both the skipper and his boat.

None of the reports stood up under the most cursory investigation. One of the Newfoundland eyewitnesses proved to be a woman of seventy who had never before seen an airplane. But on Monday, she said, she had seen not one but two *White Bird*'s. She had wondered why they made so much noise.

Some people were undoubtedly deceived by Canadian or American planes, others by their own imagination. They wanted to believe that the *White Bird* was passing overhead, and it seemed to them that she was.

The fliers' mothers, pathetic victims of the false reports, continued to hope. Mme. Nungesser, informed that the first happy news was not true, recalled her son's career as a French ace. "Look at the miraculous escapes he had during the war," she told a reporter. "If he has not succeeded in getting to New York, I am certain that he and Captain Coli will be picked up safe and sound somewhere in the Atlantic. Perhaps they were forced to come down in an isolated part of Canada or the United States. I shall pray all night, and in the morning I know I shall have good news."

She didn't. In fact, there was no news of the first men ever to

59

attempt a nonstop flight across the Atlantic from Europe to North America in an airplane. Perhaps after all the years that have passed since that sad Monday somebody will still find a rusty engine and a couple of skeletons in the wilderness. Until that happens no one will know the fate of the *White Bird*.

4

When it was certain, on May 10, that the *White Bird* had run out of fuel and was down somewhere, Levine overruled Bellanca and announced that the *Columbia* would start for Paris the next morning. The weather outlook for flights from west to east was good and the plane was ready, down to her earth inductor compass. Last-minute adjustments had been made to this tricky device by Maurice Titterington and Brice Goldsborough, both of the Pioneer Instrument Company, the manufacturer. Goldsborough, a flier and navigator who was liked by everybody on the field, was later to take off for Europe in one of the efforts that followed Lindbergh's triumph.

The heart of the earth inductor compass was a dynamo driven by the air stream outside the plane. It was mounted as far from metal as possible—usually atop the fuselage—and was connected to an indicator on the instrument board. Theoretically it enabled a pilot to set his course at any angle to the earth's north-south magnetic field which he desired, and when functioning properly, it did not swing and jiggle with the motions and vibrations of the plane. It had just been introduced, however, and had not been perfected. Moreover, the earth's magnetic field is so weak that the device often failed to operate satisfactorily on long flights.

The wives of Chamberlin and Bertaud were going to make sandwiches for their husbands. Takeoff time was set for 1 A.M. This, it was said, would enable the fliers to reach Le Bourget in daylight. Everything seemed favorable for a successful flight.

But everything wasn't favorable. The old row about the insurance was still going on. Levine didn't want to pay for it, and that was that. What's more, he had some new ideas about the whole enterprise which he had incorporated in a new contract. He brought it around to the hangar the night the airmen were making final preparations for a morning takeoff.

Under the terms of this remarkable document, Levine would become the fliers' "manager" for the twelve months following a successful flight. He would arrange all vaudeville, motion picture, lecture, literary, testimonial and other agreements in which the two men would be involved. He would pay each of them $150 a week and would split the money from the Orteig and Brooklyn Chamber of Commerce prizes and from gasoline, oil and accessory manufacturers, taking half of it himself and giving each of them one-fourth. If their earnings exceeded by a large margin the weekly $150 they were receiving, Levine would award them such "bonuses" as he considered appropriate. No mention was made of the main cause of dissension—insurance protection for the fliers' wives.

"You can sign it or not," said Levine. "But if you don't sign you don't fly." They talked it over briefly. Levine undoubtedly could keep them on the ground. Maybe they could insist later that the provisions be changed. They signed. But the weather turned nasty and they couldn't take off, after all.

Chamberlin revealed later that Levine wasn't enthusiastic about the looks of the man who had saved his little girl by his one-wheel landing. He said Chamberlin wasn't a "movie type" and wouldn't film well after the transatlantic flight. And the flier from Denison, Iowa, did look more like a farmer or a store clerk than a man who for years had made a precarious living by stunt flying. Chamberlin was indeed a clerk for a time, when he worked in his father's jewelry store, and he could have had a half interest in it.

But he liked stunt flying and rebuilding old planes better than fixing watches and selling rings.

Bertaud, grounded by the weather, had time to get mad. The more he thought about that contract the madder he got. He didn't feel any better about it when Levine told reporters that every cent of the prize money would go to the brave pilots in his employ. Bertaud engaged a lawyer to protect his interests and the story got into the newspapers, further embittering his relations with the backer. In the meantime Bellanca scotched Levine's plan to ditch Chamberlin by insisting that the man he had known for years go along.

While the biting and backbiting continued, Lindbergh got his plane built, tested it for a week and flew from San Diego to St. Louis. He completed the 1,500-mile journey in 14 hours and 5 minutes, an average of about 107 miles an hour and a speed record for the run. The next day he completed the 950 miles from St. Louis to Roosevelt Field at an average of 120 miles an hour.

The same day, May 12, Bernt Balchen ferried the rebuilt Byrd plane from the Hasbrouck Heights factory to Roosevelt Field and taxied it up to the main hangar. Above the door, big white letters announced that the shed belonged, at least temporarily, to THE AMERICA TRANS-OCEANIC CO., INC. Above the sign flew the Stars and Stripes.

The arrival of the Lindbergh and Byrd planes on the same day stirred even the ordinarily staid *New York Times* to excitement. "What promises to be the most spectacular race ever held—3,600 miles over the open sea to Paris—may start tomorrow," it proclaimed. "Three transatlantic planes are on Curtiss and Roosevelt fields, within a short distance of each other, ready to take the air.

"Yesterday was a hectic day at Curtiss Field, with the secret work being done on the Bellanca and men scanning the sky for the appearance of Byrd's and Lindbergh's planes. The air was tense with expectancy, and there was no letdown as night came on. In all three hangars workmen were busy and it seemed to be anybody's race between Lindbergh and Chamberlin, although Lindbergh said he did not believe he could get away for a day or two."

The following morning the *Times* announced that bad weather had delayed all the fliers but that Byrd's plane had made its final tests. "Now it is anybody's race," the newspaper continued, "and the possibilities are that Commander Byrd will be ready as soon as the weather clears up. By that time his broken wrist will be out of its splints and he will have chosen his pilot. As the Fokker, with its three motors, is fully as fast as the other two ships when loaded and Byrd is one of the most skillful navigators in the world as he proved on his North Pole flight, he may be able to get away and cut corners on the way to Paris so effectively that he may outdistance the others. And Byrd is one of the most dashing men when in action who ever flew a ship on a dangerous course."

Despite its obvious predilection for Byrd, the *Times* was also enthusiastic about the young National Guard captain. "Yesterday all the thousands of people who crowded Curtiss Field, where the Bellanca plane and Lindbergh's silver monoplane were being over-hauled, were hoping that the tall, handsome blond youngster from the Middle West would get away first and stay in front. Lindbergh has won the hearts of New Yorkers by his bashful smile, his indomitable pluck and his impetuous flight here from the Pacific. Everyone half expected yesterday to see him wheel his plane out on the field, fill her up and take off munching a sandwich."

But even with two dangerous rivals on the scene, and the press screaming about them, the *Columbia* group continued to squabble. Presently Bertaud got some financial backing and offered to buy the plane. But Levine refused to part with the machine.

Despite the headlines he didn't appear to believe that there was any great urgency to take off, now that the Frenchmen no longer constituted a threat. The Byrd plane probably wouldn't be ready to go for weeks, and besides, it wasn't entered for the Orteig prize. As for the young man from St. Louis—well, Levine and many others, including some reporters, didn't take him too seriously. Lindbergh certainly wasn't the flier Chamberlin was—they thought—and his plane wasn't as good as the Bellanca. He couldn't even see ahead without sticking his head out the window or pushing out that ridiculous little horizontal periscope. And as for his plan to fly alone —why, he'd fall asleep over the ocean and that would be that.

There were millions who did not share this view. And thousands of them came to Curtiss Field to see the handsome young man from the Midwest. As he walked across the field, women closed in on him from all directions. One middle-aged matron rushed up and put her hand on his jacket. "I touched him! I touched him!" she cried.

Other people tried to put their hands on the plane. One man asked a guard at the hangar to let him past the rope that stretched across the entrance. "Just let me touch his plane," he pleaded. "Why?" the guard asked. "Just for luck," the visitor said. He had been reading about "Lucky Lindy" and apparently felt that some of the luck would rub off.

Crank letters poured in to the flier, as well as requests from many people who wanted to go along as passengers. One girl wrote that she was "not bad" to look at and sent her photograph to prove it. An amateur navigational authority advised Lindbergh to change his course often, as he said birds do, and sometimes to fly in a circle.

Some of the reporters and practically all the photographers irritated the flier. The tabloid journalists badgered him with questions like "Have you got a sweetheart?" and "How do you feel about girls?" And their editors annoyed him with headlines referring to him as a Flyin' Fool. Apparently he didn't understand that "Flyin' Fool" meant that he was a fool for flying, i.e., a master hand.

Some of the photographers enraged him. Two of them broke into his bedroom at the Garden City Hotel and told him they had come to get pictures of "Lindy" shaving and sitting on the bed in his pajamas (they didn't get them). And once when he was coming in from a practice flight, a couple of cameramen got in his way so that he had to swerve sharply on landing, a maneuver that damaged his tail skid. The part was quickly repaired but the incident could have been serious.

For several days weather forecasts for ocean flights were unfavorable. The condition that was needed, the new breed of transatlantic air experts said wisely, was a high-pressure area over Newfoundland. Then winds and storms wouldn't rush in and foul up the atmosphere, as they delighted to do when low-pressure areas prevailed.

But the bad weather didn't stop the flow of statements from the Bellanca and Byrd hangars. At the former it was announced that the *Columbia* would carry two homing pigeons. One of them would be released 500 miles out as a sign that all was going well. The other would be freed only in the event of trouble. It might thus become a hero bird that would be worth thousands of dollars.

At the Byrd hangar it was announced that the Fokker—soon to be christened the *America*—had completed two more load tests in addition to those final trials already reported. Her total weight at takeoff would be 15,000 pounds. So far it hadn't reached this figure but soon, no doubt, it would. "Not a minute will be lost," said Commander Byrd on May 15. "We'll wind up these final tests in the morning and then we'll be set." It wasn't the first such announcement, nor was it the last. Bulletins were issued intermittently until the plane started for France on June 29.

As the weather outlook continued to be bad, Lindbergh took a day off to fly the Wright company's experimental biplane to Hasbrouck Heights to inspect the Fokker factory. He didn't intend to make any further tests or even any further announcements. He'd be ready to go as soon as he got word from Dr. James H. Kimball, who served tirelessly as chief weatherman for all the ocean fliers in the New York area.

Chamberlin and Bertaud didn't make any tests, either. They were now spending hours in daily and nightly conferences with their lawyers and with Levine and Bellanca. The Italian designer was trying, as a reasonable and trusted friend of both airmen, to act as peacemaker. The trouble was that Levine, who was neither reasonable nor trustworthy, controlled the plane.

By this time Balchen and Acosta, who had joined the Byrd enterprise, had run off more tests on the Fokker and it now appeared ready to move out across the Atlantic. But neither Byrd nor his backer, Wanamaker, seemed to be in any hurry. Indeed, there were banquets at the Garden City Hotel, with distinguished guests on hand, on several occasions. And while news stories about the plane and its backer seldom mentioned the department store as a Wanamaker property, the publicity certainly wasn't hurting sales.

The big hangar had been decorated with colorful chintz curtains in the windows, and red, white and blue bunting all around. When press conferences and other functions were held there instead of at the hotel, the plane was poised outside, sometimes on a sloping ramp with wooden planking for its wheels and the greased tail-skid slide which Fokker had devised to give the machine an initial impetus equivalent to 500 feet of additional runway. The ingenious designer's plan was to rope the tail skid to a stake, hold the plane stationary until the engines were roaring at full throttle, and then chop through the rope with an ax.

Fokker often drove over from the New Jersey plant just across the Hudson to see how the tests were coming along. He had a low-slung Lancia sports car with shock absorbers like those on an airplane. With this speedy machine he could roar over the hummocks on Roosevelt Field as if they didn't exist, the wheels bouncing up and down but the body remaining level. The car had a big bulb horn, which Fokker liked to honk loudly.

A small, dynamic man whose apple-red cheeks and bright, sharp eyes made him look somewhat like a goblin, Fokker loved Balchen and detested Byrd. He had been angry at the commander ever since the April 16 crash, when the plane was nose-heavy. His wrath had been swelling a bit more every time Byrd failed to take off in what Fokker considered perfectly suitable weather.

Balchen writes in his fascinating book *Come North With Me* that Uncle Tony (as he called Fokker) again considered the weather suitable on May 17. "If we don't get going soon," he quotes Fokker as fuming, "I myself will buy the plane and fly it over the ocean, by Gott! Look at that sky! Just a little mist only. Any fool could fly it blindfold with both eyes shut!"

That same afternoon, Balchen relates, he and Acosta went up to recheck the plane's rate of climb. Uncle Tony came along. The clouds threatened to close in as they got higher, but Balchen thought nothing of it. He was an experienced instrument flier, like Lindbergh, and could keep a plane level and on course by looking at the dials in the cockpit and acting on their readings.

He and most other people around Roosevelt Field thought Acosta could do this too. The man who had succeeded Bennett as Byrd's number-one pilot had been flying for years and was the best-known plane aerial acrobat in the East. Big, handsome and jovial, he sported a close-cropped black mustache and wore his sleek hair parted down the middle. His Latin allure and his low "come-hither" voice wrought havoc among the fair. In the movies he might have been another Valentino.

As they flew over Long Island, with Balchen at the controls, Fokker directed the Norwegian to take the plane into a cloud and keep it level. Once in the cloud, the designer told Acosta to take over. Soon after, Balchen felt himself forced down into his seat. The plane was banking sharply. Fokker was shouting at Acosta, "Keep your eyes on the instruments!" Acosta shouted right back, "They don't mean anything to me."

Balchen glanced at the bank-and-turn indicator; the needle was all the way over on one side. He reached quickly for the wheel and Acosta surrendered the helm gladly. "You don't know anything about instrument flying, do you?" Fokker demanded. "No, and I don't believe in it," Acosta replied. "I'm strictly a fair-weather boy. If there's any thick stuff, I stay on the ground."

When they got down, Balchen writes, Uncle Tony was very quiet —until he maneuvered the Norwegian into a secluded corner of the hangar. Then he exploded in staccato German, a language Balchen understood well. It was now clear to him why the flight had been delayed so long. With Acosta as pilot, the Fokker would have to have perfect weather all the way across the ocean.

The little Dutchman kept stabbing Balchen's barrel chest with a fierce finger. There was only one thing to do, he yelled. "You, Bernt, must go along in the crew to handle instrument flying and bad weather or all summer the plane will still be waiting here and I am the laughing stock of the whole United States!"

Balchen pointed out that he was a Norwegian citizen and that Wanamaker would only sponsor an all-American crew. "Poof! That's nothing," said Fokker. "Go out and take your first papers." Then he went after Byrd.

"I've just made a flight with Acosta," he told the commander. "He doesn't know anything about instrument flying. If you're going to make this flight and come through alive, I offer you Balchen. If you don't take him I'll buy the plane and fly it with him myself."

Byrd said he would take the Norwegian on the flight.

That night Balchen, who had a cot in the hangar, lay awake for hours. He realized that he loved America and that its ideals were the same as those of Norway. Would he be unfaithful to the land of the fjords if he became a citizen of America?

He was still uncertain about what to do when he walked into the Bureau of Naturalization in New York the next morning. There a girl smiled at his heavy Norwegian accent. "My mother comes from Oslo," she told the impressive stranger. "You want to be a citizen of this country, too?" Balchen picked up the Declaration of Intention form. "You bet!" he said.

The same day Fokker and Balchen got the bad news about

Acosta, General M. V. C. M. Duval, aviation expert of *Le Figaro,*
sounded the first of what was to become a chorus of sour notes about
ocean flying. Pointing out that in the past two weeks three fliers
had apparently been lost trying to cross the South Atlantic and that
Nungesser and Coli had no doubt perished in the North Atlantic,
the general declared that ocean flights were no good for sport, nor
did they serve to promote aviation. The airplane as then developed,
he said, was not efficient enough to justify further transatlantic
attempts.

He added a thought that sometimes occurs to those who watch
the throngs at international airplane, auto and motorboat races.
"That the crowds of two countries should be passionately roused to
a fever of excitement by the possibility of the airman's succeeding
and living or failing and dying is both immoral and shameful."

That day Bertaud made Levine a public offer. He was ready, he
said, to forgo any part of the prize money. The mail flier explained
that his greatest desire was to make the transatlantic trip and that
he was willing to have his share go to the families of Davis and
Wooster. The announcement reflected his fear that Levine was
planning to ease him out.

Levine didn't reply, and the following day Bertaud obtained
a temporary injunction restraining the backer from supplanting him
as pilot and navigator. Service was held in abeyance so that Bellanca
could make another effort to persuade his partner to let Bertaud
stay on. And that evening not only Bellanca but Bertaud and Frank
Tichenor, publisher of the magazine *Aero Digest,* also conferred
with Levine at the latter's house in Belle Harbor, Long Island. A
white-painted frame dwelling of about eight rooms, it hardly qualified as a millionaire's mansion and caused some reporters to wonder
just how much money Levine had.

The four men talked most of the night. When Bellanca, Bertaud
and Tichenor returned to the Garden City Hotel at three in the
morning and announced that everything had been settled satis-

factorily, the morning-newspaper reporters rushed to telephones. Reporters for afternoon newspapers didn't have to hurry, and later one of them decided to call Levine at home and ask him for his version of the settlement.

"Well, Mr. Levine, I hear you buttoned things up at that conference you had last night," the journalist said. There was a short pause. "What conference?" Levine inquired.

Later on he declared that he had fired Bertaud three days earlier and that the navigator was apparently trying to get back into his good graces. He added that he still expected the *Columbia* to take off as soon as weather permitted. Also, that he had a new co-pilot. When asked who the man was, Levine turned secretive again. "He is known only to three persons," he said. "The three are the man himself, Chamberlin and me."

There were rumors that Balchen might step into the cockpit in place of Bertaud. They were persistent but nothing came of them. Not until years later did the Norwegian reveal that Chamberlin had invited him to be co-pilot and navigator of the *Columbia,* offering to split the Orteig prize with him. Balchen refused because he was still chief pilot for Fokker, a rival of Bellanca, and also felt an obligation to Byrd.

The day the offer was made, a Thursday, the *Columbia* stayed in her hangar while rain drummed on the roof. There wasn't much doing at the Lindbergh hangar, either. With that high-pressure area still absent, Lindbergh had gone with some friends to meet one of his backers who was arriving from St. Louis. Thereafter they visited the Wright engine factory in Paterson, New Jersey, and in the evening they planned to see the musical *Rio Rita* and meet some of the stars backstage.

At the Byrd hangar things were more active. The big plane was to be christened on Saturday and two thousand people had been invited to the ceremony. A speaker's platform had been erected outside and workmen were putting up more patriotic bunting inside.

Byrd had already stocked the plane with enough pemmican and other concentrated food to last four men for three weeks, and six gallons of distilled water per man were to be put in later. Some reporters wondered why he had stored a foul-tasting substance like pemmican. Cynics among them replied that it made for more publicity than baked beans.

The rain continued all day. In the evening, returning from Paterson, one of Lindbergh's friends called up Dr. Kimball for a late report. The man atop the Whitehall Building said that while rain and mist hid the stars over New York, the weather over the ocean was clearing. Lindbergh decided to take off in the morning.

Before daylight on May 20 the rain had become a gloomy drizzle. A truck towed the Ryan, tail first, to the west end of the 6,100-foot grass-and-dirt runway at Roosevelt Field, which Wanamaker had leased for the Fokker but which he had invited the other ocean fliers to use. Mechanics poured gasoline from 5-gallon cans into the wing and fuselage tanks until they topped off an overload that seemed to make the wheel struts bow out. The little silver-colored monoplane now weighed 5,000 pounds, more than half of it gasoline. She was heavier by half a ton than she had ever been before.

News of the impending takeoff got around and a small crowd collected at the field. Byrd, Acosta, Noville and Chamberlin turned up to wish their young rival well. Police cleared photographers off the soggy turf runway. Lindbergh got into his plane. He revved up the Whirlwind and the machine started to move.

To those of us who watched the *Spirit of St. Louis* that dismal morning it seemed that she was staggering hopelessly under her load. She got under way so slowly that some of us felt she never would attain takeoff speed. Gradually the roll quickened—but not nearly enough to lift her off the rain-drenched field.

Now she was going faster. She lurched past the halfway mark of 3,000 feet and then struggled a few inches into the air—only to squash down again. A few hundred feet farther on she rose briefly again—and again squashed down.

Beyond the end of the runway, to the east, stretched a net of telephone wires. Would they catch the poor overladen bird and hurl her to the ground? Once more she struggled up with her terrible load. This time she got into the air. She cleared the wires by about ten feet and kept going straight ahead toward Paris.

5

Lindbergh's takeoff caught many reporters by surprise. One of those most embarrassingly caught was Charlie Murphy, a leading member of a team of four *Evening Post* reporters. Thinking that nothing was going to happen at the field for several days, Charlie had gone to Larchmont on Thursday to call on the girl he later married. On Friday morning he made the mistake of telephoning the office. He got the city editor. "This is Murphy," he began.

The editor seemed excited. "Just a second. I'll give you a rewrite man!"

"I haven't got anything," Charlie said. "What's up?"

The editor's voice turned harsh. "Lindbergh's just taken off."

"Oh my God!" said Charlie.

There was some talk of Charlie's being fired, but his colleagues had given the paper good coverage and within a day or so he was writing lead stories again. The slip certainly didn't blight his career. Later he became a star reporter for the *Morning World,* thereafter went to Antarctica with the second Byrd expedition, and still later became an editor of *Fortune* and *Life* magazines.

Lindbergh's sudden departure was also a surprise—and a heavy blow—to his rivals on the two fields, especially to the *Columbia* group. Their only hope was that the young man from St. Louis would turn back. And indeed, for a short time after the Ryan labored into the air, there seemed to be a chance that he would come back because at Curtiss Field we began to get reports of bad weather over Newfoundland.

These reports, which later proved false, impelled us to interrogate Chamberlin. "I feel very sorry for the boy," he told us. "I think he will turn back—as he should turn back. If he's running into bad weather it's the only sensible thing to do."

In the afternoon Levine came up with another announcement. The *Columbia*, he declared, would take off at dawn. He said he had engaged an "expert naval aviator" to accompany Chamberlin, but he wouldn't reveal the man's name.

Nothing came of the contemplated dawn takeoff. At one-thirty Saturday morning Chamberlin got word that there were headwinds all the way to Newfoundland.

Some hours later Giuseppe Bellanca decided he had had enough of Levine and announced his resignation from the company. After recalling his efforts to settle the controversy between Levine and Bertaud, Bellanca added, "I was helped in my efforts by many friends, including the American press, but I found the obstacles too great to surmount. All this convinced me that two characters such as Mr. Levine and myself could not continue together in the same enterprise." He ended his statement with an eloquent tribute to Lindbergh.

Meanwhile Bertaud's injunction had been dismissed, and Levine had concluded an agreement with Chamberlin which none of the reporters knew about at the time. As the pilot reveals in his book, Levine had offered to pay him $25,000 and put up $50,000 insurance on his life if he would take the backer along instead of a co-pilot or navigator. In addition, Levine had promised to pay Chamberlin $150 a week for a year and to give him half the money accruing from any source as a result of the flight.

On Saturday afternoon Levine ordered the *Columbia* dragged over to Roosevelt Field and filled with gas, announcing for the second time in twenty-four hours that the plane was going to start for Europe. A Colonial Air Transport pilot appeared at the field with Chamberlin, starting rumors that he was to be the co-pilot.

As was usual with any Levine aeronautical effort, things began to go wrong right away. First, Chamberlin couldn't find Carl Schory, chairman of the National Aeronautical Association's contest committee, who was needed to install a sealed barograph, or self-registering barometer, to keep an official record of the flight. Then the Nassau County Police refused to let him use the Roosevelt Field runway without the permission of Grover Whalen. Chamberlin couldn't find Whalen, who later explained that the *Spirit of St. Louis* and the *Columbia* groups were authorized to use the field only after having given sufficient notice to enable the police to rope off dangerous areas and keep spectators off the runway. There were still people at the east end of the field, where several thousand had attended the christening of the Byrd plane.

That ceremony had been about as elaborate as Byrd and Whalen, who reveled in such events, could make it. It brought Governor Harry Flood Byrd of Virginia, brother of the commander, to the flag-draped speaker's stand and opened with a flag-raising ceremony conducted to the music of a military band. As the brass gave out with "The Star-Spangled Banner," Mr. Wanamaker hoisted a successor to that famous emblem above the roof of the bunting-bedecked hangar. Then the band broke into the stirring strains of the "Marseillaise," as Pierre Mory, the French vice consul, hauled the Tricolor aloft.

Thereafter Mr. Whalen asked the assemblage to remain silent for a few moments while a squad of soldiers from Fort Totten fired a salute in honor of Nungesser and Coli. And then to the front of the platform stepped Mrs. Gurnee Munn and Mrs. Ector Munn, daughters of Rodman Wanamaker and granddaughters of the great John Wanamaker, founder of the famous department store.

There would have been ample reason, it was indicated, to select the Mesdames Munn for the part they were playing in the christening solely because their arteries throbbed with Wanamaker blood. But there was another circumstance which made their participation even more appropriate. Mrs. Ector Munn had been born in America, but Mrs. Gurnee Munn had been born in France, whither the plane about to be christened *America* was bound.

In those days Prohibition, which made it impossible to use champagne, hampered many a christening ceremony in this country. But Whalen—or Byrd—had surmounted this obstacle in brilliant fashion. Each Mrs. Munn wielded a bottle that contained water; yes—but what water! It came from the Delaware River, taken from the very spot where George Washington had crossed it a century and a half earlier. It was conceivable, though perhaps unlikely, that it was the very same water that had supported Washington's boat, for the historic 1776 fluid could have flowed down to the sea, been transmogrified into vapor, circled the world a few hundred times and returned to the Delaware as rain at just the right time and in just the right place to be bottled for the christening ceremony.

The Mesdames Munn broke their bottles over the Fokker's middle propeller without scattering glass into anybody's eyes. "I christen thee *America!*" they chorused. Thereafter came another dramatic display. As Commander Byrd prepared to speak, three New York National Guard biplanes from Miller Field, Staten Island, roared overhead, dropping hundreds of tiny silk American flags.

The great transocean plane had been officially christened. Soon she would soar over the Atlantic, to advance aeronautical science and promote friendship between great nations. As Byrd spread his notes on the lectern, somebody rushed up and handed him a slip of paper. He read it and raised a hand.

"Ladies and gentlemen," he said. "Charles Lindbergh has landed at Le Bourget at ten twenty-two Paris time."

At the other end of the field the chunky Bellanca plane looked like a yellow butterfly in the deepening dusk. Everybody knew about Lindbergh now, and a happy crowd had formed around the plane to see what the crew intended to do. John Carisi and the other mechanics thought that this time she was really going. They fussed around her, getting ready to empty more 5-gallon cans into her thirsty tanks.

Chamberlin came up and learned from newspapermen that Bellanca had resigned from the company. Levine didn't appear. He already knew about Bellanca's action and was suffering from what might be called well-deserved shock. But he sent somebody to the field, and presently his emissary arrived. "Mr. Levine says the flight's off," he said. "Take her back to the hangar."

Carisi couldn't believe it. He refused to do anything until Chamberlin assured him that the messenger really was in Levine's employ. Chamberlin looked for a moment at the fine, able plane and at the words "NEW YORK ⟶ PARIS" painted on the sides. Then he opened the dump valve of the main gas tank to lighten the plane on her jolting trip back to the hangar. The liquid—150 gallons—which might have propelled the *Columbia* one third of the distance to Paris lay in a big silver puddle on the ground. After the plane had been backed safely away from it, Chamberlin tossed a lighted match into the puddle, which became a little burning lake. People far away saw the blaze and the rolling clouds of black smoke, and came running, sure that the Bellanca was ablaze. Somebody turned in an alarm and the fire engine from Westbury and the ambulance from Mitchel Field came careering toward the scene.

Beyond the bright flames they were hauling and pushing the monoplane back toward her hangar at Curtiss Field. She no longer resembled a butterfly. Now she seemed like a giant bird that should have been soaring above the dark ocean on a magnificent flight to another continent. They had caught her and were dragging her, tail first, back to captivity.

John Carisi was heartbroken. He realized at last that there would be no flight. Thinking of Levine, perhaps, he praised the marvelous Lindbergh. "What a boy!" he kept saying. "I'd do anything for him. What a boy! What a wonderful boy!" He reached up and patted the propeller of the plane he had worked on so faithfully.

Before the little parade reached the hangar, Giuseppe Bellanca came running up. He had heard that the plane was at last going to leave and he wanted to see her take off, even if he was no longer connected with the company. "She is my work and I want to see her go," he had said. But when he reached her he was told that the flight had been postponed again. The column of black smoke which stood over the distant blaze seemed to rise from the funeral pyre of his hopes. He gazed at it for a while and then followed the plane into the hangar. He stood there in the shadows for several long minutes until Carisi saw him. The two began to talk in Italian. When I joined them Bellanca turned again to the tongue that was foreign to him.

"No, I have no plans," he said. "I am glad to have taken the step that I have in resigning from the company, but I have no plans. Only of this I am sure, that I shall build planes till I die. What else can I say? That is all I can do."

He went out and got into his cheap little car, where his wife sat waiting at the wheel. Chamberlin came up and they talked briefly. Then they shook hands.

Bellanca looked at us fondly. "Good night. Good luck to us," he said.

The little car rolled away in the darkness.

6

THE ARTFUL MR. LEVINE

Lindbergh's spectacular flight, which brought him world fame overnight, did not dampen the enthusiasm of his rivals. For the aviators he had left behind at Roosevelt Field there still seemed to be several aerial goals whose attainment might make them heroes in their turn. The Bellanca, holder of the endurance record, could probably fly farther than Lindbergh's Ryan and might be used for a trip to Berlin, Rome or Vienna. And the three-engined Fokker could symbolize the big safe airliners of the future, thus advancing the cause of aeronautical science. Lindbergh was already carrying out Byrd's second announced purpose—that of strengthening the ties of friendship between great nations.

Levine had the last word of the legend NEW YORK ⟶ PARIS on the *Columbia*'s flanks painted over, as well as the name *Bellanca* on the tail. The machine was going to fly to Europe, all right, he said, but he refused to specify where or when. He added that she would remain in the hangar for some time.

Mr. Whalen declared that Lindbergh's feat had failed to demonstrate that ocean flying was safe. He contrasted the trimotor Fokker —the probable prototype of future airliners—with the single-engined Ryan and announced that the principal goals sought by Mr. Wanamaker had not been achieved by the *Spirit of St. Louis*. It appeared that Mr. Wanamaker's aim of advancing the cause of aeronautical science had numerous important ramifications. Many things of great value, said Whalen vaguely, remained for Commander Byrd to prove.

That same day Postmaster General Harry S. New revealed that he had refused to let the New York–Chicago air-mail contract go to a Cleveland concern because Levine appeared to be connected with it. The Postmaster General reviewed the disputes Levine had had with Acosta, Bertaud and Bellanca, and added that Department of Justice agents were investigating the arrangements under which Levine had bought and sold back to the government those surplus shell casings and ammunition.

Levine replied sharply, "He can't prove anything against me. The plain truth is that the Postmaster General wanted to give the contract to some of his friends."

Four days after Lindbergh landed in Paris, James Dole, the Hawaiian pineapple king, came up with some prize offers of his own. He announced a first prize of $25,000 and a second of $10,000 for the first nonstop flights from America's Pacific Coast to his island Elysium. He invited Lindbergh to enter the contest, which was to begin about August 12.

Levine promptly announced that the *Columbia* might go after the money. In the meantime, he said, she might fly nonstop to Rome. On June 2 he had Chamberlin take him up on a climbing test in which they reached an altitude of 9,000 feet. During this and other flights Levine took over the controls to familiarize himself with the plane's performance. He had already had a few flying lessons, and both he and Chamberlin felt that he could take the stick for a while on a transatlantic flight.

Mr. Wanamaker let it be known that he wasn't interested in Dole pineapple money. The increasingly famous merchant seldom if ever was quoted directly. His views, like those of God's, were interpreted and publicized by those who received—or expected to receive—his favors. Presumably with his approval, the Fokker was put through additional tests. The day the Bellanca was climbing, the Byrd plane droned over Long Island along a measured course. This, it was explained, permitted Commander Byrd to test his instruments with the help of known landmarks. The commander later said that both speed and fuel-consumption tests indicated that the plane was performing satisfactorily. It was a state of readiness that the Fokker had by then maintained for more than three weeks.

On June 3, however, the craft was subjected to still another test. With 6,050 pounds of gasoline, oil, men and ballast added to her own weight of 5,550 pounds, she got off the ground after a run of 1,000 feet. She had carried heavier loads than this in earlier trials, but Commander Byrd seemed to think the latest effort proved something. On the same day Chamberlin flew the Bellanca across the river to Teterboro Airport, where Wright engineers installed a new carburetor heater.

Rumors were spreading that the *Columbia* was about to start for Germany, which Levine denied, but shortly after midnight on June 4 Chamberlin announced that he would take off in a few hours. He refused to name his destination, but at the hangar he received a radiogram from Lincoln Eyre, Berlin correspondent of the *New York Times*, saying that all Germany was awaiting the *Columbia's* arrival. Chamberlin grinned. "Well, we'll be glad to drop in on them on the way back," he said, leaving reporters with the impression that he hoped to fly even farther. He did say he would keep the plane in the air as long as the engine functioned and the gasoline supply held out.

This time he gave the Nassau County cops the takeoff notice they wanted so that they wouldn't thwart the project. In fact, a squad of motorcycle police escorted the *Columbia* as she was towed tail first to Roosevelt Field. The police also kept a small crowd at bay while mechanics loaded the main gas tank with 390 gallons and put aboard fifty-five additional gallons in 5-gallon cans.

Who, if anybody, was going along with Chamberlin? When

reporters asked the airman, he only smiled. Nobody paid much attention to a black limousine that rolled up near the starting area at the west end of the runway. In it were Mr. and Mrs. Levine, but they had come, it was assumed, just to see the *Columbia* take off.

Levine, in a pin-striped blue business suit and without a hat for his balding head, got out of the car with a roll of charts. He walked over to the plane and thrust the charts through the window. "Are you going?" somebody asked him. Levine merely looked at the questioner. Somebody also inquired who was going to be the navigator. "He's not here yet," Levine replied. A few minutes later he disappeared in the crowd.

Harold Kinkaid asked that the engine be started. Kinkaid, known generally as "Doc," was a Wright engine man who had accompanied Byrd to Spitsbergen and tuned up Lindbergh's engine. Now he listened with an expert ear to the roar of another Whirlwind. "Never heard a motor sound better," he said. A mechanic shut it off.

Another mechanic discovered that the main gas tank would hold ten more gallons. These were poured in to make the total gasoline load 455 gallons, five more than Lindbergh had carried. Then Carisi, who had worked on the plane devotedly for months, started the engine again. Although he had often declared that he was not "one of those emotional wops," he was so overcome by the apparent certainty that the *Columbia* was really going at last that he climbed up to the window and planted a resounding kiss on Chamberlin's cheek.

Chamberlin idled the engine for a few minutes and then opened it up. The roar resounded down the field and the plane trembled and strained against the wheel chocks. Chamberlin throttled it down again, looked at a knot of persons behind the ropes and nodded. And suddenly out of the crowd darted Levine. Keeping his head down and looking at nobody, he ran around the plane to the other side, opened the door and climbed in. Quickly he closed the door and slumped down in the seat next to Chamberlin, keeping his gaze averted from his wife.

Grace Levine was once known as "the Belle of Williamsburg," having won two beauty contests in that section of Brooklyn. She had been a good wife to Levine, had borne him two children and stood by him in the face of criticism and ridicule. She and her husband had discussed recent rumors that he might fly to Europe with Chamberlin, and together they had laughed at the absurdity. Once she had said she would burn the plane if he tried to fly across the ocean in it.

Now she turned to some friends who had come with her to see the takeoff. "What's all this foolishness of Charles getting into the plane?" she asked. Nobody knew. She became frightened and started to get out of the car.

Carisi ran up to reassure her. "It's all right," he said. "It's only a test run." And indeed, for a while it seemed to be only that. When the wheel chocks were removed Chamberlin gunned the plane down the runway for several hundred yards. Then, to avoid hitting some people whom the police hadn't kept back far enough, he turned off the course and returned to the starting area near Curtiss Field. He handled the heavily laden craft as if she were a highly maneuverable fighter plane.

Carisi sprinted over to the machine and stood beside the window, one foot on a wheel. "What are you doing, Mr. Levine?" he yelled. "Your wife is going out of her mind! She has got the idea that you are going to Europe in the plane!"

But Grace Levine was now smiling happily. Her husband wasn't going to fly, after all. She laughed at her former nervousness. How foolish she had been! She was still laughing when Chamberlin opened up the engine again. The propeller blast blew Carisi away and the *Columbia* started to roll.

Now the monoplane was roaring over the same path Lindbergh

had taken, a runway that was dry instead of soggy. With six inches more wingspread—forty-six and a half feet—and a load some 500 pounds heavier than the Ryan had had, the *Columbia* took off in 2,000 feet, less than half the distance her rival had used.

It was a beautiful Saturday morning. The sun was a glowing red ball and the light clouds above it were edged with gold. But Grace Levine was sobbing hysterically as the small plane climbed into the air shortly after six o'clock. "He isn't really going!" she cried. "He isn't really going!" And then, as the plane became a dot and disappeared, she began to weep bitterly.

The faithful Carisi came over and put his arms around her. "He'll make it," he told her. "You should be proud of him. He's a brave boy."

Only a few people besides Chamberlin had known that Levine was planning to go. Bellanca had suspected and opposed the project because he felt that Chamberlin needed a competent navigator. Still another who had had an inkling of Levine's intention was Samuel Hartman, his attorney.

Hartman told reporters later that Levine had sat up most of the night before the takeoff writing notes to his wife and his lawyer and making a will disposing of an estate of $5,000,000. The note to Hartman said: "Well, I'm off. Bet you'll be surprised, but don't worry. We will make it. Will cable you first moment I can and wish you would sail over to join me when I dine with Mussolini. Have arranged to have you continue checking out the monthly allowance checks should anything happen, but I am sure I'll be back soon enough."

The monthly allowance checks, Hartman explained, referred to various charities and needy individuals. They amounted, he estimated, to $30,000 a year. He didn't name the recipients. The statement that they existed startled many persons who had been exposed to Levine.

This tale, and the courage Levine was showing in attempting

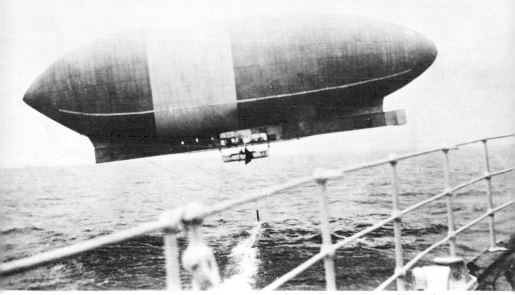

1910. Walter Wellman had to abandon his airship and his effort to cross the Atlantic about 400 miles east of Hatteras.

"Safe" in Ireland. John Alcock and Arthur Brown's flight from Newfoundland in 1919 ended like this. Their reward for the first successful transatlantic aerial journey was £10,000.

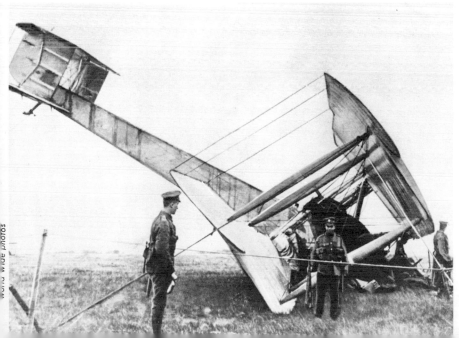

Risky prelude, 1926. Lt. Commander Byrd
ferried his plane ashore on an improvised raft
at Spitsbergen.

Goal: the North Pole. The *Josephine Ford,*
Byrd's three-engined monoplane, takes off from
Kings Bay, Spitsbergen. Floyd Bennett was at
the wheel of the ski-equipped Fokker.

Amundsen congratulates Byrd and Bennett after their return to Spitsbergen.

From Spitsbergen to Alaska. In 1926 the *Norge* carried Roald Amundsen, Lincoln Ellsworth, Umberto Nobile and thirteen other men in the first flight over the North Pole.

Success and failure. This big Sikorsky was to
have carried René Fonck, top ace of World
War I, and three companions to Paris, but the
overloaded biplane crashed on takeoff. Fonck
and his navigator escaped miraculously.

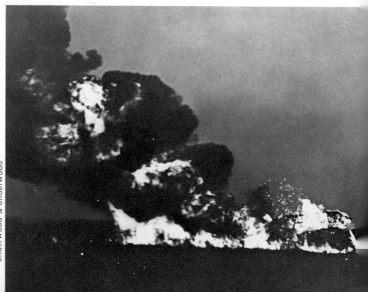

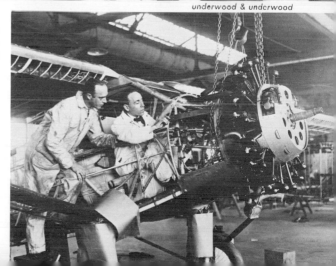

Top: The *White Bird,* in which French war ace Charles Nungesser and Captain François Coli disappeared forever in the Atlantic.

Center: Start of a flight to fame. A monoplane called the *Spirit of St. Louis* is hauled toward the runway at Roosevelt Field. The next stop after that was Paris.

Bottom: Giuseppe Bellanca (right), who built the most efficient planes of his day, works in his factory on Staten Island.

Left: Charles A. Levine startled everybody, including his distraught wife, by climbing into this Bellanca at the last minute and taking off with Clarence Chamberlin for Germany in June 1927.

underwood & underwood   *culver*

Wingtop conference. From left: Anthony Fokker, Brice Goldsborough, Bernt Balchen and Commander Byrd make final checks on the *America*.

smithsonian institution

Before and after. At Roosevelt Field the *America* was poised on an inclined ramp to aid her takeoff. Off Ver-sur-Mer, near Deauville, Balchen had to ditch because of bad weather and lack of fuel.

Levine (left) and Chamberlin came down in a wheat field near Eisleben, Germany, birthplace of Martin Luther. Their flight of 3,905 miles set a new distance record.

Art Goebel (left) and Bill Davis tuned up in a bit of jubilation after winning the $25,000 first prize in the "pineapple race" to Hawaii.

The Flying Schoolmarm, Mildred Doran, prepares to climb into the plane which was to take her to Honolulu. She and her two male companions, as well as seven other fliers, died as a result of the ill-conceived Dole contest.

"Why couldn't I have been with him when he fell?" Constance Erwin and her husband Bill. He was lost with a companion, Alvin Eichwaldt, searching for Dole fliers downed in the Pacific.

From Georgia to____? Paul Redfern (right) with Paul Varner, chairman of the local flight committee, before the young flier started for Rio. He was never found.

brown brothers

wide world photos

Ed Schlee (left) and Bill Brock were still damp from an Atlantic rainstorm when they arrived at London. Later, relatives intervened to prevent them from completing their attempt to circle the globe.

Princess Anne Lowenstein-Wertheim took off at the age of sixty-two with two male pilots on a flight from England to Canada. Their fate constitutes another Atlantic mystery.

DEHAV

Top: *Old Glory's* last flight. Lloyd Bertaud, J.D. Hill and Philip Payne take off from Old Orchard Beach, Maine.

Center: Sex across the sea. Ruth Elder, prettiest aviatrix of the day, infused new interest into transatlantic flying when she took off with George Haldeman. They were forced to ditch in the Atlantic near the Azores.

Bottom: Ruth posed fetchingly with her husband, Lyle Womack, on her triumphant return from Europe. But her attitude toward him, he said sadly, had changed.

"I am going to be the first woman to fly across the Atlantic," said Frances Grayson, a Long Island realtor. She and the male crew of her amphibious plane were lost at sea.

Amundsen called their flight incomparable. Ben Eielson (left) and George Hubert Wilkins, later knighted by King George, flew 2,200 miles from Alaska to Spitsbergen.

The semi-rigid dirigible *Italia* arrived at Spitsbergen in May 1928 for a series of flights over the Arctic wastes. Returning from the Pole she crashed, costing the lives of seventeen crewmen and rescuers.

General Umberto Nobile, commander of the *Italia*, on the catwalk of the airship.

The last photograph ever taken of Roald Amundsen. The famous White Eagle of Norway used this French seaplane to search for *Italia* survivors. He and five companions in the plane were lost.

Queen of the Air. This German Junkers plane was named for Mabel Boll (center), who was constantly frustrated in her attempts to fly the Atlantic. With her are Bert Acosta (left) and Levine.

Pilots for Antarctica. From left: Harold
June, Dean C. Smith and Bernt Balchen,
who flew Commander Byrd over
hundreds of white miles at the bottom
of the world.

In this trimotor Ford, named for Floyd
Bennett, Byrd, Balchen, June and
McKinley reached the South Pole on
November 29, 1929.

Belly-landing. Clyde Pangborn and Hugh Herndon, Jr., dropped the undercarriage of their Bellanca after taking off from Japan in September 1931. In the first successful transpacific flight, they came down at Wenatchee, Washington, after a journey of 5,041 miles.

In front of 450 horsepower. Amelia Earhart and Bernt Balchen took off in this sleek Lockheed-Vega for Newfoundland in May 1932. Thereafter Miss Earhart went on by herself to make the first transatlantic solo by a woman.

a transatlantic flight, caused many to wonder if he wasn't a good fellow, after all. There was talk that whatever his faults, he had vindicated himself. Now that he was at least temporarily famous, people wanted to believe in his essential nobility, an attribute they had already accorded Lindbergh and which on lesser occasions Americans bestow on baseball players, prize fighters and football stars.

The *Columbia's* takeoff made big headlines both in the United States and Europe, although the plane's destination was uncertain. The two most likely objectives seemed to be Berlin or Rome, though there was also speculation about Warsaw, Vienna and Prague.

The German capital prepared for a welcome that would outdo Paris' greeting of Lindbergh. High government officials, it was said, would meet the gallant fliers at Tempelhof Airport, where three thousand police would keep the immense crowd from storming the plane. The Berlin field, as well as airports at Cologne, Hamburg and Bremen, would be kept lighted through the night. And Lufthansa, the German air trust, would have planes flying along the western border to meet the *Columbia* and escort her in.

Newspapers ran off extras about the flight, and hotels set up information bureaus to provide excited guests with the latest news on the plane's progress. Attention centered on Chamberlin rather than on Levine, who was then known to few Europeans. It was considered a happy omen that the last two syllables of the pilot's name spelled the name of the city toward which the Bellanca seemed to be headed.

But Rome saw itself, not Berlin, as the fliers' goal. After all, for a plane designed by an Italian, what could be a more appropriate destination than the Eternal City? Italian newspaper presses whirled out extra after extra. But even these weren't enough. Crowds collected in front of the newspaper offices demanding even later intelligence about the machine that was supposedly speeding toward them.

Aboard the plane all was not entirely well. After the first hundred miles Chamberlin noticed that the earth inductor compass was misbehaving. He was attempting to follow a great-circle course modified, in accordance with last-minute weather forecasts, by Goldsborough and Balchen. Setting the indicator to match his course, he tried to keep the pointer at zero, but it wouldn't stay put. At Newport, Rhode Island, they were four or five miles off course, and when they reached what appeared to be Cape Cod the needle began swinging from side to side in a meaningless and maddening dance. Moreover, there seemed to be an extra hook on the arm of land below that didn't appear on their chart. They couldn't be sure they were really over the Cape.

Chamberlin circled about, hoping that the aberrant compass would return to normal. They had flown about 200 miles and had 3,400 to go. Should they rely on their $50 magnetic compass to guide them? Or should they return to Roosevelt Field and have the $1,000 earth inductor adjusted? They talked it over and decided to go on.

Chamberlin kept circling until he got a bearing on what he thought was the tip of Cape Cod and had oriented himself with the help of the sun. Then, steering by the magnetic compass, which was jiggling from the engine vibrations, he headed out over the water toward Nova Scotia. The air was smooth and they went along a few hundred feet over the ocean, sighting several sailing yachts and fishing smacks and waving to their crews. But a northeast wind was rising and slowed them down.

In two hours, Chamberlin figured, they ought to hit Yarmouth. But the second hour passed with only blue water below. A third hour faded into the past. What if the magnetic compass had failed too and was prompting them to fly in circles on a crazy course that would end in a splash and a hiss and a silence?

The main gas tank was shaped like an upright piano and the eleven 5-gallon cans were strapped on its ledge. Levine now emptied the first of these into the tank. Each can was fitted with a petcock and the tank had a rubber hose connection, so the operation was simple. When a can was emptied, Levine threw it overboard to clear the space on the tank shelf and give access to the rear of the cabin.

Finally, to their relief they sighted Nova Scotia. Their magnetic compass was doing its stuff, after all. Chamberlin took the new bearing his charts called for and pointed the *Columbia's* nose toward Newfoundland. The wind had now veered from dead ahead to quartering from the east and southeast. To counteract its thrust and to keep the plane on course, Chamberlin had to crab sideways into the wind. As the plane flew on, her position in relation to the magnetic pole varied, but Goldsborough and Balchen had taken this into account on the charts. Chamberlin followed the magnetic bearings they had given, compensating for his estimated wind drift.

Soon he let Levine take the stick and reached for the food Mrs. Chamberlin had prepared. There were ten chicken sandwiches on toasted rye bread, two vacuum bottles of chicken soup, a vacuum bottle of coffee and half a dozen oranges. The hot soup tasted fine, Chamberlin reported later. But he took only a bite or two from a sandwich.

By the time they reached Halifax the wind was blowing across their course from the south, necessitating more crabbing and slowing their progress eastward by about 30 miles an hour. They were now two hours behind schedule because of the head and quartering winds, but the air currents were at last shifting in their favor and starting to push the plane along. And since the magnetic compass seemed to be working satisfactorily, things began to look up.

Chamberlin climbed to 2,000 feet to let the plane take advantage of the tailwind, and headed for Trepassey, Newfoundland. He had decided to go slightly south of the great-circle route to avoid a storm area shown on the weather map. By the time they reached Trepassey, Levine had emptied and thrown out the last of the 5-gallon cans and the way to the rear of the cabin was open. Chamberlin let his companion take over the plane again and went back to put on his cold-weather clothing—heavy woolen drawers to be pulled over trousers and a woolen shirt with parka hood. Then he stretched out on the gas-tank ledge to get a little rest before the coming night over the ocean. But he couldn't sleep.

Some 2,500 feet below them stretched the last of Newfoundland they would see—rough, desolate country blotched with swamps and wasteland. After a while they sighted the ocean and, a few miles offshore, what seemed to be the white sail of a fishing boat. The red sun was sliding down behind the world to the west and its last rays picked out the white triangle and turned it a luminous pink. It was like a great jewel risen from the blue of the sea. Then they saw it was an iceberg. Chamberlin took a final bearing and headed east across the Atlantic. Levine grinned. "Europe next stop," he said. "Well, here goes nothing."

7

THREE-MILE DIVE

They flew on toward the night which was creeping over the northern sea. Soon they were looking down on a scatter of icebergs. While admiring their beauty, Chamberlin used them to check the drift of the plane until they faded like ghosts into the darkness.

The air was now so calm that the remarkably stable plane was flying itself without the touch of human hand or foot. Chamberlin had attached a spring to the rudder bar which he had devised to compensate for propeller torque, and left the controls alone for as much as two hundred miles at a stretch.

Presently they were soaring above clouds. And then, through a rift, they saw the lights of a ship three or four thousand feet down. Levine blinked a flashlight but there was no answering signal. The incident depressed them. They wanted to be sighted and reported often; it would reassure their wives and facilitate a search if they had to come down at sea. But after an hour or two, when they were flying at 3,000 feet, they saw the lights of another ship. And this one instantly answered Levine's flashlight blinkings. Immensely cheered, they flew on. Only later did they learn that no report from either vessel was ever received on shore.

Soon clouds blanketed the world below and then the gray mass started up toward them. The Bellanca climbed until she could climb no more. With her still-heavy load of gasoline she couldn't struggle higher than 15,000 feet, and the cloud bank ahead of her loomed three or four thousand feet higher. The short northern night was fading ahead of them and giving way to a slow dawn. In this meager light the plane entered the gray mist. The temperature was one degree below freezing. A thin layer of ice began to form on the cabin windshield and on the leading edges of the wings.

Wing ice was a terror to the fliers of those days, since they had no equipment to melt it or break it up. And many a plane crashed because the thin film changed the contours and destroyed the lifting effectiveness of wings, as well as adding to the load the machine was carrying. So Chamberlin cut the throttle and headed down through the blankness, hoping for a space between the underside of the cloud bank and the sea. He also hoped that the altimeter would continue to work—a faulty reading could plunge them into the waves.

Ten thousand feet. Six thousand. Three thousand. Two. Still nothing visible below but gray. One thousand. Chamberlin flattened out a little. He would ease her down to a hundred feet but no farther. Then he would pull up and fly on and perhaps leave the mist behind.

He had been revving up the engine at intervals to keep the spark plugs free of oil so that the Whirlwind would run smoothly when he needed it. And suddenly he did need it. Below 800 feet the gray ghostly stuff thinned, and whitecaps appeared. There was enough light now to see that it was raining.

Apparently this was the storm area shown on Dr. Kimball's weather map. They could run out of it, he had said, by turning south. Chamberlin banked to the right, but for an hour the rain continued to beat against the windshield. Then they emerged into beautiful clear weather.

The ocean had a brown appearance and the air was so warm that both men discarded their heavy clothing. Chamberlin decided they were over the Gulf Stream and coursing the steamer lanes to Europe. He set a new great-circle course for Land's End on the southwest coast of England.

Their watches were still running on New York time, five hours behind London's, so when the sun appeared out of the sea they did some quick figuring. This sunrise was two and a half hours earlier than the June 5 sunrise would be in New York. Hurrah! They must be halfway across the ocean.

The wind was still behind them and the Bellanca was moving toward Europe at a speed which was probably around 120 miles an hour. The magnetic compass, as far as they could tell from the position of the sun, was still giving accurate guidance. They celebrated with a Sunday breakfast of oranges, chicken soup and coffee.

They were flying at an altitude between 2,000 and 3,000 feet now, so that the tailwind could do its best for them. About nine o'clock they sighted a Scandinavian tramp, though they couldn't make out her name. Chamberlin came down to 300 feet, but the name was still only a jumble of letters to the fliers. They circled the ship and the crew waved. They felt sure that the ship would report them—and learned later that she didn't. After a couple of hours they sighted another tramp, and again couldn't make out the name. Again they thought that she would report them; they were wrong this time too.

But at four-thirty that afternoon they got one of the big thrills of the trip. The liner *Mauretania* appeared so suddenly and so close that it seemed as if she had sprung out of the sea. She had come over the horizon under the plane's nose at 25 knots or so, and the Bellanca, with a quartering 25-mile wind behind her, was doing 120 miles an hour or better. The big Cunarder, with her four red funnels, white superstructure and black hull, and with flags flying and decks lined with passengers, was a glorious sight. Chamberlin pointed the plane down toward her and flashed by at the height of her top deck. Then he banked sharply and came up on the opposite side.

Throttling the plane, which was now slowed further by the wind, he kept just abreast of the liner, while her wildly excited passengers tossed hats, books and umbrellas into the air. They had read about the *Columbia*'s progress in the ship's news bulletins and could readily identify her from the Department of Commerce experimental license numbers on her wings—NX 237—and the number 140 on her fuselage, given her for the national air races a year earlier.

As they flew along abreast of the liner, Levine noticed a group of officers on the bridge. He leaned out the window and made motions with his hands as if he were punching a telegraph key. The officers stopped waving and nodded and the *Mauretania* did what was asked, giving the United States the first news that the plane was nearing Europe.

Levine leafed through a copy of the *New York Times* which they had aboard. On the marine page he read that the liner had left Southampton at noon the day before. Then he looked again at the chart, which showed the lanes that transatlantic liners were using that month. From these data he and Chamberlin calculated they were 400 or 500 miles west of Land's End (actually the distance was about 350) and pretty well on course.

Then Chamberlin opened the throttle, pulled ahead of the liner, banked and came back right over the ship and along her wake. This invisible air path would lead him to Land's End. He had to crab into the wind to stay with it. The maneuver gave him what he needed—both the compass heading and the correction to compensate for the wind.

The *Mauretania*'s passengers were still waving when the *Columbia* was a speck in the sky. They had had another unforeseen excitation earlier the same afternoon: the Cunarder had passed the U.S. Navy cruiser *Memphis,* which was bringing Lindbergh home. Now her passengers had seen two more heroes in the making.

Half an hour after leaving the *Mauretania,* Chamberlin sighted the *Memphis.* But she was about ten miles to the south and he turned down Levine's suggestion that they fly over and "jazz her up" a bit. The afternoon was waning and so was the perfect weather. A haze dead ahead was thickening, low-hanging clouds had appeared and flashes of lightning heralded rain squalls. Before sunset they saw the *Transylvania* and circled over the liner. Thereafter they passed a tanker but didn't come down to identify her. And then, through the haze, they saw the low cliffs of Land's End, lit by the long rays of the setting sun.

The wind behind them had strengthened, and while their air path over the sea was smooth, it became turbulent as they circled above the coast, checking its outlines against their charts. Dusk was moving in over the green countryside. With a black, stormy night in prospect there was a great temptation to land on the hospitable Cornish shore.

Now the clouds were becoming thick. Chamberlin climbed above them and headed eastward. Through a rift in the rack he saw Plymouth and got another bearing: they were about five hour's flying time from Berlin. However, the clouds were rising higher and Chamberlin realized that he was very tired, that he might not be able to find the German capital, that if he did find it he might have trouble landing in the dark. He headed in the direction of Berlin but decided that even if he reached it he would stay aloft until dawn. There was plenty of gas to last through the short night.

The Bellanca had climbed to 15,000 feet. Now, with the cloud mass still rising straight ahead, she had to go higher. Chamberlin nursed her up to 18,000, then 20,000 feet. Still the cloud barrier towered above them.

Should they try to fly through it? Up ahead they might hit a mountain while their altimeter showed they still had plenty of altitude. The only thing to do, Chamberlin felt, was to fly along the western edge of the cloud range and kill time until it became light enough for him to see if it extended all the way down to the earth. So he flew north for fifteen minutes, then turned and cruised south for another fifteen, repeating the turnabout over and over. Several times he felt sure he was flying over the North Sea, for great black canyons in the cloud range indicated the presence of water far below. The moon had slipped down beneath the sea of clouds but a glittering spangle of stars provided both welcome company and golden gauges to steer by.

Chamberlin was nearing exhaustion. The thin air was making the plane hard to handle; he had to work the controls almost continually to keep her level. And insufficient oxygen, added to nearly forty hours of sleeplessness, was making him light-headed. Dawn paled the east again and Chamberlin realized that he would pass out soon unless he got some rest. They were still flying at 20,000 feet or higher, with the cloud floor visible below them. Surely Levine could handle the ship for a while.

"See what you can do with her," Chamberlin told his companion and eased himself onto the gas-tank shelf. Levine managed to keep the plane level for about ten minutes; then, either by losing altitude or by following a box canyon in the clouds, he got into the bewildering mist. As inexperienced pilots sometimes do, he tried so hard to keep the Bellanca horizontal that he pulled the nose up too far and the plane stalled. Unable to rise higher, she pointed the left wing toward the earth and went into a deadly spiral. Since Levine could see nothing but mist, he had no idea what was happening.

But Chamberlin, half asleep, sensed disaster. He slid off the tank and into his seat. The Bellanca's wings had started to shiver. The rudder was flapping violently back and forth, shaking the rear end of the plane as if it would tear it off, at the same time whipping the rudder bar to and fro so viciously that Chamberlin didn't dare try to stop it all at once.

The second memorable event of the trip affected the two men in different ways. Chamberlin was badly scared but Levine enjoyed the situation. He had taken his hand off the quivering stick and his feet off the jerking rudder bar and was sitting there chuckling at the antics of the plane. She was behaving, he said later, like a bucking bronco.

These antics, the rush of air and the instruments told Chamberlin that they were plunging toward the sea at terrifying speed. The altimeter needle was racing past hundred-foot marks as if they represented inches. The needle on the airspeed indicator was jammed against the pin which marked 160 miles an hour, the most the instrument was capable of showing.

Chamberlin knew that if he tried to pull out too suddenly he probably would rip the wings off the plane, and if he pushed too hard against the rudder bar it would break the control cables. He set about the latter task gingerly, pushing at the bar with increasing strength as it neared the end of its swing. Gradually he tamed the berserk bar and was able to steer out of the spiral. Then he slowly flattened the dive until the plane lost her dangerous speed.

By this time the altimeter showed 4,000 feet. They had dropped more than three miles. Heading east, they were still in the gray mist. All they could see through the windshield was the blue spurts from the Whirlwind's exhaust pipes. The flames turned the haze into an eerie blue blur.

Chamberlin figured they were now flying over Germany. He thought they must be somewhere near the Harz Mountains, and although he knew these were several thousand feet high, he decided to go lower to try to find some landmark shown on their chart. They slid down below 1,000 feet before they came out of the gray to find themselves flying in rain over a river. Soon they saw the glare of blast furnaces. Chamberlin thought they must be over Essen. Levine disagreed. He said the lights below were those of Bremerhaven. As proof, he added that he had been in Bremerhaven once.

They flew around in the rain, looking for a name on a factory roof. From the air the scene looked like the traditional concept of hell. Flames flared up from the blast furnaces, painting the low clouds a lurid red. Almost as soon as the fire gushed up, the rain-filled gusts slapped it down and spread it over the ground. Even if they had wanted to land in the area it would have been well-nigh impossible in that storm. Not until the next day did they find out that the city was Dortmund.

Soon they saw white flares being fired into the air not far away. They headed toward them and saw a flying field. On it, in the growing light, they spotted a few men. Chamberlin idled the engine, came down to about twenty feet, stuck his hand out the window and yelled downward at the top of his voice, *"Nach Berlin? Nach Berlin?"* He swept over their heads and banked around to see if they had understood him. All of them pointed in about the same direction. Chamberlin headed that way.

It was just after four-thirty and the fuel was getting low. They were pointing eastward from Dortmund on a course that would take them south of the German capital. But both men thought they were heading for Berlin and Chamberlin held the course until the gasoline gauge neared zero. He wanted to land near some village while he still had enough fuel left to use the engine in landing. But Levine wanted to go on until the last drop was used, so Chamberlin told him to go to the rear of the cabin and act as ballast, for with empty tanks the Bellanca was nose-heavy. A few minutes later the faithful engine coughed and stopped. Chamberlin brought the plane into the wind and came down in a pretty, dead-stick landing. Shortly before six o'clock the Bellanca rolled to a smooth stop in a small wheat field near the town of Eisleben, birthplace of Martin Luther.

They had been in the air for almost forty-three hours and were still 110 miles short of Berlin, but their straight-line distance from Roosevelt Field was 3,905 miles, 295 miles longer than Lindbergh's. Actually their zigzag course had taken them well over 4,000 miles. Indeed, Chamberlin estimated later that in the last ten hours of their journey they had moved eastward only 300 miles, though they must have flown 1,000 miles in that time.

They had come down safely, however, and there was plenty of reason to be thankful. In the sudden silence they heard the singing of birds. They got out of the plane and stretched their stiff limbs. Chamberlin found he couldn't stand upright unless he kept moving. When he stood still he swayed like a drunk.

Nobody was in sight. Nearly half an hour passed and the bird song was beginning to pall. Then a woman with two boys crossed the field and came up to them. She spoke to them in German, seemingly complaining about the wheat they had smashed. Chamberlin responded with some phrases he had learned in high school. Then Levine tried. Suddenly the anger on the woman's face gave way to fear. She spoke urgently to the boys and all three turned and ran. Long afterward Chamberlin learned that she had taken them for kidnappers who had been terrorizing the neighborhood, though presumably the criminals had not heretofore been equipped with planes.

Other field workers appeared. Within an hour a small group of men, women and children were looking curiously at the strangers and the plane. They didn't seem to believe that the two men were *"von New York gekommen,"* but they finally comprehended that the *Columbia* needed fuel. One of the boys volunteered to bicycle four miles and arrange for ninety liters of benzol to be sent to the field. Chamberlin wanted to ask him to fetch a map, too, but couldn't think of the German word for it.

After an hour a truck appeared with the benzol—twenty-two gallons of it. It wasn't gasoline but it would run the Whirlwind. The truck driver had a funnel but it was too big for the cabin tank, and the wing tanks had been sealed, as they always were, to make any distance flight official. One of the women had a solution: she walked a mile across the fields and came back with a long-necked teapot which Chamberlin used to fill the main tank. It took him an hour and a half and he must have poured in a hundred potfuls of the benzol, which filled the cabin with fumes. He paid $15 for the fuel, and they were ready to go.

A boy who spoke fair English came forward to act as translator. He told them they could get a map in Eisleben but they didn't recognize his version of the word "map" and they started without one. Everybody agreed that Berlin was "that way," so why not get going? Unfortunately, they had left the inertia starter behind because of its weight. The propeller would have to be turned by hand and Chamberlin was so weak he could hardly stand up.

A fellow who said he was an airplane mechanic offered to throw the propeller over, but he was so awkward that he might have been killed if the engine had started. Chamberlin hauled the blades around to give the engine a charge of fuel and then tried to give the propeller the quick pull-through needed to do the job. With Levine manipulating the switch and throttle, he toiled for half an hour—yelling "Contact!" and "Switch off!" time and again—before the Whirlwind took hold and began to roar.

The farm people held the wheel struts and tail skid while Chamberlin tested the engine with its new fuel. It seemed to be all right and he signaled them to stand clear. Then he opened the throttle. The field was damp but not soggy, and the *Columbia* rose from it easily. She circled around the field and headed for Berlin, or at least in the direction the farm workers seemed to have pointed.

But exactly where had they pointed? The two men couldn't agree. Levine thought they ought to bear more to the northeast; Chamberlin, more to the east. The weather was clear and Levine was now flying the ship some of the time. When he had the controls they went northeast; when Chamberlin had them they went east. It was one of the few times he was wrong and Levine was right.

They should have picked up Berlin in an hour. But after ninety minutes they saw only a small city with the name COTTBUS marked on its flying field. A map would have shown them that they were already past Berlin and about seventy miles south of it. They flew on for about twenty-five miles. The country under them was getting

100

swampy and the benzol was about to run out. Chamberlin banked around and headed back toward the Cottbus airfield.

Five miles short of it, the engine stopped. Levine got behind the gas tank again. The landing place was a soggy pasture. As the plane rolled more and more slowly toward a stop, one of the wheels sank in to the hub. The *Columbia* stood up on her nose and the walnut-wood propeller, which was in an up-and-down position, snapped off at the bottom. Every loose object in the cabin surged forward. Powdered milk and chocolate—part of their emergency rations—cascaded down on Chamberlin, giving his head and shoulders a chocolate-milkshake hue.

It was now about eleven-thirty. As Levine and Chamberlin slid out of the uptilted plane, a peasant woman ran up to them and began to jabber in German. Pointing to the wheel ruts the *Columbia* had made in the field, she screamed, "*Bezahlen! Bezahlen!*" (Pay! Pay!) A crowd quickly gathered around them.

They had come down near the village of Klinge, whose *Bürgermeister* soon arrived to welcome them. Apparently the *Columbia*'s presence in Germany was now well known. But before Klinge's mayor could drive them into town, *Bürgermeister* Kreutz of Cottbus drove up. Frowning terribly at his fellow dignitary, he told the fliers it was all a mistake about Klinge; they had really landed in Cottbus, a town capable of giving them appropriate entertainment. Soon he had shoved his rival from Klinge into the background, feebly protesting.

When the *Columbia* was eased down to her tail skid, *Bürgermeister* Kreutz assigned two Cottbus policemen to ward off souvenir hunters and then whisked the Americans into town. At the Hotel Ansorges, the best hostelry Cottbus afforded, he plied them with crab soup, fried eel, roast goose and beer. While they were eating, fifteen planes from Berlin arrived, eight of them carrying newspapermen and photographers. Cheering citizens of Cottbus massed outside the hotel, many of them to remain there until late at night. *Bürgermeister* Kreutz hastily recruited police reinforcement from neighboring communities to keep his countrymen from storming the place.

The planes from Berlin brought sacks of telegrams and mail for the fliers. One of the messages in them was from Grace Levine: FOLLOWING YOUR FLIGHT WITH PRAYER, LOVE, PRIDE AND CONFIDENCE. LOVE FROM FAMILY. CABLE PROMPTLY. WILL LEAVE TO MEET YOU. Both men cabled their wives.

Lufthansa offered to fly the Americans into Berlin, but both wanted to arrive there in the *Columbia*. In the afternoon Chamberlin went back to the plane and asked that she be towed to a nearby soccer field. He also asked for a new propeller and some gasoline.

The Lufthansa men were amazed at the puny size of the Bellanca; beside some of the German planes she looked like a toy. But they were positive that, small though she was, she couldn't take off from a regulation soccer field. They wanted to dismantle the machine, take the parts to the Cottbus airport and reassemble it there. Chamberlin finally convinced them that he knew what he was talking about, and the plane was towed to the drier ground. They also wired for a propeller to be taken from an experimental Heinkel plane which was fitted with two Whirlwind engines.

Back at the hotel Levine, basking in his sudden fame, was talking volubly to newspapermen while the hastily assembled Cottbus band serenaded him in the street below. At his very first press conference on German soil he was unwittingly giving evidence of the difference that can exist between heroes.

Lindbergh had done everything right. He made a magnificent flight—alone—to his announced destination and arrived on schedule. Thereafter he was modest, generous and gracious. He made his first call in Paris on Mme. Nungesser to tell her how much he admired her son and to express his hope that the famous French ace might yet be found. He took the 150,000 francs (then worth about

$5,850) which a French aeronautical club had awarded him and donated it to swell a fund for families of lost French fliers. He turned down a $1,000,000 purse which some Americans wanted to raise for him. And he refrained from publicly criticizing his transatlantic rivals and from disparaging their often questionable activities.

The *Columbia* group's performance—thanks largely to Levine —had been a comedy of errors for months. He had battled with associates, schemed and lied, and nearly killed himself and Chamberlin in a fatal spin. Yet in spite of everything—thanks largely to Chamberlin—the *Columbia* had crossed the Atlantic. Now Levine was close to exhaustion after eighty hours without sleep, and from the excitement and alarms of the journey. Characteristically, however, he was still able to say the wrong thing. "We've made a record even if we haven't reached Berlin," he told the first American newspaperman who got to him. "Believe me, if we had had Lindbergh's luck we would have reached Berlin with enough gasoline for three or four hundred miles more." Then he added with a grin, "We had plenty of luck, only it was all hard."

When Chamberlin returned from the field they had a big dinner and after that cased themselves into hot tubs. Then, oblivious to the booming of the band outside the hotel, they slipped into bed and sleep. Lincoln Eyre of the *New York Times*, who had flown down to Cottbus to greet them, wrote that their sleep was sound and happy because they had carried through to completion "one of the most splendid enterprises ever achieved by man on land, on sea or in the air."

The next day, everybody agreed, was the greatest in all the history of Cottbus, whose age was just three years short of a millennium. Outside the Hotel Ansorges, people massed on all sides of the square, and some of them—doubtless friends of the police—managed to push their way into the room where Chamberlin and Levine were having breakfast. Those already present included *Bürgermeister* Kreutz, local officials and most of the hostelry's porters, clerks and chambermaids, for whom the fliers signed numerous autographs.

The Americans emerged from the building to a tremendous ovation from the men, women and children in the square. *"Hoch! Hoch!"* the admiring townseople shouted. Then the airmen rode in state to the *Rathaus*, where they signed the Golden Book, whose pages are opened only to distinguished visitors. The old building's reception hall was bursting with still another crowd, which cheered them from the floor and from the galleries. On the wall above the rostrum hung a new flag, made during the night. It had thirty stars and no stripes, but its colors were red, white and blue.

Bürgermeister Kreutz led the heroes to seats on the rostrum. "Has the music arrived?" he asked an aide. The music had, and the band which provided it had been working—like the flag makers—far into the night. It burst into a rendition of "The Star-Spangled Banner" with an enthusiasm that almost drowned out various inaccuracies.

The *Bürgermeister* made a speech of welcome and praise. The counselor of the American embassy, who had flown down from Berlin, read a speech of acknowledgment in German. After that the band again broke into its rendition of "The Star-Spangled Banner" and everybody stood up in honor of the anthem.

Then the mayor presented the visitors with two splendid silver salvers and made them honorary citizens of the town. This meant, he explained, that they could come back to Cottbus and live rent-free for the rest of their lives, presumably buying their own food.

The band was so pleased with its performance to date that it now attempted to play "The Star-Spangled Banner" again. But the *Bürgermeister* shushed it before the assembly could rise again. Several other dignitaries made speeches, and the ceremony ended with "Deutschland über Alles," which the Germans sang with great volume and verve.

The crowd outside the *Rathaus* gave the visitors another big hand, and two little girls curtseyed and presented them with bouquets. Then they drove to the soccer field, where Lufthansa mechanics had replaced the broken propeller and put some gasoline in the *Columbia*'s tanks.

Chamberlin found that the new prop, which was larger and more sharply pitched than the other, would turn up only 1,350 revolutions per minute, 300 fewer than its predecessor. He wasn't sure how well it would work, so he left Levine on the ground. The Lufthansa men, who had thought he couldn't take off in such a small area, were amazed when he used hardly one third of the available space. He flew to the Cottbus airfield in about three minutes.

At the White Horse Hotel they were luncheon guests of *Bürgermeister* Kreutz. Autograph hunters besieged them wherever they went. The most personable of these were three girls in the folk dress of the Speewald region, who presented them with more flowers. The *Fräuleins* wanted to be photographed with the daring Americans and the cameramen readily obliged.

The officials in Berlin wanted the reception at Tempelhof Airport to start at six o'clock. So fearful was *Bürgermeister* Kreutz that they might be late for it that he got them off the Cottbus airfield at four-thirty for the seventy-mile flight to the capital. This time the Americans had an escort of fifteen planes, so they could hardly get lost. In fact, they reached Berlin ahead of schedule and had to circle over the city for twenty minutes before the official ceremony of welcome could properly begin.

8

"CHAMPION OF THE AIR"

A crowd of 150,000 people, one-third larger than the gathering which had greeted Lindbergh at Le Bourget two weeks earlier, was waiting at Tempelhof when the Bellanca touched down at 5:51 P.M. on Tuesday, June 7, 1927. Some of the Germans had been there Sunday night, when the plane was originally expected, and again on Monday. This time they were not disappointed.

The same could not be said for twenty thousand Poles who were waiting for the Americans at the Warsaw airport. Somehow a rumor had got abroad that when Chamberlin and Levine took off from Cottbus they were heading not toward the German but toward the Polish capital. Warsaw papers headlined these glad tidings in afternoon extras, which said that the government had ordered all planes to stand in readiness to meet the American airmen at the border. People had rushed to the airport and didn't disperse until darkness settled down and news of the Berlin reception began to trickle in. Foreign correspondents got word later that the false story probably had been circulated to get many people out of the center of town lest news of the assassination of a Soviet official trigger a riot.

In Berlin, where no recent assassinations had been staged, the three thousand police at Tempelhof were barely able to prevent the huge crowd from rushing the *Columbia* to hoist the aviators on German shoulders and parade them around the field—and perhaps also to rip a few souvenirs from the plane. When Chamberlin and Levine stepped out, cheers filled the evening air and the crowd surged forward. But the police lines around the plane held, and the enthusiastic Teutons could only watch and listen while U.S. Ambassador Jacob Gould Schurman clasped each man by the hand and Suzanne Hausler, the fourteen-year-old daughter of the chairman of the Board of Aldermen, presented a huge bouquet of Whitsuntide roses. The *New York Times* said it was a great occasion for the little maid who the day before had stood on the field in a thin festive dress, so chilled by a strong wind that her teeth chattered.

Ambassador Schurman delivered himself of some elegant elocution. Addressing Chamberlin rather than his companion, he said, "Welcome to the aviator who made the first nonstop flight from New York to Germany and covered the greatest distance ever made in continuous flight. In accomplishing this wonderful exploit you have at the same time enlarged our vision of the possibilities of human achievement. We Americans here are proud of you. The American people are proud of you. We all congratulate you most enthusiastically, congratulate you and salute you as the conqueror of the ocean and the champion of the air."

It was pretty powerful stuff. And there was more: "I hail you also as the celestial messenger of good will and friendship from the American people to the German people—friends united over the ocean through the eighteenth and nineteenth centuries and now, please Heaven, also more closely through the air in the twentieth century and all centuries to follow."

Finally the ambassador got around to Levine. "I am delighted that you and your companion in your flight, Levine, arrive in Germany in such excellent condition and beg you both to come with me to the American Embassy, where you will be my guests."

Minister of Commerce Julius Curtius and *Bürgermeister* Scholz of Berlin also were on hand to welcome the Americans at

Tempelhof. The mayor presented them with a huge laurel wreath, and somebody else draped a wreath of German oak leaves around Chamberlin's neck. Floral wreaths also appeared—a gift of German aviators in World War I. Two of these were hung over the *Columbia*'s propeller.

A band in flaming-red hussar uniforms marched around the field playing German and American airs. More cheers rose from the crowd. Then, while mechanics hauled the Bellanca into a hangar, Chamberlin and Levine got into a car belonging to the German Aero Club's president. It circled the field to shouts of *"Hoch"* from the crowd. Then they transferred to the ambassador's car, festooned with American flags and bearing a big wreath on its radiator. As they took their seats a great chorus of auto horns filled the air.

Finally, preceded by the car of the chief of police, the ambassador's automobile threaded its way through streets thick with frenzied people. Berliners hadn't shown such enthusiasm since 1925, when Paul von Hindenburg made his triumphal entry as President-elect. Nor would they surpass the display until the advent of Adolf Hitler.

Even after the Americans had reached the embassy a big crowd outside cheered until they appeared on the balcony. In the rooms the ambassador had assigned to them they found several tons of gifts, including cigars, cigarettes, silver loving cups, a chest of tea, numerous cases of beer, and dozens of bottles of still wine and champagne.

DeWitte Poole, the embassy counselor who had met them at Cottbus, now took informal charge of the airmen to see that they acted as good-will envoys should. As a starter he broke the bad news to the reporters who flocked in to interview them that the *New York Times* had bought the fliers' personal stories and that they therefore couldn't answer questions about their experiences during the trip. To newsmen not associated with that magisterial daily, this was an infuriating practice which the *Times* pursued with most of the prominent aviators of the day. As an *Evening Post,* and later *Evening World,* reporter, I saw the results when foreign airmen began gliding into Roosevelt Field. And there was nothing I could do but swear.

The next morning the ambassador drove his guests through cheering crowds to the Presidential Palace, where Von Hindenburg greeted them. The German President, then eighty, received them in his workroom, where his old-fashioned frock coat contrasted oddly with Chamberlin's doeskin jacket, plus fours and golf stockings, and Levine's somewhat rumpled business suit. But nobody objected to their attire. Indeed, officials in German, Austrian and other cities repeatedly requested them to appear at all social functions in the clothes they had worn on their flight.

Ambassador Schurman translated the President's remarks. Von Hindenburg, who had already cabled President Coolidge to express his admiration for the two men, now compared their feat to the voyage of Columbus. The Americans, like the Genoese navigator, had set out in the same spirit of adventure, he said, without knowing what goal they would reach. He voiced the usual hope on such occasions that the bold exploit would bring two great nations closer together. Then he gave each a signed photograph of himself, set in a silver frame.

Back at the embassy, after bucking more crowds, the two men shook many small hands at a reception for the children of German and diplomatic officials whom the youngsters had been pestering ever since the *Columbia*'s arrival. Then they attended to the case of Karl Klotsche, who had sold them the benzol near Eisleben and who had come to the embassy in pathetic agitation.

A story was going around Eisleben that Klotsche had sold the fliers such bad benzol that they had been forced to come down near Cottbus instead of going on to Berlin. If the canard wasn't scotched, Karl would be a ruined man. He had brought along a testimonial he had prepared, which stated that the fuel was good. He hoped the Americans would sign it. They did, and Klotsche went out with tears coursing down his cheeks.

In the afternoon Chancellor William Marx and Foreign Minister Gustav Stresemann gave a tea in honor of the airmen. The chancellor also expounded the Columbus theme. He assured the fliers that their marvelous performance would stand for all time as a monument in the history of human progress. "What you have done," he added, "will serve to unite the peoples of the earth as well as to expand the scope of human relations."

After the tea Chamberlin went out to Tempelhof to see how repairs on the old propeller were coming along. He found the *Columbia* surrounded by German pilots, mechanics and other airport workers who couldn't understand how such a small plane could carry such a heavy load so far. They asked about her wing area, horsepower, weight and other features, did some elaborate figuring and came up with the conclusion that the Bellanca was more efficient than any airplane in Europe. To make them feel better, Chamberlin told them that the machine also excelled its American rivals.

In the evening the airmen were guests of honor at a big dinner in the embassy attended by Chancellor Marx, Papal Nuncio Pacelli, and other distinguished eaters. The fliers also prepared their personal by-line story—with the help of Mr. Eyre—for publication in the *New York Times* (they didn't mention the three-mile spiral), and discussed the numerous offers they had received from film companies and vaudeville chains. One impresario wanted to present them in a circus.

The rest of the week kept them going at the same dizzying pace. They were luncheon guests of Foreign Minister Stresemann, who gave them inscribed gold and silver cigarette cases. They were tea guests of the German Aero Club, dinner guests of the American

Club and of Air Navigation and Transportation Minister Wilhelm Koch. It was noted that among the three hundred other guests at this impressive function was *Bürgermeister* Kreutz of Cottbus.

They visited the Siemens-Halska motor works, the UFA movie studios, the Rohrbach airplane factory, the palaces in Potsdam. They signed Berlin's Golden Book and received its Medal of Honor. But they saw little of the city's night life. Mr. Poole discouraged every effort on their part to go out on the town, and shepherded them into their own bedrooms every night.

During the week Berlin renamed one of its thoroughfares "Columbia Strasse" in honor of their plane. And from Pilsen came the announcement of a new Chamberlin Beer. Levine, who had been widely billed as a millionaire, discovered he had relatives all over Europe. They wrote to him out of a deep distress. Practically all of them needed money.

Perhaps as a substitute for painting the town red, Levine began to issue statements. Three days after their arrival he announced that he and Chamberlin intended to start a transatlantic airline. He was prepared to put $2,000,000 into the enterprise, he said, and predicted it would start operations within a year.

Levine also found himself in a controversy with Charles Colvin, president of the Pioneer Instrument Company, which had made the *Columbia*'s earth inductor compass. In the fliers' personal story they said that the compass had run "wild." Mr. Colvin told the *Times* that he was not surprised at the unfavorable report on the instrument; Levine, he explained, had been greatly annoyed when the company didn't give him the compass free. Moreover, he had refused to let Brice Goldsborough give it a final checkup.

Levine was soon involved in still another dispute—with a Dr. Julius Puppe of Pittsburgh, who was suing him for $10,000, allegedly due for expert advice on a Ruhr steel plant given three years earlier. A court bailiff turned up at Tempelhof and tried to attach the plane, but Lufthansa officials chased him away.

112

Vienna, Moscow and several other European capitals had invited the airmen to come for gala visits, and they had agreed to fly to Austria the following Sunday. Late Saturday afternoon Chamberlin began to test the engine. He found that one cylinder was missing, while two others were not turning up full power. He also learned that the weather forecast for the next day was unfavorable.

The engine disorder was due to a cracked cam follower, which caused an intake valve to stick and permitted air to leak into two other cylinders. To the amazement of the Lufthansa men, Chamberlin asked them to remove a push rod from the bad cylinder to give it an automatic intake. This, he informed them, would provide the engine with eight good cylinders and one that probably would function at full throttle.

The Lufthansa experts were aghast. For a pilot to take off with a crippled power plant was unthinkable to the methodical Germans. They tried to talk Chamberlin out of the project. He pointed out that the *Columbia*'s scheduled arrival in Vienna the next day had been widely publicized in the Austrian press. The Germans spoke of the bad weather; Chamberlin said he would fly through it. Finally his hosts cited the air regulations against flying with a disabled engine. It became apparent that, if necessary, they would invoke them against the *Columbia*. The Austrian trip was postponed for a week.

On June 17 the fliers' wives arrived at Bremerhaven aboard the North German Lloyd liner *Berlin*, on which they occupied suites as guests of the German government. After the Whirlwind on the *Columbia* had been repaired, Chamberlin and Levine took off for Munich and Vienna, their wives and newspaper correspondents following in big Lufthansa planes. Both the city of Munich and the state of Bavaria were their hosts at a beery luncheon. In the afternoon they flew on to the Austrian capital, where they were received by President Michael Hainisch and Chancellor Ignaz Seipel and decorated with the Golden Cross, the highest honor the little nation could bestow. The usual ceremonies followed, enlivened by an event not on the official schedule. This was a demand for $1,500 from the local frankfurter vendors' association for losses allegedly incurred because of the week's postponement of the flight. The airmen refused to pay and the association later asked the government to reimburse it for the hot dogs that had to be thrown away.

The two Americans flew down the Danube to Budapest and then up the Moldau to Prague. They took off for the Czechoslovak capital in thick weather that had forced several commercial pilots to turn back. Then, after sorties to Pilsen and Marienbad, they started for the airport to leave for Warsaw, where twenty thousand Poles had waited for them vainly three weeks earlier. Their wives remained snugly in Marienbad.

It was a rainy, windy Monday. The Czech pilots who were to have escorted them didn't show up at the airport for the scheduled departure at eight o'clock. Surely sane aviators would stay on the ground in such weather, they thought. The tops of the hills were hidden in low clouds, and mountains straggled across the route to Warsaw. But the Americans had received a telegram from the Polish capital that this time they should arrive on the appointed day—that is, Monday.

Upon learning that Chamberlin and Levine were at the airport, the Czech pilots arrived there shortly before ten-thirty. They said they would fly if Chamberlin insisted, but were greatly relieved when he told them he didn't want company. He'd have enough on his mind with those mountains along the route, he explained, without worrying about smacking some escorting machine.

When he started he had a ceiling of about 200 feet. He felt his way along a valley beneath the gray clouds and above a railroad track which threaded the mountains. At about the halfway mark the weather cleared a little, though not enough for Polish welcoming planes to find them. After five hours they reached Warsaw, where several thousand people were waiting for them in a driving rain. At the airport they found there was a mistake in the telegram they had received. It should have said they didn't need to arrive in Warsaw until Tuesday.

On June 30 the airmen headed for Paris, arriving at Le Bourget in the evening after flying through rainstorms and thickening mist. They were welcomed by Clifford Harmon, the man who had planned to fly out over the ocean to guide them in, and a delegation from the International League of Aviators, of which he was president. A crowd of three thousand persons had gathered, some to greet Chamberlin and Levine and some to welcome the *America*, which had taken off from Roosevelt Field the day before.

The big Fokker was now expected at Le Bourget at nine or ten o'clock. Mr. Wanamaker's representatives in Paris and a welcoming committee were celebrating the expected triumph with a dinner in one of the airport buildings. Chamberlin and Levine had their dinner in town, then came back to the airport to greet their trans-atlantic colleagues. Workers at the field were playing searchlights on the clouds, and firing rockets and star shells at regular intervals. The clouds were low, Chamberlin said later, but not too low for the *America* to have come in safely at that time. The rain amounted then to only a slight drizzle.

The crowd had grown larger now and was increasing in size every minute. Nine o'clock came, and then ten. But there was no news of the plane. There was nothing for the people at Le Bourget to do but wait. They waited and waited.

9

PRECURSOR OF FUTURE AIRLINERS

"I just want you to know what you may not realize, that you are the world's prize boob to get left at the switch as you did." Thus a gentleman from North Carolina to Commander Richard Evelyn Byrd, a gentleman from Virginia, after Lindbergh had arrived in Paris. It was typical of hundreds of messages, many of them anonymous, which the retired naval officer received after both the *Spirit of St. Louis* and *Columbia* departures from Roosevelt Field.

Such criticism, which often included accusations of cowardice, didn't change Byrd's plans. He continued to subject the *America* to manifold tests. In his book *Skyward* he explains that the effort to compile useful data for the transatlantic airliners of the future required him to ascertain the most efficient engine speeds for various loads. Also, he says he didn't want to detract from Lindbergh's glory by starting for France until the nation's current great hero had been welcomed home.

At any rate, the tests continued—and continued to enrage the plane's designer. In his book *Flying Dutchman,* Fokker recalls angrily that the operations at Roosevelt Field, "where Wanamaker had trimmed up an old hangar like a boudoir," constituted "the most interminable series of test flights it has ever been my grief to witness. They dragged on for days. It seemed to me that every possible excuse was seized on. The absence of Bennett, who was laid up in the hospital for months, seemed to take the heart out of the expedi-

117

tion. I began to wonder whether Byrd really wanted to make the transatlantic flight, which was basically hardly more than an elaborate advertisement. Instead of eagerly trying to push ahead it seemed to me every possible excuse to stall was seized upon."

If the tests continued, so did the statements. On June 12 the commander announced that the plane would go through its final tests the next day and might take off on the fifteenth. On June 14 he said the *America* was ready and would start on the first favorable day after the Lindbergh celebration ended. On June 15 there was another delay of two days because of storms over the Atlantic.

On June 19 the storms were still raging, but Byrd came up with an item which the *Times* saw fit to print. The *America*, her skipper said, would be run like a ship. The instruments would give her crew a choice of courses above the sea, and on the way over they would study ocean winds, fogs, icings and other perils which future airliners might encounter. In short, the flight would promote aeronautical science. And, incidentally, it might begin the next day. The plane was hauled up on Fokker's incline ready for the flight.

It didn't begin then, but when that day arrived, Byrd said it would start the day after—if the storms abated. And on June 21 he said it would be going on the twenty-second—if the weather cleared. The *Times* of that date was even more specific, giving a 7 P.M. starting time for the great scientific experiment, though it was again possible the departure might be delayed.

Byrd also revealed in another interview that catwalks had been built from the Fokker's fuselage to each outboard engine so that if either power plant broke down in flight somebody could move out and try to repair it. He designated Balchen for the job, which would entail ministering to a stricken Whirlwind while exposed to an air blast of 90 or 100 miles an hour.

Storms or fog over the Atlantic persisted. Instead of taking off on June 22, Byrd went to New Haven to get an honorary M.A. from Yale. But the next day the outlook was better and a start was scheduled for the morning of June 24 at about four o'clock. The plane was hauled up on the incline again and the tanks partially filled. About a thousand people turned up to see the long-delayed departure.

Fokker had gone over the plane carefully when, shortly after midnight, he learned that the flight had been postponed. The *Times* reported he said "Hell!" Other sources described his remarks as considerably more emphatic.

Byrd said he regretted the delay. "If I were on my own I probably would take off," he told reporters. "But I've got three men with me and there is a responsibility there. And if we should fail by disregarding weather advices it might do a serious injury to aviation."

Two days later the Atlantic weather forecast was favorable. Takeoff was set for dawn on June 28. Again the big plane was hauled up the incline and the tanks partially filled. Fokker looked her over carefully once more and pronounced her fit. Balchen, Acosta and Noville walked over the Roosevelt runway. It was wet from recent rains but they decided it would do. But Doc Kinkaid, the engine expert, opined it was too soggy.

The two pilots advised Doc to stick to his engines. They knew more about getting planes airborne, they said, than he did. They convinced Whalen that the runway was satisfactory. He called Byrd at the Garden City Hotel. At five forty-five that morning Byrd told them he couldn't sanction a takeoff if Kinkaid didn't approve.

Acosta wept with exasperation. Uncle Tony blew up. Balchen later described the scene between the designer and the commander. "The *America* is being towed back to the hangar for the third time," the Norwegian says in his book, "and Tony Fokker has been up all night, waiting vainly for the takeoff. When Commander Byrd strolls into the hangar later that morning, Uncle Tony flies into a Dutch rage. His round pink cheeks blow in and out, like the rubber-bulb horn on his Lancia, as he honks with fury.

"He is sick and tired of all this damn stalling. Byrd can fly the *America* non-stop to Hell, for all of him—he is through right now, by Gott. He roars off in his sports car in a cloud of mud and flying grass, and goes for a long cruise on his yacht to cool off."

The same day Byrd revealed that if the transatlantic trip was successful he intended to fly back to New York, making the eastward trip that had so long balked ocean aviators. Late that night he received word from Dr. Kimball that while the weather over the Atlantic wasn't perfect, it was probably as good as it would be for some time. A cold front was building up over the ocean but there should be good visibility this side of it, and thereafter a plane should be able to fly under the clouds.

Byrd decided to chance it on the morrow. The airliner of the future, he told reporters, must be able to cross the Atlantic even in bad weather. Perhaps the big Fokker—which after all was the prototype of such ocean planes—would contribute more to aeronautical science if it flew to France through snow, rain, heat and gloom of night.

After that long wait for weather that would be perfect all the way across, Byrd's decision came as a surprise to Balchen. But he lay down on his cot in the hangar to get a little rest. About three in the morning Byrd and Noville appeared. A drizzle was soaking the field. But this time, it seemed, they really were going. The *America* was poised on her little hill again, her tail skid tied to its stake by a rope. Mechanics topped off her gas tanks with 1,295 gallons.

To many of the thousand people who turned up at Roosevelt Field that gray morning, the three-engined Fokker really did seem like the forerunner of future airliners. Certainly she dwarfed the two single-engined aircraft that already had flown from Long Island to Europe. Her wingspan of seventy-one feet was about twenty-five feet longer than that of either the *Spirit of St. Louis* or the *Columbia*. She was going to carry four men instead of one or two. Her total weight—over 15,000 pounds—was three times that of either of the others.

At the last minute Byrd decided that this was too much. He had the mudguards removed from the front wheels and took out two 5-gallon cans of gasoline, four pairs of moccasins and a 5-pound vacuum bottle of hot tea for himself. This lightening action ended a plot of Doc Kinkaid's to stow away with Acosta's help. Doc decided that if Byrd felt he had to dispense with his tea, he probably would not welcome 160 pounds of engine expert.

Before getting into the plane, Byrd handed the reporters a message to the public. It emphasized a theme which, some of the recipients felt, had already been aired at some length. "Whereas I am attempting this flight for many reasons," it said, "I hope our countrymen will appreciate the fact that my shipmates, Noville, Acosta and Balchen, are flying over the top today totally for the progress of aviation to which they are devoting their lives. There is, they realize, little glory in the undertaking. There are no prizes awaiting them."

Whalen also had a message. It was addressed to Byrd but there were more than enough copies for the reporters. This document, a letter, termed the flight "a scientific research and good will expedition." It reminded the commander—if he needed reminding—that the plane was carrying a "precious bag of United States mail" which had been given to him some days earlier, while the cameras clicked, by Postmaster John J. Kiely of New York. The letter also said that Mr. Wanamaker had entrusted to Byrd's care a strongbox containing a letter from the merchant to President Doumergue of France; a copy of the first American flag, made by a great-grandniece of Betsy Ross—also to be given to Doumergue; and the flag which Byrd had carried on his North Pole project and later given to Mr. Wanamaker. This was to be carried across the ocean and then brought back and given to Mr. Wanamaker again.

By five-fifteen all the messages had been delivered and everybody was aboard the plane—Acosta in the left-hand seat of the cockpit to handle the takeoff; Noville in the other seat with his hand on the dump valve, ready to jettison gas and lighten the ship if necessary; Byrd and Balchen in the navigator's compartment aft of the main gas tank. The plane was facing the same way Fonck's overloaded Sikorsky faced when it failed to get off the ground nine months earlier. Now the Fokker was overloaded too, and Noville was ready to dump some of the load if Acosta thought they couldn't get into the air.

Acosta revved up the engines until they produced a steady roar. He wanted to warm them up thoroughly. But suddenly the plane lurched forward down the incline. The rope to the tail skid had snapped. The effect of Fokker's invention was lost. Instead of getting the equivalent of 500 or more additional feet of runway, the plane was rolling with inadequately warmed-up engines toward the place where the Fonck plane had crashed.

Acosta made a quick decision. He could have shut down the engines and rolled to a safe stop. Instead he shoved the throttle forward. The big plane gathered speed. She lumbered past the halfway mark. Too late to stop now. She roared on a little farther. Then, 3,270 feet from the starting point, she left the ground.

Everybody relaxed. At 300 feet above the earth Acosta began a slow climbing turn. At 400 feet he had the plane pointed to the northeast, heading over the tip of Long Island toward Cape Cod. Favorable winds came along to give a welcome boost. Soon the *America* had a groundspeed of 95 miles an hour.

After the April accident, Fokker had put in a narrow passageway between the cockpit and the rest of the cabin. Now it was almost blocked by 5-gallon cans of gas. But Balchen squeezed past them to spell Acosta at the helm. Noville went back to his radio operator's cubicle behind the two pilots. There the automatic transmitter started sounding the plane's call letters.

122

The weather improved. Over Maine the offshore wind grew stronger. Balchen altered course 5 degrees left to compensate for drift. Noville began pouring gas into the main tank and dropping the empty cans through the trap door in the floor. He also jotted down figures on the amount of gas being used.

Over Newfoundland, Noville handed the pilots a slip of paper. It was enough to alarm anybody who knew about engines. Their gas consumption, it said, was much greater than had been expected. Balchen stared at the figures his shipmate had written. They contrasted shockingly with the computations based on the many fuel-consumption tests he and Acosta had made.

Byrd, who had also seen the figures, ordered the engines throttled back to their most economical speed. But the clouds closed in and he said he couldn't navigate unless they could see something more than mist. So they turned up more power and climbed to 5,000 feet. But they couldn't rise out of the gray vapor.

They asked Noville to recheck the gas gauges. Again he announced that the Whirlwinds were sucking up fuel at a ruinous rate. Byrd eased into the cockpit. If Noville's figures were correct and the plane encountered headwinds, they would never reach France. How did everybody feel about turning back?

The mist swirled around them. The land below was invisible. They couldn't come down at either St. John's or Harbour Grace. And between Newfoundland and the United States there wasn't any other place for the Fokker to land. Perhaps Noville was mistaken. They decided to keep going.

By eight o'clock that night they were flying at 6,500 feet but still could see only blank gray. Acosta was dozing in his seat. Balchen, piloting the plane, began to get hungry. He thought of some chicken sandwiches he had tucked under his seat. "Take the plane for a minute, will you, Bert?" Acosta nodded and gripped the wheel. Outside the windows the mist still swirled.

It was pleasant, thought Balchen, to be able to look away from the instruments. He bent down and groped under the seat for the sandwiches. He felt himself pulled strongly down into the seat. He tried to rise against an invisible force. He realized the Fokker was in a spiral and diving toward the sea. It was the kind of situation Chamberlin had met earlier in the Bellanca.

The instruments confirmed Balchen's fears. The altimeter and bank-and-turn indicator showed that they were spiraling nearly out of control. The airspeed indicator showed 140 miles an hour. Balchen knew that if the heavily loaded plane reached 160, the wood-veneered wing would rip off.

He suddenly remembered that Acosta didn't "believe" in instruments. He grabbed the wheel on his side and waved Acosta off the other. Already the plane had lost a thousand feet and the airspeed was rapidly increasing. Balchen eased back gently on the wheel. Then, as Chamberlin had done, he ruddered the Fokker slowly out of the spiral and leveled off at 5,000 feet. By this time the plane was heading toward North America. Balchen had to make a 180-degree turn to get her back on course.

Byrd pushed in through the passageway, tearing his jacket in his haste. "What happened?" he demanded. "Oh, nothing much," Balchen replied. "At least, everything is okay now." Acosta slumped in his seat. "This instrument flying is one thing I've never bothered with," he said. "You'd better handle it from now on, as long as we're fogged in."

Watching the dials on the instrument panel, Balchen started a long climb to regain the lost altitude. He also pondered the glass tubes that showed gasoline levels in the tanks. Perhaps they weren't telling the truth. After all, the tail of the overloaded plane was down a bit and that would affect their accuracy. With the engine speeds and gas mixtures they had been using so far, it didn't seem possible that fuel could be running out so prodigally. He consulted his slide rule. Noville must be wrong. He had to be wrong.

At about one o'clock in the morning the Fokker roared out of the haze at a height of 8,000 feet. The friendly moon illuminated a solid layer of stratus below them. Above them golden stars spangled the dark blue. Perhaps the commander would take some shots and give them their position. He hadn't given them any positions since they started.

Balchen leveled off at about 500 feet above the cloud floor and again turned the ship over to Acosta. After seven hours at the wheel he was tired. He stood up, stretched his stiff limbs and started toward the rear. Noville was fiddling with the radio, trying vainly to raise a ship. He gave up after a while. Balchen tinkered with the set but had no better luck. Noville began to recheck his fuel-consumption figures. Balchen crawled farther back, to the navigator's compartment, sat down and stretched out his numb legs.

Byrd was poring over a chart. The roar of the three engines up ahead now sounded like a distant waterfall. How much fuel were those Whirlwinds really using? Balchen wondered about it drowsily. Presently Noville came in with another slip of paper. This one said: "Made mistake in first estimate. Have enough gas to fly all the way."

It had taken him over eight hours to discover he was wrong.

During the next few hours they flew above the fleecy floor, and the two pilots continued to spell each other at the wheel. But toward dawn, walls of cumulus rose ahead of them and they were again in the mist. Acosta turned the helm over to his companion and crawled back to the navigator's compartment for a nap.

Alone in the cockpit, Balchen watched the luminous instrument dials in the darkness. With their help he held the big plane on an even keel through updrafts and downdrafts. Sometimes she would race out of the murk for a few moments and he would look up between the cloud mountains and see their sides touched with the first golden light of faraway sunrise.

On and on toward the east they droned until they flew into a joyous day where the sunlight turned the cloud floor a brilliant white. Acosta crept back to the cockpit and the two men sat gazing at the beauty stretching in all directions around them.

After an hour, in which Balchen got another nap, the mist rose around them again. He took over the wheel and tried to climb out of it. They were supposed to be following the same compass course Lindbergh and Chamberlin had taken. But were they really on it? The commander still hadn't give them any positions, even though the stars had been visible for hours. Balchen wondered why the flight leader hadn't used his sextant. The pilots hadn't been able to determine their drift, for there had been a haze below them, and their smoke bombs, designed to ignite when they hit the ocean, were of course useless as long as the water couldn't be seen. With a wind from the north pushing the Fokker southward they might be hundreds of miles off course.

At 15,000 feet, the highest the plane would climb, they were still in the clouds. In the thin air the controls felt mushy. Soon Balchen heard a rattling against the fabric sides of the fuselage. It was ice, forming on the propellers and breaking off to be hurled at the ship. Ice was also forming on the wings, starting to change their contours. "Get a load of this," it seemed to say. "Get a load of this and see what happens."

It was midafternoon. Noville had been trying all day to get into Morse conversation with somebody. Now he got a message from a ship nearly three miles below them. It reported a broken ceiling of about 2,000 feet, with northwesterly winds.

Balchen pushed the wheel forward and started down. They had to go to 1,000 feet before they saw the ocean. It was dark blue and rough, with whitecaps, and it stretched away to a circling horizon. There was no sign of either land or ships.

They flew on toward the east for nearly two hours longer. Finally, at five o'clock, they saw a faint smudge ahead of them. They were rapidly approaching Brest, the arm of land which France stretches toward the New World.

They were more than 200 miles off course. They should have been approaching Le Havre, for a quick trip up the Seine to Paris. Well, at least they had reached the Continent.

They crossed a margin of white breakers and were over green fields and red-roofed farmhouses. The weather was bright and clear. Perhaps everything was all right, after all. Paris was only 300 miles away. They should reach it in less than three hours.

But Noville had received a message from a French station, sent especially for the *America*. It predicted low ceilings and rain squalls for the evening. And now, over Brest, they got another radio message direct from Le Bourget. This one reported heavy drizzle and lowering ceilings, and predicted the murk would close in by nightfall.

Still, by that time they should be at the airport. They could follow the railroad from Brest to the capital, Balchen reasoned, and land at Le Bourget before dark. But he was in for a shock. He was astounded when Byrd told Acosta to fly northeast along the coast to Le Havre, then turn right and use the Seine as a guideline into Paris.

Byrd does not mention this incident in his various published descriptions of the voyage. But Balchen reports it at some length. He explains that he was familiar with northern France and that he had last flown in and out of Le Bourget only two years earlier.

Now he told Byrd that if they used the coastline–Seine River route it would take at least two hours longer than if they followed the railroad. The Brest–Paris route, he pointed out, would get them in while they could still see the field, ahead of the thick weather. Byrd did not act on the suggestion. Again he ordered Acosta to stick to the coastline.

Over Cherbourg it began to get dark and Acosta relinquished the helm to Balchen. Rain started to fall. The little lights below grew dim as the plane twisted above the winding coastline. The radio reports had proven very useful, but about this time they ceased—Noville, shifting his position in the cramped little cubicle, had ripped some wires off their terminals with his foot.

They reached Le Havre and set a course up the sinuous Seine toward Paris. Now Balchen was alone in the cockpit again. Some 2,000 feet below, in the last light of the gray day, he could see the bright river beaded with black barges. As the light faded he came down closer to the ground, and over Rouen he was only 200 feet above the wet cobblestone streets. Then the rain blotted out the earth and he tried to climb above the weather, setting a course for Paris from the town he had just left.

For forty-five minutes he flew on at 4,000 feet, watching the glowing instrument dials and sometimes looking out the windows at the blue flames from the Whirlwinds' exhaust pipes. The engines were still roaring without a miss after nearly forty hours from Roosevelt Field.

Perhaps the *America* was now somewhere near Paris. Had they had a radio to guide them the surmise would have been surer—but they had neither radio nor river any more. Balchen eased the big plane down through the rain rattling on its fuselage, hoping to find some hole in the clouds. But there was no hole through which he could see lights or reflections on the ground.

He banked and turned for fifteen or twenty minutes, peering down through the black, then easing down a little lower and circling again. It was now ten o'clock. He decided that the only thing to do was fly back to the coast, which had had a fairly high ceiling ninety minutes earlier, and try to steer for the capital again.

After an hour and a half at 4,000 feet he slanted down again and broke out of the overcast 1,500 feet above the water. He picked up the lights of Le Havre once more and started again for Paris. The gauges showed that the gas was getting low, and this time the readings were correct.

·   ·   ·

Meanwhile, as the Fokker was probing blindly through the rain over France, the sponsors of the project, the wives of the crew and numerous hangers-on were celebrating the supposed triumph in the bunting-bedecked hangar the plane had left at Roosevelt Field. The America Trans-Oceanic Company had decided to combine a buffet supper for the reporters, who had covered its great effort, with some well-bred elation over a successful flight. A jazz band had been hired and lively music echoed through the big barnlike building. Mrs. Byrd had gone to Boston after watching the takeoff but Mrs. Acosta, Mrs. Noville and other guests were on hand. Whalen, as usual, was in charge of proceedings.

Near the hangar entrance two bulletin boards displayed messages about the plane, whose automatically transmitted call letters had been picked up by ground stations and ships. Herbert Sussman, former navigating officer of the *Leviathan*, stuck red-headed pins in a big map to show the Fokker's progress up the coast, across the Alantic and over France.

Near Whalen's office a Western Union telegraph instrument tinkled musically from time to time to dot and dash another message about the splendid voyage. The manager of the special hangar office typed out the messages and handed them over to be thumb-tacked on the bulletin board with the others.

At seven-thirty that evening, June 30, the instrument clicked especially happy news. And it came from no less an authority than the superintendent of the Western Union office in Paris. The *America*, he said—no doubt after analyzing the latest intelligence available to him—was expected to land in Paris in thirty minutes.

Later another message announced that the plane was over Le Bourget. Mrs. Acosta, a shapely, vivacious woman, leaped to her feet. "They're there! They're there!" she cried. Mrs. Noville giggled. "Of course we knew they'd make it," she said.

A motorcycle policeman fired five shots in the air. Mechanics who had worked on the plane slapped each other on the back. Even reporters grinned and talked excitedly about the achievement. They telephoned the glad news to Mrs. Byrd in Boston. Then everybody fell on the food.

Still another message said the plane had actually landed—not at Le Bourget but at a place called Issy-les-Moulineaux. It seemed this Issy-whatever-it-was was a suburb of Paris. Well, what the hell? They were down safe and everything was jake.

Sussman and Tom Mulroy, Byrd's chief mechanic, came up with armfuls of flares and rockets. Whalen organized a parade. With the band playing "My Bonnie Lies Over the Ocean" and "Madelon," and with French and American flags waving, he marched out on the field, accompanied by Mrs. Acosta and Mrs. Noville and followed by most of the people from the hangar. They ended up at the ramp from which the *America* had prematurely started her run.

The Reverend Henry Meiser of Grace Church, Jamaica, Long Island, who had come over for the celebration, climbed up on the ramp and raised his hand for silence. Then, as the company listened with heads bowed, he offered a prayer of thanksgiving. After that the French and American flags were hauled to the tops of improvised flagpoles and the band played the "Marseillaise" and "The Star-Spangled Banner." Then Whalen proposed three cheers for Byrd and his gallant companions. They were given in the traditional manner; i.e., with right hearty good will.

Rockets and Roman candles, whizzing up in front of the hangar, illuminated the happy throng as it returned to the big building. By this time most of the bulletins had disappeared from the boards. Souvenir hunters had quietly removed them, along with most of the red-headed pins.

But now another bulletin was coming in, and this one refuted all the others. It was from a reliable news agency and said that earlier reports about the plane's having landed safely were false. Far from being down, the Fokker was probably somewhere over

France, flying around in rain and clouds which blacked out all landing fields.

For a while people tried to be cheerful. "I'm not worried," said Mrs. Acosta. "Bert will bring them down. They're probably down right now and nobody knows where they are." "Certainly," rejoined Mrs. Noville. "There's nothing to worry about." But they agreed that Mrs. Byrd should be notified.

An Associated Press dispatch from Winchester, Virginia, didn't allay anybody's fears for the fliers. It quoted Tom Byrd, another brother of the commander's, that he wasn't worried at all. If they couldn't land in the dark, he declared, they could always parachute from the Fokker and float gently to earth. He apparently didn't know that there weren't any 'chutes aboard the plane. To have taken four would have added eighty pounds to the total load.

It was past midnight now, and still there was no word of the *America*. The hours dragged on. It became cold. There was nothing to talk about and nobody wanted to sleep. The two women looked more and more anxious.

In the black skies over France, Balchen wasn't sure where they were. He calculated that they were over the French capital again at about one o'clock in the morning. Watching the instruments, he went down to 4,000 feet. He didn't dare come lower. The altimeter might not be accurate, and somewhere in the darkness the ugly skeleton of the Eiffel Tower reared up nearly a thousand feet above the city.

The plane circled and circled in the dark, rainy night. Once Balchen thought he saw a flash below the wing. He peered down anxiously but it was not repeated. Later he learned that a big crowd had been waiting for them at Le Bourget and that at one o'clock people there had heard engines overhead. The ceiling at the field at that time was 75 feet.

131

The fuel gauges showed that the tanks were almost empty. The airmen couldn't come down blindly in the dark lest they kill both themselves and people in the city. At the coast there had twice been a little visibility. So back to the coast they started. As the plane droned on, Balchen listened apprehensively for ominous coughs from Whirlwinds that had whirled faithfully for over forty-two hours but which had to have fuel to keep on whirling.

Around two o'clock he thought they must be over the coast again. He came down through the clouds and saw scattered lights along the shore. Then he noticed an electric sign on the roof of a building. It read DEAUVILLE. They were a few miles south of Le Havre.

Byrd crawled through the passageway, and shouting over the noise of the engines, asked what their position was. Balchen told him of the sign and added that they would have to come down soon. The commander asked him if they would crash. The pilot replied—with more confidence than he felt—that the fuel might hold out until they found a landing site.

The first faint light of oncoming day enabled the worried Norwegian to see a sandy beach as the plane flew southwestward along the shoreline. But the beach was littered with fishing boats and offered no space to land the Fokker. Ahead of the plane the yellow beam from a lighthouse swept around the horizon. Balchen banked around behind it as he and Byrd examined the ground below. There were meadows but they were blocked out into little fields by stone walls. There was a small beach but it was studded with boats.

Only the water offshore seemed to offer reasonable space. Shouting at each other, the two men agreed that their only chance was to ditch. As the plane banked over the water the starboard engine coughed. Balchen asked Byrd to toss out three carbide drift flares, about a hundred yards apart, to give him a target on the water. The commander crawled back to the navigator's compartment, opened the trap door in the floor and dropped the flares. As the plane came around again, Balchen saw them burst into flame on the water. He decided to set the plane down on the middle flare.

The crew got ready for the shock. Acosta squeezed into the radio operator's seat. Byrd and Noville braced themselves in the navigator's room. Balchen eased the Fokker down almost to the wave tops. At three or four feet above the water he cut the three engines. The big plane splashed into the black sea. Her voyage was over.

The front part of the plane and the engines sank beneath the surface, but the depth was only a few feet. Cold water poured around and over Balchen. He unfastened his safety belt and kicked open the door of the radio room. He pulled himself up through the hatch above it and drew in deep breaths of fresh air.

Byrd and Noville had come up through the hatch in the roof of the navigator's compartment and crawled up on the wing. The empty main gas tank held part of the fuselage above the surface. Byrd helped the Norwegian up on the wing and asked him where Acosta was, in a voice that sounded high and shrill to ears stunned by the roar of engines.

Acosta was in the darkness behind them, shouting in a shrill voice. He had trouble clambering up on the wing, for his collarbone was bruised, but with the help of the others he made it. As Balchen's hearing began to return to normal he listened in a strange silence to the lapping of the tide running out along the sides of the plane. The wing was awash and the heavy nose was on the bottom. The landing gear had been cleanly sheared off.

They hauled out a rubber raft, inflated it with a foot pump and put into it the strongbox and some of the mail. Then they got in themselves and paddled the 200 yards to shore. By this time it was half past four of a dismal, rainy morning.

They trudged up a hill to a village about a mile away. All the houses were dark and still. The only person they saw was a boy on a bicycle. He took one look at the bedraggled apparitions from the sea and pedaled rapidly away.

They climbed farther up the hill to the lighthouse and pounded on the heavy door. Finally Jules Lescope, the keeper, poked his night-capped head out of an upper window. Noville, who spoke some French, explained their peculiar appearance. The keeper and his wife unbolted the door. They told the Americans they were at Ver-sur-Mer, near Caen, a place which became known to American GI's seventeen years later as Omaha Beach.

Lescope put Noville and Acosta, the most exhausted of the quartet, to bed in the lighthouse, and lent Byrd and Balchen dry clothing. Then the commander and his companion walked back down the hill to the broken plane. The tide had rolled out and the machine lay on its belly. The wheels were a hundred yards down the beach.

Excited villagers ran up to see the wreck of the plane from *les Etats-Unis*. They helped the airmen take it apart and carry sections above the tidemark. One man brought tools from the local machine shop and helped unbolt the engines and carry them onto the beach. Later he helped unbolt and carry the big wing.

Some of the villagers wanted souvenirs. Balchen saw one group staggering away with an engine. When he and Byrd protested, the Frenchmen shrugged in surprise but abandoned their project without apparent resentment. But another group, possibly working quietly while the airmen were retrieving the Whirlwind, got away with a big strip of fabric from the side of the fuselage. Eight feet high and forty feet long, it bore the name the plane had been christened. Neither Byrd nor Balchen saw it go.

Finally the weary Americans were able to quit. They were put to bed in the Norman cottage of Mme. Josephine Cossier, a mother of five. "These men will remain as dear to me as my five children," Mme. Cossier later told a reporter. "Not for many years have I had as much joy as today, this greatest day of my life."

.   .   .

134

While the four airmen slept or salvaged what was left of the plane, wives and friends in America thought of them with increasing apprehension. Finally, at 3:30 A.M. in New York, a call from a newspaper to the hangar disclosed that the plane had reportedly been forced down off the French coast and that the crew was safe. After that the telegraph instrument began relaying more bulletins. They supported the dispatch which had been sent by the newspaper and it was finally confirmed by Mr. Wanamaker's representative in Paris.

Mrs. Acosta and Mrs. Noville went home shortly before six o'clock. Mr. Whalen, before leaving, made a statement. "This was a scientific flight, undertaken for a scientific purpose and the forcing down of the ship could not possibly end the undertaking," he told sleepy reporters.

"The America Trans-Oceanic Company," Mr. Whalen resumed, "will continue this experimental work to the point we originally considered. I cannot tell you what our immediate plans are, for we haven't decided yet. But you may be certain that we will continue along the same path, building for those other pioneers yet to follow us in this field. Commander Byrd did the best he could. So did Acosta, Noville and Balchen. The wrecking of the ship is an inconsequential matter so long as the men are safe.

"I have ordered our representative in Paris to proceed immediately to Ver-sur-Mer, give whatever assistance he can to the fliers and cable us the extent of the damage. We shall then salvage her."

Within the next few days the America Trans-Oceanic Company saw to it that the remains of the vehicle to promote aeronautical science were packed into ten big boxes and shipped home.

10

AMBASSADOR OF GOOD WILL

More than ten thousand people swirled in the St. Lazare Station and in the streets outside when the express from Caen brought the four survivors of the *America* into Paris. Those in the admiring throng included Chamberlin and Levine, who were to participate in many of the welcoming ceremonies scheduled over the next fortnight.

From the station the fliers rode through cheering crowds to the Hotel Continental, where Mr. Wanamaker maintained a suite. There Gurnee Munn, nine, shook Commander Byrd's hand and said, "On behalf of my grandfather, Rodman Wanamaker, I heartily congratulate you on the success of your flight and welcome you to France."

The fact that the Fokker's flight had ended with the plane almost a total wreck did not dampen world acclaim for the transatlantic crossing. Many adults, among them no less a personage than Premier Raymond Poincaré, seemed to be under the impression that Byrd had scored a great triumph. In attaching the rosette of an officer of the Legion of Honor to the commander, the statesman said that the French people considered the voyage to have been perfectly successful. He also told the four men that they had provided a splendid example of discipline and patriotism in thinking less of saving their lives when their ship smacked into the sea than they had of saving the precious flag they were bringing to President Doumergue and the mail destined for distinguished persons in France.

A similar evaluation of the flight, made by a dozen manufacturers of American aircraft and aircraft equipment, appeared in a full-page advertisement published in the *New York Times* the day after the Fokker splashed. Captioned THE AGE OF WONDERS and addressed to Commander Byrd, it said: "Your thrilling accomplishment, your splendid enterprise, is another link in the chain of America's aviation progress. Your pioneer effort in charting the trackless airways under such adverse conditions has earned the esteem of leaders in science and commerce alike as well as all humanity."

But if Byrd's performance in the air didn't approach that of Lindbergh's, his behavior after he landed did not suffer by comparison. Like Lindbergh, he said and did all the right things. He called on Mme. Nungesser, who had surrounded a photograph of her son with flowers in a pathetic shrine. He laid a wreath on the tomb of the Unknown Soldier. He praised the prowess of French aviators and the excellence of French planes. And he repeatedly emphasized the greatness and glory of France.

Before boarding the *Leviathan* for home, some of the *America* fliers stopped at the casino in Deauville, where the Prince of Wales and a few friends were dining at a center table. Balchen and Acosta were introduced, and His Royal Highness, then a handsome young man of thirty-two, asked them to join his party. With the prince was a beautiful Hungarian dancer, a chilly blonde whom Acosta eyed with lively interest. Next to Balchen was a very British general with a drooping mustache and a monocle dangling on a black ribbon.

Wine flowed freely and Acosta's glass was refilled several times. Couples were waltzing around the floor to seductive music. Suddenly Acosta pushed back his chair and slapped His Royal Highness on the shoulder. "Say, boy, can I dance with your girl?" he asked.

The British general stiffened and put his monocle into his eye, measuring Acosta as if he were a worm. The pilot took a five-franc piece from his pocket, squeezed it into his own eye, and returned the glare. There was a moment of dead silence. Then the prince laughed. "Go right ahead, old chap." Everybody relaxed.

Before Balchen left the casino, he noticed a new wall decoration forty feet long. It was a familiar piece of fabric; it bore the name *America* in big white letters. Balchen returned to the room he and Acosta shared, but his companion didn't show up. Balchen assumed the aerial sheik was out on the town.

When he walked into the hotel courtyard the next morning Balchen found the prince sitting alone at a table looking morose. When he saw Balchen he asked, "Aren't you one of the chaps who was on the *America?*" Balchen admitted he was. "Where is your friend?" the prince demanded. "He went away with my girl."

Balchen made inquiries and found a bellhop who said he knew where Acosta was. Encouraged by a small fee, the boy led Balchen to another hostelry. There, in answer to a knock, Acosta made a sleepy reply but didn't open the door. It turned out that he had spent the night with a fair companion who had proved less chilly than she had at first appeared to be.

All the *America* fliers—along with Clarence Chamberlin—got an enthusiastic welcome in New York. And Balchen got several welcomes all to himself when he returned to Norway in August to see his mother and discuss with Roald Amundsen the equipment for the coming Byrd Antarctic expedition, which he expected to be a member of. He had been wondering if he'd be able to find a hotel room in Oslo but when he arrived there was a suite reserved for him at the Grand Hotel, and a car and driver at his disposal.

During the festivities, which to the modest airman were totally unexpected, King Haakon welcomed him at the Royal Palace and questioned him about his flight and future plans for an hour and a half. Balchen also had a long talk with Amundsen, whom he had idolized for years. The renowned explorer arranged for a veteran sailmaker and tailor to get leave from the naval base at Horten so he could make garments and tents needed for the Byrd expedition. And he also helped Balchen get the sealer *Samson,* which later accompanied Byrd south under the name *City of New York.*

If Byrd, Balchen and the others had made friends for the United States by their exploits and conduct abroad, the situation was different with Levine. The former used-car salesman, who with Chamberlin shared some the the *America* crew's Parisian honors, was busily undoing his compatriots' work of strengthening those bonds of friendship between two noble republics.

On July 6 Levine announced that he would fly back to the United States in the *Columbia* with someone other than Chamberlin. He also said he had engaged a suite for his family on the August 9 sailing of the *Leviathan* so he could fly over the liner and wave to his wife. Then he disclosed that his new aviator would be Maurice Drouhin, a famous French World War I ace.

This announcement burst on French *amour-propre* like shells from one of their celebrated 75's. Even before the Nungesser-Coli tragedy French aviators and aircraft manufacturers had been talking of westward flights, and now three local planes were being readied for the trip. Byrd had been flattering the French by stressing the magnificence of such a flight against prevailing winds, and expressing confidence that some Frenchman would make it. The achievement had become a matter of Gallic pride. If Frenchmen were able to fly to America first, it would make up for the humiliation some of the citizenry felt at seeing the eastward passage dominated by Americans.

Of the three French planes scheduled for the great effort, the most likely candidate was the *Blue Bird,* a big specially designed Farman biplane powered with two Hispano-Suiza engines. Drouhin had been on the Farman payroll for half a year and had put the plane through so many tests that it was just about ready to go. There was need for haste if the French were to be first, because some German

140

fliers were known to be getting a couple of Junkers planes in shape for a westward flight.

And now Levine had bought Drouhin's fealty. He had contracted to deposit 300,000 francs (then about $12,000) in a French bank for Mme. Drouhin, just in case; he would pay Drouhin 3,000 francs weekly expense money while he prepared the *Columbia* for the return trip, and give him half the movie, literary and other profits if the flight was successful. Further, Levine would hand over 100,000 francs if he failed to carry out the agreement.

"We are very much disappointed," said Henry Farman when he got the news. "There was nothing in Drouhin's attitude to make us feel he would drop the *Blue Bird* within forty-eight hours. For six months we have been preparing to make the flight from Paris to New York. We have trained him to use charts and taught him all he should know for making a flight of this importance. Today everything is ready and Mr. Levine takes him away.

"It is not that Drouhin is indispensable. Many other pilots will be very happy to make the transatlantic flight in our plane. But there is a way of doing things in all matters, and Mr. Levine's way of doings things has certainly taken us by surprise. He did not consult us either by letter or by telephone."

French newspapers denounced the deal. "We must declare emphatically," said *L'Echo*, "that however flattering Levine's proposition is for our aviators, it will not satisfy French public opinion. We know that German aviators are preparing for a Berlin–New York flight with a German crew in a German plane with German engines. The Paris–New York flight must be accomplished by French aviators in a French plane with French engines. It is up to the French government to do its duty. The national interest is at stake."

The French might better have braced themselves for further affronts from one of the men to whom Paris had given its gold medal. In mid-July, Levine called on Captain Frank Courtney in

England. The Briton had a Dornier-Wal seaplane which he wanted
to fly to America. Levine, after inspecting it, reportedly offered
Courtney $10,000 to take him along as a passenger.

Nothing came of this proposal or indeed of Courtney's project,
and when Levine failed to put up that 300,000 francs for Mme.
Drouhin, a coolness developed between him and the French flier.
Paris newspapers accused the American of trying to goad Drouhin
into breaking the agreement so that he could hire a British pilot.
Drouhin threatened to fly to New York with a countryman if the
American did not show some good faith.

John Carisi had come to Paris with a spare Whirlwind for the
Columbia. It was kept in the hangar at Le Bourget. One day while
Drouhin was absent, Levine had the engine removed. Thereafter
Drouhin's friends stood guard in relays over the plane.

Adding further spice to a pungent situation was Mabel Boll,
who was now living in Paris. Miss Boll had offered $25,000 to any-
body who would fly her westward across the ocean. She wanted to
make the trip in her new gold sweater, a garment fashioned by a
Parisian jeweler who had created it from link gold and topped it
off with a platinum collar. The lady had approached both Levine
and Drouhin, and each suspected that the other would take her to
America and leave him in *la belle France*.

They were now quarreling constantly. Levine claimed that
Drouhin had refused to start several times when the weather was
favorable. Drouhin retorted that Levine was the one who had shown
reluctance. Neither spoke the other's language and friends of
Drouhin had to act as interpreters. This, Levine felt, gave the flier
an unfair advantage. He started to study French—both for quarreling purposes and for possible use on the possible flight.

On August 28 Levine went out to the airport and asked
Drouhin to fly him to Deauville to see the Grand Prix. Drouhin
replied that he was not an air taxi driver. The two nearly came to
blows. Then Levine ordered the gas tanks of the *Columbia* partially

emptied in order to prevent the Frenchman from making off with the plane. After Levine had gone, Drouhin ordered mechanics to have fuel on hand at all times so that the tanks could be quickly refilled. He also arranged for a young mechanic and an airport policeman to keep an eye peeled on the machine.

This none-too-bright pair were in the hangar when Levine sauntered in at lunchtime the next day and said he wanted to taxi the plane around the field. He wouldn't take off, he said. He just wanted to see if the engine was still running well and get the feel of the controls again.

Mais oui! Certainement! said the watchdogs of the hangar. They obligingly helped push the *Columbia* out. The mechanic even started the engine. Levine waved his thanks, taxied over to the military section of the field, tested the engine a few minutes and then opened the throttle.

He took off, everybody said, quite skillfully. The hangar watchdogs were astounded. They implored airport officials to stop the *Columbia.* A military pursuit plane roared into the air. So did a machine carrying two of Drouhin's friends. Neither machine could catch the speedy Bellanca.

Drouhin, notified by telephone, drove furiously to the field. A plane was placed at his disposal. He had taken up the *Columbia* several times and knew that nothing on the field could catch her. He also knew that she had enough gas in her tanks to fly out of France. He decided to consult his lawyer as to his next move.

Major Ange Renvoise, commandant of Le Bourget, suspected that Levine was headed for London. He telephoned Croydon and suggested that they make preparations to receive a flier who had never soloed before. The manager of the hangar in which Levine had kept the *Columbia* also telephoned Croydon. He told his agent there that Levine had departed without paying his bill.

Mrs. Levine, who had been left behind in a Paris hotel, was panic-stricken at the news. Her husband had told her merely that he would attend to some business at Le Bourget. Fliers had warned him repeatedly, she told reporters between sobs, never to take the plane up alone. And now he was headed for the Channel!

Before long the *Columbia* was sighted over Abbeville and then over Boulogne, on the coast. But not until four-thirty that afternoon did she swoop down on Croydon. Apparently Levine had got lost along the way, for he had traveled some 350 miles and the Paris–Abbeville–Boulogne–London air distance is only about 220 miles.

He arrived at a time when airliners were coming in from and taking off for cities all over Europe (cross-Channel passenger service was quite advanced, more so than air traffic in the United States). But Croydon had done what it could for the incoming fledgling. A long north-south runway was kept clear, and a fire truck and an ambulance waited nearby with engines running.

The airport siren hooted loudly to alert all hands and stop all runway traffic. Levine had been seen approaching the field. He sped in low over a row of houses, doing 90 miles an hour. He was coming in so fast that he didn't get down close to the runway until he was halfway along it. The fire truck and ambulance started for the north end of the field where it seemed likely that the *Columbia* would crash and burst into flames.

Levine had slowed down for a landing. Now, seeing he couldn't make it, he tried to climb and turn at the same time. Experienced fliers on the ground were appalled. Abrupt climbing turns, which often result in a stall, have caused more deaths than almost any other aerial maneuver. When flying speed is gone, planes just drop. And at low altitudes nothing can be done.

In this case one of the wings was tilting down so far that it almost hit the ground. But somehow the stable plane managed to lurch along. Then it started upward. A veteran cross-Channel airman swore softly. "It takes a jolly good pilot to do that," he told a companion. "It's the engine, the engine," his friend muttered.

Whether it was good engine, good plane, good luck or a combination of all three, Levine regained speed and then raced at a crazy tilt almost into the roof of a nearby building. Spectators waited for the crash. It did not come. Instead the Bellanca zoomed up and away. She circled prettily and droned around the field, with Levine looking down from the cockpit window.

On his second try he came down as before toward the field's south end, but again too fast and this time too steeply. Seeing that he couldn't make it, he zoomed up sharply, and as before, almost lost flying speed. The wings wobbled and the plane seemed about to slide back on its tail and crash. Fire truck and ambulance roared down toward the probable scene of disaster. But once more Levine escaped death. The plane nosed upward, gathered speed and was safe in the air—temporarily—a second time.

The Croydon Airport staff was fascinated. But airline officials were aghast. What would passengers think of such goings-on? This kind of thing was enough to scare off the most intrepid prospective customer. After Levine's second thrilling exhibition, the manager of a company whose airliner was waiting to start for central Europe took action to shield his clients from further shocks. He had the passengers kept in the waiting room—out of sight of the drama on the field—until the situation was resolved.

The Levine menace was finally averted by Captain Frederick Smith, pilot of a local air taxi service. Jumping into a small plane, Smith flew up near the American, led him away from the airport and then turned back. At the right distance from the field he nosed down, glided in and landed, with Levine obediently following. Then the English plane dodged off sideways toward the hangars, like a scared chicken evading a pouncing hawk.

The Bellanca came in too fast again, hit the ground hard, bounced thirty feet in the air, came down and bounced again. After several more bounces she rolled to a stop. Everybody began to breathe normally.

Relieved by Levine's landing, Air Ministry officials turned wrathful. They rushed forward to meet the hatless pilot. And the amateur airman, the *New York Times* reported, was the least shaken man on the field.

"Oh, hello," he said as the officials converged upon him. He rubbed his stubby chin and grinned. "You know, I think I need a shave. I didn't know I was coming here till I started." An Air Ministry official looked at him stonily. "You have had a shave—a very close one," he said. Thereafter he led Levine swiftly into the Air Ministry office beyond sight and hearing of newspaper and camera men.

In the office Levine learned that he had broken numerous rules, regulations, ordinances, laws and enactments of both France and England, beside scaring years off the lives of flying-field employees. "By leaving France without proper clearance papers he had broken the customs laws of both England and France," said *The Times* of London. "He had not observed the flying rules of Britain, which say that no plane shall be flown more than three miles from any airdrome by any other than a licensed pilot. He had not made the proper circlings of the air field."

There were many other infractions, too, but in the end the Britons forgave Levine and set his exploit down as a good joke on the French. That evening, when the airman went as a guest of honor to the musical *Blue Skies*, the audience cheered him. He was called onto the stage, where he said he was glad to be on British soil.

The correspondent of *The Times* described Levine's performance as "the most alarming experience which has ever happened in the memory of the civil aviation traffic officers, regular pilots and airdrome staff." They all stood there helpless, he added, while Levine "committed every possible error, any one of which might have cost him his life." And he emphasized that Levine's life was saved by the prompt action of the air taxi man.

Levine declined to acknowledge this debt. Instead, he declared he hadn't even seen the plane that led him in, and attributed his landing difficulties to his failure to adjust the plane's stabilizer, or horizontal tail surface. He also issued a statement accusing the French of obstructing his effort to conquer the Atlantic from the east, and repeating earlier charges that Drouhin had declined to take off when weather forecasts were favorable. "I saw that my flight from France would be subject to French control and that did not seem quite just to me," he added. "Finally, when I could see no other way out I decided to bring my plane to British soil and start from here homeward." He made the whole escapade sound almost reasonable.

In Paris Mrs. Levine received the news of his safe landing when she was on the point of collapse. Drouhin said he didn't know exactly what to do. "But I'm not going to chase Levine over to London," he added, "because if I saw him I would feel like killing him and then the English would put me in jail."

Before Drouhin left Le Bourget it was noted that he had a long talk in a luxurious limousine with none other than Mabel Boll. What they discussed was not revealed but it aroused speculation, for the heiress was believed to be financially capable of buying several ocean planes.

Two days later Levine engaged Walter Hinchliffe, a pilot for Imperial Airways, to fly the *Columbia* and him to America. Hinchliffe, a war ace with twelve German aircraft to his credit, had lost an eye in combat but was reputed to be one of the best pilots around. To overcome the handicap of headwinds, the *Columbia* now had additional gas tanks, which, Levine said, would enable her to stay in the air for sixty-five hours.

Thereafter Levine went back to Paris, and to the surprise of practically everybody, paid Drouhin $3,200, since he had failed to carry out his part of the agreement. Rumor now had the French pilot ready to fly Miss Boll and her sweater to America in a plane soon to be bought by the heiress. Six days later, however, the fame-crazed frail turned up in Cranwell, England, where adverse winds had been delaying the Bellanca's takeoff. She renewed her offer of $25,000 for a place in the plane and became hysterical when Hinchliffe turned her down.

She regained some of her composure when Doc Kinkaid—who had come to England to help two other fliers—explained the facts of flight, and in later converse with reporters seemed to believe that by agreeing to sacrifice her ambition she had cast herself in a heroine's role. "How could I endanger their lives?" she asked almost tearfully. "I was just dying to fly but they told me it would be impossible for any additional weight to be taken. Mr. Kinkaid showed me the figures and I said, 'That will do. You can count me out of this entirely. I wouldn't risk the lives of those two brave men.' "

The day Miss Boll saved the airmen's lives, Mrs. Levine arrived in New York on the *Ile de France* and announced that when her husband came home she was going to put her foot down and be the boss for a change. She had protested many times against his westward project, she said, but it hadn't done a bit of good.

The weather over the ocean didn't improve. Finally Levine gave up the transatlantic flight for the nonce and announced that he and Hinchliffe would fly to India. On September 22 they set out for a nonstop journey to Delhi, but an unruly new steel propeller and trouble with the Whirlwind's fuel system forced them down in Vienna.

After repairs they changed direction and headed for Venice and thereafter for Rome, where Levine wanted to meet the man he most admired—Mussolini. But first he had an audience with the Pope and was so awed by the pontifical presence that he couldn't utter a word. His Holiness was the only person Levine met in Europe, it was said, with whom he didn't argue. All he could do was kiss the papal ring in silence.

With Mussolini, a less God-oriented person, Levine felt more at ease. They chatted at some length and Il Duce opined that his admirer's greatest achievement was his solo flight from Le Bourget to Croydon. Levine revealed that he had a silver watch for Musso-lini's latest baby and wanted to parachute it from the *Columbia*. It was arranged that a white sheet should be spread on the lawn of the dictator's suburban villa to facilitate the reception of this gracious tribute.

Emerging from the meeting, Levine announced that Mussolini was the greatest statesman in the world. He also said he was negotiating with two Italian companies to build a fifty-passenger transatlantic plane. If the companies' estimates of costs were satis-factory, he added, he would award contracts at once. If they weren't, he would erect his own plant in Milan.

The watch-dropping ceremony did not take place from the *Columbia*. When Levine and Hinchliffe took off, with Prince Louis Ferdinand of Orleans as passenger, the engine died and the Briton had to bring the plane down on a rocky field. Nobody was hurt but the machine was badly damaged. Levine finally made the drop from a regular passenger plane to Venice whose pilot he persuaded —without much difficulty—to detour over Mussolini's house. The little parachute became entangled in telephone wires, but peasants retrieved it so that the bambino's life—as the inscription on the watch said—could be "filled with happiness."

The watch-dropping ceremony about ended Levine's opera-tions in Europe for 1927. In October he went home by ship and re-ceived a subdued official welcome. The *Columbia* came home the same way. A government claim against her owner for payments still due on his World War I surplus acquisitions was settled out of court for $150,000. And his long-suffering wife, forgetting to put her foot down, declared, "He is a hero in my eyes no matter what anyone else can say."

11

TO PUBLICIZE PINEAPPLES

After Byrd had shown the way to the airliners of the future, American ocean fliers focused their attention, for a time, on the Pacific. Nine men and one woman were to die because of the cash prizes offered by Mr. Dole before the little planes of the day resumed their by now practically meaningless exploits over the stormy Atlantic.

When the pineapple promoter announced his project on May 25 it had seemed to him and to many others that the flight wouldn't be unduly difficult. The distance from San Francisco to Hawaii—2,400 miles—was 1,200 miles less than Lindbergh had logged. But the over-water distance was 600 miles longer than on the great-circle route from New York to Paris. Moreover, the air currents over the Pacific were reportedly tricky. And the target to be hit was far smaller than the Continent—by comparison almost infinitesimal. The slightest error in navigation would lead a plane past the tiny group of islands and out over the world's widest ocean.

Dole set the start of his contest for August 12 to give Lindbergh time to enter it. But five fliers—in three planes—planned to defy the Pacific before that date. They were Lieutenants Lester Maitland and Albert Heggenberger of the United States Army; Ernest Smith, an air-mail pilot, and Captain Charles Carter; and Richard Grace, a movie stunt flier who wanted to be the "Lindbergh of the Pacific."

Maitland had persuaded his superiors to let him and Heggenberger attempt a San Francisco–Hawaii flight in the Army's recently acquired Fokker—a trimotor plane like Byrd's but with slightly more powerful engines of a later model. Smith, who hoped to beat the Army men to Hawaii, had a single-engined Travel Air monoplane. And Grace, who expected to fly the other way—from the Hawaiian Islands to San Francisco—had a Ryan monoplane like Lindbergh's. It had been transported to the Islands by ship. All three planes were fitted with Whirlwinds.

Both the Army men and Smith readied their planes at Oakland. And on the morning of June 28 the lieutenants were ready to go. The olive-drab Fokker, inappropriately named the *Bird of Paradise*, warmed up with a total load of 13,404 pounds, 6,240 of them representing 1,040 gallons of gas. Smith, whose plane—the *City of Oakland*—was several miles an hour faster than the Fokker, yelled at Maitland just before takeoff, "I'll wave to you boys as we go by." Then he hurriedly prepared to catch up.

By the time Smith and Carter got going, their big rival was out of sight. Ten minutes later the two men returned to the city whose name their Travel Air bore. The windshield on Captain Carter's side of the cockpit had collapsed, and the fierce blast made it impossible for him to navigate.

Smith scurried around the airport looking for a windshield pane that would fit, tears of exasperation coursing down his face. Nothing could be found that could be used to replace the broken pane. Finally Carter decided that so much time had been lost that they would never overtake the Fokker. So Smith, broken-hearted, postponed his great project.

Meanwhile Maitland and Heggenberger sped on toward their goal. The Army had set up radio beacons whereby the officers would ride a beam out of San Francisco and another into Hawaii. But their receiver soon failed and the beacons became useless. However, Heggenberger did a masterly job of navigation and the two men reached the main island in 25 hours and 50 minutes. Both were hungry, for they had mislaid their chicken sandwiches, hot coffee and soup and didn't find the food until after they landed.

The next of the pre-Dole fliers to take off was Grace. He got into the air above Kauai Island before dawn on July 4 but soon ran into heavy rain. Then the Ryan began to vibrate and went into a dive. Something was wrong with the tail surfaces. Grace extricated the plane from the dive, but she promptly went into another and then a third. He turned back toward the island, fighting the ship. He was able to reach Kauai, but in landing hit a tree and wrecked the plane. Without enough money to finance repairs, he abandoned his Operation Lindbergh.

Ten days later Ernie Smith was ready for another try—this time with Emory Bronte, a steamship-line navigator, as his companion. The Army had the radio beacons going, but the *City of Oakland*'s receiver, like the Fokker's, soon failed. So the new navigation aid again was unable to function.

To make things worse, a cloud floor obscured the water and prevented Bronte from calculating their drift. For four and a half hours the men didn't know exactly where they were. At six the next morning they figured they were still 700 miles from land, with the gas gauge showing enough fuel for only another hour's flying. So at six-thirteen Bronte sent out an S O S, giving their position and saying they would be landing in the sea and using their rubber raft. Half an hour later he sent out another message saying the plane had enough fuel to stay up for another four hours, but repeating the call for help.

Then the transmitter went as dead as the receiver and Bronte couldn't send out any more messages; they now realized, however, that the gauge had been giving them false readings and that they had enough gas to reach land. By this time several ships were heading toward the last position Bronte had given. They never found the plane, for it came down in a clump of kaiwi trees on

Molokai, the island southeast of Oahu, a fact which the skippers didn't learn until hours later. In its descent the *City of Oakland* was damaged, but Smith and Bronte were unhurt.

As mentioned before, none of the four men who had flown to Hawaii were eligible for the Dole prize money. Moreover, their success obscured the dangers they had faced, so now several dozen fliers prepared to enter the contest. The new Aeronautical Branch of the Department of Commerce ruled that each plane must have sufficient fuel range to reach Hawaii and that no pilot was to fly alone or without a capable navigator. Department of Commerce inspectors converged on Oakland's airport—from where the contest would start—and began to test the planes for airworthiness and the pilots for ability, and to issue provisional licenses for the flight.

One of the first airmen to sign up for the Dole Derby, as the contest came to be called, was William Erwin of Dallas, America's first ace in World War I. Captain Erwin, who had shot down nine German planes, was also trying to win a prize of $25,000 put up by William Easterwood, a Dallas broker, for a flight from the Texas city to Hong Kong in an elapsed time of 300 hours with no more than three stops. One of those stops, Erwin thought, could be Hawaii.

His machine, a Swallow monoplane called the *Dallas Spirit* (there wasn't much originality in most of the nomenclature of the time), had been provided by local businessmen and built by a Witchita concern which had turned out several mail planes. Like all the other entrants except one, it was fitted with a Whirlwind. Erwin expected that his wife, Constance, would go along with him as navigator and radio operator. An attractive girl just short of twenty-one, with big blue eyes and black bobbed hair, she had studied radio communication and navigation so she could help him in his effort to win $50,000 (the Dole and Easterwood prizes) in 300 hours.

Another woman who hoped for Dole prize money was Mildred

Doran, twenty-two, a schoolteacher from Flint, Michigan, who had learned to fly and was crazy about planes. As a schoolgirl she had often stopped at the gas station of Bill Malloska for friendly greetings, and when Malloska got rich and bought several planes she became acquainted with his two pilots, John Pedlar and Captain Eyer Sloniger. When Malloska agreed to finance a Dole contest entry, she pleaded with him to let her go along. But she didn't know navigation, and a navigator was essential. Finally Pedlar and Sloniger decided to flip a coin to determine which one should be pilot, and thereafter get a navigator. Pedlar won the toss. After that they named the machine—a Buhl biplane—the *Miss Doran* for the girl who was going along for the ride.

Perhaps the fastest plane in the race was a little monoplane called, both redundantly and inappropriately, the *Angel of Los Angeles*. It was a tricky machine designed by Leland Bryant, who expected to go along as navigator, and fitted with two Bristol-Lucifer engines of 120 horsepower each, mounted in tandem. The pilot was Captain Arthur Rodgers, a British war ace with thirty-two German planes on his list. The machine was reportedly capable of 145 miles an hour and was said to cruise at 125.

Another speedy entry was the *Golden Eagle*, a prettily streamlined Lockheed-Vega entered by Jack Frost and sponsored by George Hearst, publisher of the San Francisco *Examiner* and son of William Randolph Hearst. By far the oddest machine of the lot was the *Spirit of Los Angeles,* a clumsy twin-engined triplane. But this craft did not have a long life. On a flight from Long Beach to Oakland before the contest she dived into San Francisco Bay, precipitating her three occupants unhurt into shallow water but wrecking herself beyond repair.

The number of entries had been cut to fifteen, and then, when two fliers were unable to get planes, to thirteen. And this, in the opinion of some authorities, was still too many. It became evident, as starting day approached, that there hadn't been nearly enough time to test and equip planes, tune engines and make other necessary preparations for such a hazardous flight. One pilot, Martin Jensen, said later, "Five days before the start of the race not even the fuselage was on my plane, but in those five days I worked night and day, making preparations, always against great odds."

On August 10, two days before the scheduled start, Navy Lieutenants George Covell and Richard Weggener took off from the North Island Naval Base at San Diego for the 450-mile flight to Oakland. They had pulled Number 13 in an earlier drawing for takeoff position in the race and had laughed about it. But some other aspects of their case were less amusing.

Their machine, the *Humming Bird*, was a low-wing monoplane of the Junkers type which was new in this country. It had been designed by a little-known Austrian engineer, and Covell had doubts about it. Moreover, there had been trouble with the fuel system, and mechanics who had worked on it most of the previous night advised against starting for Oakland before additional tests of the engine could be made. But the two officers didn't want to wait.

Airmen who watched the takeoff said the plane was in difficulties from the start. The *Humming Bird* ran a mile and a half across the island before she rose from the runway. Even then she merely skimmed above the water beyond, apparently unable to gain altitude as she headed for Point Loma. Then, seemingly attempting to turn, she crashed into a sand bank, rolled down to the bottom and burst into flames. Both men were cremated.

Most of the other planes in the race also needed more tests. And so did many pilots. Some of them were not qualified to make a 2,400-mile ocean flight to a tiny group of islands. A few had log books showing they had flown the 200 hours required for the Department of Commerce's new transport pilot rating, but many others hadn't. And none had the new licenses which the Department of Commerce had begun to issue. As a result, Department inspectors at the field had to test each airman and then issue provisional licenses. They also had to set up tests for aerial navigators, for up to then only mariners had been licensed in this field. The navigator tests included a written examination, and one or more trial flights in which the candidate had to prove he could fly a course well enough to hit the distant islands.

It soon became obvious that most planes and airmen would not be ready for the scheduled start on August 12. So the contest committee in San Francisco requested a two-week postponement. The group in Honolulu, which was making plans for a big reception celebration, refused to sanction a delay. But on August 11 the airmen at Oakland held a meeting and agreed unanimously to put off the start until August 16. The Honolulu group didn't like this defiance by men who were going to risk their lives to advertise Hawaii and its pineapples, but there was nothing it could do but acquiesce.

The next day another pilot who didn't trust his plane prepared to give it a tryout. Captain Rodgers, twenty-nine, had flown in the Lafayette Escadrille, where he had become a friend of Nungesser's. Later, when he was old enough, he had transferred to the Royal Flying Corps. The two engines that powered his plane were on struts above the fuselage, one driving a tractor and the other a pusher propeller. Perhaps this made her top-heavy. Anyway, the plane wasn't stable.

Rodgers told Leland Bryant, the designer, who wanted to go up with him on this test, that the plane was so new and untried that only one man should take her aloft. And he put on a parachute, just in case. Then, as Bryant and Rodgers' young wife watched, he coaxed the machine into the air. But he couldn't keep it from slipping off to one side.

As he approached the field for a landing, the aircraft dived toward the earth. Rodgers tried vainly to regain control, then jumped and pulled the rip cord of his 'chute. But by now he was only 150 feet above the ground. The parachute didn't open in time. Anna

157

Rodgers saw her husband die. When she could speak she said, "Thank God he left me a daughter."

Now, four days before the rescheduled starting time, the Dole death toll was three. Pineapples were getting profitable publicity. People were flocking to the Oakland airport from all over California to see the planes and pilots that were left. On Sunday, August 14, the number who came during the day and evening was estimated at one hundred thousand.

Two of the thirteen planes entered had already crashed with fatal results to their occupants. A third—the triplane—had transformed herself into junk. Two other machines had been ruled out as unsafe, one of them on the eve of the contest, when Department of Commerce inspectors determined she wouldn't carry enough gas to get to Hawaii. That left eight planes, in which fifteen men and one woman would try to land on some dots in the ocean 2,400 miles away.

Fifty thousand people were at the airport for the start of the great ocean race—the first of its kind—at noon on Tuesday, August 16, 1927. The first to get away, in accordance with the earlier position drawing, was the *Oklahoma*, a Travel Air monoplane piloted by Bennett Griffin, with Al Haney as navigator. She rose nicely, but after a few minutes returned to the field with an engine whose sickly condition would have furrowed the brow of Doc Kinkaid. The Whirlwind had overheated rapidly and its red-hot cylinders were firing out of phase. The Travel Air wasn't going to travel to Hawaii.

Next to speed down the runway was *El Elcanto* (The Charm), a monoplane designed by Lieutenant Norman Goddard. His navigator was another naval officer, Lieutenant K. C. Hawkins. The homemade craft ran for 4,800 feet but was unable to rise with her heavy load of gas. Finally the right wing tipped downward, throwing the machine into a ground loop. She skidded to the right and came to a halt in a slight hollow off the runway, her nose pointed back toward the starting line. The unplanned maneuver demolished the right wing and caved in the fuselage, but there was no fire and the two Navy men stepped out of the wreck uninjured.

Third at the line was a Breese machine called the *Pabco Pacific Flyer,* containing Major Livingston Irving, who worked for the Pacific Paraffin Paint Company. The company was sponsoring the monoplane, and many of its employees had contributed dollars toward its purchase price.

Irving, who was another war ace, had qualified as his own navigator and had persuaded the racing committee to let him fly the orange-colored machine alone. He revved up his engine and started off but couldn't get the heavily laden plane off the ground. Later he made another attempt. His second run was like an unsuccessful rendition of Lindbergh's takeoff. Irving nursed the Breese up a few feet and then she squashed down, splintering the tail skid and damaging a wing. Fellow fliers quickly drove Irving's wife, with their small daughter in her arms, to the scene of the wreck. Irving was standing beside it, unhurt. "Well, my dear," he said sadly, "I won't get to Honolulu now."

Since the crash of the little Bryant, the undisputed speed king of the race had been the *Golden Eagle,* with Jack Frost at the controls and Gordon Scott ready to do the navigating. This handsome craft, whose round fuselage was painted a bright yellow, took off without trouble at twelve-thirty and sailed away toward her goal. She was the first of the Dole planes to get out of the San Francisco area.

A minute later the *Miss Doran,* the only biplane in the race, sped away toward the same destination, with John Pedlar, pilot; Navy Lieutenant V. R. Knope, navigator; and the "Flying Schoolmarm"—as newspapers had dubbed her—as passenger. The red, white and blue Buhl rose to about 800 feet when a gasoline feed line clogged. Pedlar brought the plane back to the field, and mechanics probed feverishly for the trouble while Miss Doran, in a natty new uniform with Sam Browne belt, talked with friends and reporters and watched other planes leave.

The next machine out was the *Aloha*, with Martin Jensen, pilot, and Paul Schluter, a steamship-line officer, navigator. Jensen, who lived in Honolulu, had a Breese monoplane which friends had helped him pay for. The plane climbed into the air easily. Closely following was the *Woolaroc*, another Travel Air, piloted by Art Goebel, a movie stunt man and friend of Richard Grace's, with Lieutenant Bill Davis to plot the course. The *Woolaroc* flight was partly financed by an oil man; the name of the plane originated from the "woods, lakes and rocks" on the backer's ranch.

After the *Aloha* came Bill Erwin in his Swallow. Erwin's wife had been denied a license for the flight on the grounds that she was not yet twenty-one and hadn't qualified as an expert navigator. In her place Erwin had taken on Alvin (Ike) Eichwaldt. The *Dallas Spirit* raced swiftly away from the field but soon an insecurely fastened trap door in the navigator's compartment flew open. The 100-mile-an-hour draft ripped a hole in the bottom of the plane and Erwin had to bring his machine back to Oakland.

Repairs to the fabric couldn't be made quickly, so the *Dallas Spirit* was out of the running. But the *Miss Doran* wasn't, for her engine was now purring happily. The Flying Schoolmarm was airborne again ninety minutes after her return to the field, and now there were four planes heading for Hawaii. Only two of them—the *Woolaroc* and the *Golden Eagle*—were equipped with radios, and the *Eagle* could only receive, for she had no transmitter.

The next day more than twenty thousand people poured into Wheeler Field, Honolulu, to welcome the fliers from the mainland. It was a colorful crowd. There were pretty little Japanese women in bright kimonos, Chinese in flowered jackets and pajama pants, Polynesians and Koreans, Filipinos and Americans, Australians and Mexicans, Negroes and Swedish blondes. A band played popular

160

airs. Flags went up. Food went down. And illegal stimulants heightened general jubilation.

The reviewing stand filled with notables, among them Wallace Farrington, Governor of the Territory, and the millionaire who had offered the prizes. The pineapple potentate's thirty-five hundred employees were not on hand. They had expected to have the day off but the pineapples had ripened so rapidly that the workers had to stay in their canneries lest the luscious fruit spoil ere it could be preserved.

Shortly after noon a squadron of welcoming planes took off from the field and headed northeastward over the water. They returned a few minutes later escorting the radio-equipped *Woolaroc*. The ocean plane circled the airport and then slid down to a landing at 12:20 P.M., Hawaiian time, after a flight of 26 hours, 17 minutes and 33 seconds—about half an hour more than the Army officers' time six weeks earlier.

Goebel emerged from the plane garbed in a plain business suit. "Say, folks, it's great to be here," he said. And then, "Honest to gosh, do you mean I'm the first one here? I thought surely some were ahead of us."

Dole gripped Goebel and then Davis by the hand. "I'm mighty happy, boys, that you arrived safely," he said. Hawaiian girls hung leis around the fliers' necks. Then Mrs. Jensen, wife of Martin Jensen, fought her way to the airmen. "Where is Martin? Is he still in the air?" she demanded. Goebel told her he hadn't seen her husband since the *Aloha* took off. He hadn't seen anything, even a steamer. Mrs. Jensen sagged and a couple of army officers supported her. She trembled and began to cry.

But two hours later the *Aloha*, with Jensen and Schluter aboard, droned in without fanfare. There was no escort because, lacking a radio, the plane had not been able to announce her coming. As Jensen climbed stiffly out of the plane his wife rushed to him, her face streaming with tears, and hugged him again and again. There were more official greetings and leis. The Hawaiian girls sang soft native songs.

Now people were anxiously watching the skies. There were two more planes to be heard from—the *Golden Eagle*, with two men, and the *Miss Doran*, with two men and a girl. They should have been in by now. Indeed, the *Golden Eagle* should have been in first of all, for she was the fastest ship in the race.

The afternoon drained slowly away with no word from the missing planes. There wasn't even a radio message from any surface craft. A big celebration had been scheduled for that evening, but nobody felt like celebrating now. The crowd's attitude, one reporter wrote, was one of anxiety, sympathy and hurt surprise that such a thing could happen. For now there was a sense of disaster. And the people of Hawaii felt that the preparations made by the fliers and the inspections made by the Department of Commerce should have eliminated the possibility of tragedy.

With a capitalist's faith in the might of the dollar, Dole offered $10,000 for the rescue of the crew of either plane, $20,000 for both. Bill Malloska offered $10,000 for the trio in the *Miss Doran*, alive or dead. And George Hearst pledged $10,000 for the men in the *Golden Eagle*.

None of the sponsors had to make good on their promises. Nobody ever claimed the money.

The usual false rumors raised flickering hopes. One report had the *Miss Doran* safe on the island of Maui at a point 115 miles from Honolulu. This story was sent out by the San Francisco *Examiner*'s Honolulu correspondent, picked up by the Associated Press and headlined all over the country. Flint newspapers rushed out extras, and managers of local movie theaters in the automobile city made joyful announcements to audiences who rose and cheered. In the streets, strangers embraced, slapped each other on the back and wept.

Another report had a plane crashing on Koko Head, about

twelve miles from Honolulu. The submarine tender *Holland* and two of her brood searched the area but found no evidence of a wreck. There was also a rumor that an object resembling a plane had been seen floating eight miles off Pearl Harbor. Other Navy craft sped out but returned with no clues.

Army planes from both Hawaii and San Francisco began flying fifty miles out to sea along both coasts, reporting by wireless every five minutes. The messages, monitored at shore points, came in with disheartening monotony: Nil. Nil. Nil. Nil. Nil.

The Navy organized the greatest sea search in history. Thirty-nine warships from both the islands and the mainland prowled the waters where the planes might have come down. Nineteen civilian vessels also took part in the hunt. And Erwin gave up his chance to win the Easterwood prize and prepared to take off with Eichwaldt on his own search for the lost planes. He made this decision despite a telegram from Easterwood that unless he started for Hong Kong before 6 P.M. on August 19, he would be ineligible for the prize if he didn't return to Dallas and start all over again.

Erwin and Eichwaldt conferred with Navy officials and worked out a zigzag course from San Francisco that would take them over areas not well covered in the 540,000-square-mile search being made by the warships. And Livingston Irving lent them the transmitter from the wrecked *Pabco Pacific Flyer* so they could report any clues they might pick up. Both men were expert telegraphers and each had his own sending key. But there was no receiver.

A big crowd at the airport cheered the two men when they appeared there on the afternoon of August 19 to take off on their rescue mission. The lost planes had now been down for at least two days. Both had carried rubber rafts, however, and there was hope that they might have come down gently enough to enable their crews to inflate and climb aboard the little craft.

Mrs. Erwin had stayed in Dallas, but Eichwaldt's mother came to the field to see him off. A reporter asked her how she felt about the impending affair. "I don't like this very much when I think of those others down in the water," she said. "But I mustn't cry, for that might unnerve Alvin." She didn't cry, either. She kissed her son good-bye and patted him and smiled.

The *Dallas Spirit* started with 460 gallons of gas, more than either Lindbergh or Chamberlin had carried. It was enough to keep the Whirlwind fueled for more than forty hours. Erwin made a skillful takeoff with this tremendous load shortly after 2 P.M. and soon he and his companion were tapping out dots and dashes in a lively account of their progress.

"Going strong. We are passing the docks. Will see the lightship soon. We are carrying the tail high at 1,700 [feet] and are making close to 100 mph air speed. Will call again when passing lightship."

"We are passing Point Lobos [the Golden Gate] now."

"We are passing the lightship and see the two flag signals, which means that you bums are getting us, and we can see the Farallones [islands] ahead."

After a while they began giving the time of each message.

"2:50 P.M. We are flying at 300 feet and under the fog with 30 miles visibility. Passing Farallones now."

"3:10 P.M. Our ceiling is increasing and the sun is breaking through."

"3:33 P.M. Just had a drink of water."

"3:49 P.M. The ceiling is now 700 feet. We are flying at 500 feet. We haven't seen anything since the Farallones and all is O.K. except Bill just sneezed. We are keeping a sharp lookout for the *Doran*, also the *Golden Eagle*. Will call you again later."

"4:20 P.M. We just passed close to a rain squall. The air is a little bumpy in its vicinity. We soon left it behind, however. Very clear ahead."

"4:35 P.M. We adjusted antenna for more radiation. The visibility is very good. We are able to cover eighty-mile patch."

"5:04 P.M. We see a ship ahead of us, presumably the *Mana*."

"5:11 P.M. Just passed the S.S. *Mana* [then 240 miles from San Francisco] and dipped to salute. They answered on the whistle. Of course we could not hear it but we saw the steam. We might pick up the squadron of destroyers before dark, but that depends on their speed. All O.K."

"5:45 P.M. Just saw a rum runner on the left and had a time keeping the Ike in. Bill."

"5:48 P.M. Just passed a destroyer going toward San Francisco. The destroyer was too far away for us to make out his number. Nothing else in sight."

"6:05 P.M. Please tell the gentleman who furnished our lunch that it's fine but we can't find the toothpicks. Bill."

"6:45 P.M. Just had a sandwich apiece and a cup of coffee and it sure went down good. We changed our course at 6:40 P.M. [Pacific time] to 244 and one-half true. Position at that time Latitude 35 degrees 30 minutes north; 130 degrees west." (This position was 459 miles from San Francisco.)

"7:10 P.M. The weather is part cloudy with a smooth sea. Visibility about 30 miles. Have seen no wreckage or anything that might be either of the ones we are looking for. The visibility is still very good. Everything with us O K. We are flying at 900 feet."

The *Dallas Spirit* roared on for nearly two hours more, sending out its cheery messages. Finally, at 9:02, Eichwaldt began tapping news of a different kind. "We went into a tail spin. S O S. Belay that. We came out of it but we were sure scared. It was a close call. We thought it was all off but we came out of it. The lights on the instrument board went out and it was so dark that Bill couldn't see the—we are in a tail spin. S O S."

After that there was only silence from the little plane from Dallas.

Her last position was calculated at 592 nautical miles out. Four destroyers, which had been sweeping the sea for the other planes, began to race toward the new area of disaster. Other warships took up the hunt, and fourteen merchant ships between the mainland and Hawaii were asked to keep a lookout for the latest Dole victims.

As usual, the women who had been left behind bore up bravely for a while. Constance Erwin said her husband had taken along a life raft and emergency rations and that she was confident he would be rescued. "He's a level-headed man," she said, "and the sort who keeps his wits in any situation." Mrs. Eichwaldt said she knew her son would be able to survive until he was picked up. "Alvin is an excellent swimmer," she added, "and if they had time to get out their life raft and climb aboard it, they will be all right. They had plenty of provisions. I know because I fixed them."

It seemed probable, however, that the spin Eichwaldt reported had ended in a crash that destroyed both the plane and her crew. A radio engineer who had logged the plane's flight from the time she left Oakland concluded, after studying the varying pitch of the radio waves she sent out, that the *Dallas Spirit* went into her final tail spin at an altitude of 2,000 feet and plunged downward at 200 miles an hour.

The same kind of fatal spin, many pilots thought, might have accounted for the *Miss Doran* and the *Golden Eagle*, killing or seriously injuring their crews in terrible collisions with the water. In that kind of smash-up, life rafts would have been useless.

Before hope faded entirely, public prayer meetings for Mildred Doran and the other Dole racers were held in both Flint and San Francisco. In the automobile manufacturing center, Chevrolet and Buick workers turned out in hundreds to bow their heads. And in San Francisco many parishioners heeded the request of Mayor James Rolph, Jr., to beseech God to save the lost ones.

But they remained lost. Even Mrs. Erwin gave up after a few days. "I felt at first that Bill would come through, but now they tell me I must expect the worst," she said. "Why couldn't I have been with him when he fell?"

12

MORE MADNESS OVER THE ATLANTIC

The deaths of nine men and a girl in a project to publicize pineapples dramatized the madness to which ocean flying had given
wing. And in the ensuing revulsion, national sanity began to return.
On August 22 Secretary of the Navy Curtis Wilbur, on a visit to San
Francisco, declared that some federal move must be made to prevent a recurrence of the Dole disasters. In Washington Rear Admiral Edward Eberle, Acting Navy Secretary, predicted congres-
sional enactment of a law to prohibit hazardous ocean flights. The
newspapers, while continuing to give such activities front-page display, rumbled editorially against them. Even aviators joined the de
nunciatory chorus—among them Lindbergh, who had started it all,
and Ernie Smith, whose effort to reach Honolulu had ended in a
clump of trees.

But more than a dozen planes were even then being tested for
flights on both sides of the Atlantic. And three days after Wilbur
and Eberle had expressed their disapproval, the first of these machines was ready to go. This was a Stinson-Detroiter, about the size
of Lindbergh's Ryan and powered with a Whirlwind engine. In it
Paul Redfern, a thin young man who weighed a scant 108 pounds,
hoped to fly from Brunswick, Georgia, to Rio de Janeiro. If he completed the 4,600-mile journey he would set a record, outdistancing
Chamberlin by 700 miles and Lindbergh by 1,000 miles.

Paul Redfern and his backers were typical products of the 1927 aviation craze. The flier was a mechanical-minded young man who had bought an old biplane, rebuilt it and barnstormed through the Southeast, taking up passengers and doing various stunts for advertisers. Then for a while he did aerial scouting for the Prohibition director for the southeastern coastal district, locating eighty stills and several offshore rum runners.

Like Lindbergh, he wanted to fly to Paris. But he couldn't obtain financial backing either for this project or for a flight to Hawaii. In July 1927 he heard that some of the businessmen of Brunswick, Georgia, wanted to put their little city of twenty thousand souls more spectacularly on the map through aviation. It was a desire common to many city fathers of the day. Boston, Philadelphia, Cleveland and several other cities were offering prizes of $25,000 for ocean flights ending at their airports. And other centers offered varied financial inducements for young men to risk their lives for the sake of local business.

The businessmen of Brunswick raised $25,000 to buy Redfern a plane, plus the equipment he might need if forced down. This included a rubber life raft, a gun that would fire both rifle bullets and shotgun pellets, mosquito netting, quinine, fishing tackle, flares and food for two weeks. It did not include a radio. But otherwise it was good equipment for a flight to South America, with whose ports the port of Brunswick wanted increased trade.

Early in August, Redfern's plane was christened the *Port of Brunswick*, and the legend BRUNSWICK–BRAZIL was lettered on her sides. Her tanks held 550 gallons of gas, nearly 100 more than Lindbergh or Chamberlin had carried. Wright engineers figured that Redfern's engine would burn eleven gallons an hour to give him a range, at 100 miles per hour, of 5,000 miles. The flier figured that even if he couldn't make that speed he would reach Rio in fifty hours. And if he didn't reach Rio he could land at Pernambuco or Pará.

These calculations didn't jibe with those of U. S. Navy navigators and hydrographers in Washington. These specialists thought that Redfern might meet both headwinds and storms, and pointed out that, because there would be no moon, he would have to fly in total darkness for more than twenty-four hours. But Lindbergh had ignored the prophets of doom, and so did Paul Redfern. Shortly after noon on August 25 he kissed his young wife good-bye, climbed into his plane and revved up the engine. Then he waved to the crowd of Georgians who had come to the field to see him off, and signaled the mechanics to remove the chocks from the wheels.

With 3,300 pounds of gas aboard, the little green-and-yellow monoplane was the most overloaded aircraft of the day. It was one of a small fleet of machines designed by Eddie Stinson, a noted pilot, which were to attempt long, dangerous voyages. And it proved that it was an able machine in the hands of a skillful airman by getting off the field without trouble and quickly fading into the sky to the south.

The next day a radio report from Nassau said the Stinson had been sighted by an unnamed steamer 300 miles east of that city. This indicated that Redfern was right on course, and led his wife and backers to express confidence that he would complete his long journey on schedule. In Rio people avidly read newspaper accounts of the flight and flocked to newspaper offices to scan late reports on the bulletin boards. And Brazilian Navy officers installed special reflectors for powerful lights at the airports to help the Americano make his expected night landing.

But after the first reported sightings there were no more reassuring tidings until August 31, when the small Norwegian steamer *Christian Krohg* reached Jamaica. There her master showed reporters the ship's log. It certified that the day after Redfern took off he flew over the ship between Trinidad and Kingston. He was then about 1,675 miles from Brunswick.

Redfern circled the ship several times, the log said, and dropped cartons containing three notes which crew members recovered. These messages asked that the vessel point her bow toward the nearest land and indicate the approximate distance from it by waving a flag once for every 100 miles. The *Christian Krohg's* master then pointed his ship toward the Venezuelan coast, which was 165 miles to the south, waved a flag twice and blew the whistle twice. After that the plane flew away.

The log, signed by the captain and other officers, said the plane's fuselage bore the legend BRUNSWICK–BRAZIL and that her wings showed the number NX 773, which the Department of Commerce had assigned to her. There seemed to be no doubt that Redfern had completed more than a third of his journey and that he and his plane were at that time in good shape.

The log of the *Christian Krohg* was the most authentic record that was made on Redfern's progress. Later reports of sightings over Venezuela were unconfirmed. Days went by and nothing more was heard of the flier. But his wife and sponsors, like those of earlier lost airmen, continued to hope. And in Redfern's case there seemed to be less cause for despair than in most similar misadventures.

"Don't lose hope of my return for at least six months or more," he had said before starting from Brunswick. "If I should be forced down in the Amazon Valley I believe I can live for months with the equipment I am carrying. I have emergency food for two weeks and after that I can bring down small game with my gun."

These facts, the mildness of the climate and rumors which filtered down to the coast from time to time kept hope for Paul Redfern alive for years. There were repeated tales that he was a captive of Indians, that he was king of a primitive tribe, that he was slowly coming down the Amazon or Orinoco and soon would reach civilization.

Numerous explorers of the great South American river basins have sought news of Redfern down the years. And rumors about him persist to this day. But no one has ever come out of the tropical jungles with either proof or credible reports that the young airman survived his effort to give the port of Brunswick the fame its residents thought it deserved.

On August 27, the day after Redfern waved to the *Christian Krohg* and headed toward Venezuela and oblivion, another Stinson-Detroiter took off from Harbour Grace, Newfoundland, and headed east. Aboard it were Edward Schlee and William Brock and they intended to fly not merely across the Atlantic but around the world.

This was no slap-dash venture involving an impecunious young flier and a group of businessmen eager to give their hometown some unwonted distinction. Schlee had been thinking about this flight for more than a year and was financing it himself. And if he didn't show conspicuous originality in naming the machine *Pride of Detroit* after the metropolis where he lived, he had made careful preparations on an international scale to ensure the success of the project.

Like Bill Malloska of Flint, Schlee had started his business career with one gasoline service station, and had run the number up to more than a hundred. It was just a case of picking the right street corners, he said. Soon he began selling automobile accessories and fuel oil, and presently obtained options on oil lands in Michigan, which added to his other profits. In 1927 he was president of five corporations, whose other officers were his three brothers.

As a sideline Schlee ran a flying service which carried passengers and freight. To manage it he hired Bill Brock, a former barnstormer, Army pilot and mail flier. In 1926 he became interested in the globe-circling activities of Edward Evans and Linton Wells, who used planes, trains, steamers and automobiles to complete their trip in 28 days and 14 minutes. Schlee felt that this mark could be beaten by a plane if suitable arrangements were made beforehand. And he wasted little time in making them. He learned to fly, enlisted Brock in the undertaking and ordered a monoplane from the local Stinson factory, which already had provided three biplanes for his flying service.

When the monoplane was delivered he took off with Stinson, Mrs. Schlee and their teen-age daughter on the Ford reliability tour, which involved flights around the country totaling 4,200 miles. The Stinson came in first in a field of fourteen, and Schlee concluded he had a good machine.

The modifications he, Brock and Stinson dreamed up made it even better. The big gas tank was designed like a seat, with a back against which the airmen could lean. The earth inductor compass—the kind that had misbehaved on the *Columbia* flight—was installed so that vibration wouldn't be likely to affect either the dial on the instrument board or the auxiliary dial located aft. Two other compasses were also installed.

The 5-gallon cans for the additional gas needed for long trips were made of aluminum, both to save weight and to minimize possible effect on the compasses. And in case instrument lights went out—as they had on the *Dallas Spirit*—powerful flashlights were strapped in handy places on either side of the cockpit.

The plane was equipped with radio and carried an emergency landing set that could be operated with a kite aerial. It also carried life preservers, a rubber boat and emergency rations for five days. Long before taking off from Detroit, Schlee had speeded the construction of a 3,850-foot runway at Harbour Grace by helping the local government and businessmen finance the undertaking. He also had arranged for Royal Dutch Shell and other companies to provide gasoline and oil at twenty points along the projected course.

Schlee's quiet explanations of the purpose of the flight, as well as his methodical preparations for it, contrasted pleasantly with the rhetoric about "advancing aeronautical science" and "bettering international relations," to which many ocean flights seemed to give rise. "We're seeking merely to demonstrate by a series of long hops that aviation has now reached a practical service position from which it will never be shaken," he told reporters who wanted to know if he and Brock had any other object than to break a round-the-world record. "We believe that such a flight as ours will demonstrate this better than anything else and that is why we are making it."

The *Pride of Detroit* started her transatlantic journey from Harbour Grace with 350 gallons in the gas tanks, leaving another 250 complimentary gallons behind for other ocean fliers. Brock used only half the new runway to get the yellow plane into the air, and with the morning sun at their backs and clouds from a recent storm ahead of them, the two men flew straight toward a rainbow. It dissolved into mist as they neared it, but it seemed a happy omen as they swung around and started over the Atlantic.

For several hours the weather held good and Schlee took a regular turn at the controls. Then they ran into a violent storm. Heavy gusts battered the *Pride of Detroit*, lifting her, dropping her, turning her half over, while rain pelted her fabric skin so fiercely that the noise could be heard above the roar of the Whirlwind. Water seeped in through cracks and joints, and soon both airmen were soaked.

After six hours they ran out of the storm and at ten o'clock that night they were sighted—and reported—by the liner *California* about 400 miles west of Ireland. At Croydon Airport, officials prepared to welcome the first Atlantic airmen to land at England's capital.

Red dawn rose ahead of the plane, but after a while it faded into fog. For three hours Brock and Schlee flew on by compass. Finally they came down close to the sea—or would it be the ground? —and after that they saw a town on the coast. That was the happiest sight of the trip.

But what coast was it? Ireland, England, France? There were people below them on the beach. They circled and dropped three notes. Two of them blew away. The third, weighted with an orange, fell near a knot of people who picked it up. It asked them to write in the sand the name of the town and the country it belonged to.

The people below them ran over to an asphalt walk and chalked letters that looked like S I F T O N. They also ran up the Union Jack on a pole. That took care of the country, but Schlee couldn't find Sifton on the map. He had misread the letters. They really spelled Seaton.

Still puzzled, they swooped down on a train, looking for clues on the sides of the cars. On the locomotive they made out the name GREAT WESTERN. That didn't help much, but they followed the railway line and presently came to a station. It was marked DAWLISH and this name they found on their map. After that it was easy to head for London and Croydon.

Doc Kinkaid was on hand to greet them. The Wright engineer had wagered friends there that he would hear the Whirlwind first— and so he did. Schlee and Brock stepped out of the plane in baggy pants and dirty gray sweat shirts. Their clothes were still damp, but aside from that, they might have flown in from Torquay. They had made the 2,400-mile trip in 23 hours and 9 minutes.

They didn't tarry for the adulation they could have had. The next morning, at 8:32, they were airborne again, eight hours before Levine made his Croydon debut. Nor did they loiter at Munich, their next stop. After one night's rest they were off once more—this time to Belgrade.

The following day—August 31—they arrived in Constantinople. On September 2 they were in Baghdad. The next day, after fifteen hours of difficulties with wind, rain and fog, they came down in Bender Abbas, Persia. The following day they reached Karachi and two days later Allahabad. Then it was Calcutta, Rangoon, Hanoi, Hong Kong and Omura, Japan, where they landed just in time to escape a hurricane which killed seven hundred people.

The next stop, on September 30, was Tokyo. Here they planned to install a new Whirlwind before attempting their longest over-water flight, the 2,480 miles between the Japanese capital and Midway. They were ahead of the record they wanted to beat. And they had certainly proved that aviation had reached a "practical service position." But despite their careful preparations they had had several close calls. And other aviators weren't doing nearly as well as they were.

The Germans, whose transatlantic ambitions had long troubled the French, had made one pretentious bid for fame even before the *Pride of Detroit* left Harbour Grace. On August 15 the *Bremen* and the *Europa,* Junkers low-wing monoplanes, each fitted with a six-cylinder water-cooled Junkers L5 engine of 310 horsepower, had taken off from Dessau bound for Chicago and Mitchel Field, respectively. The *Bremen* had been chartered by the Hearst newspapers, which had assigned their Berlin correspondent to a passenger's seat, and the two machines were to fly together across the Atlantic. They didn't stay that way. The *Europa* bored into a North Sea fog for a while and then turned back. The *Bremen* bumped into headwinds which cut her normal cruising speed of 97 miles an hour to 60. She also gave up and went home.

On August 31, the day Schlee and Brock reached Constantinople, the first woman to brave the Atlantic in a plane was ready to go. She was Princess Anne Lowenstein-Wertheim, sister of the Earl of Mexborough, and widow of a German prince who had been killed while fighting for Spain in the Philippines during the Spanish-American War. Still attractive at the age of sixty-two, the princess had a colorful past. An ardent sportswoman, she had invented a ski designed to prevent fractured ankles in falls during jumps. She was one of the first women to fly across the English Channel and once had piloted a light plane from Egypt to France.

But minor fame didn't satisfy the princess. Over her family's objections, she was determined to be the first woman over the Atlantic in a flying machine. She planned to fly from Upavon Airport in Wiltshire, southern England, to Ottawa, Canada, and she was ready to risk her life to achieve her wish.

The princess proposed to sit out the flight in a wicker armchair, for she didn't intend to do any piloting. For this task she had engaged two Imperial Airways fliers—Captain Leslie Hamilton, slight and boyish, and Lieutenant Colonel Frederick Minchin, taller, older and quiet. She also had bought a plane—a Fokker with a single 450-horsepower Bristol-Jupiter air-cooled engine which looked like an oversized Whirlwind. She had named her plane the *St. Raphael,* who was said to be the patron saint of flying.

Early in the morning of the great day she appeared at the field in an outfit she deemed suitable for the occasion. It consisted of a black toque, a loose-fitting bright blue suede jacket, blue riding breeches, high-heeled yellow fur-lined boots and black silk stockings. She carried two attaché cases, a small wicker basket and two red hatboxes.

The two pilots supervised the intake of 800 gallons of gasoline. This should be enough for about 4,000 miles in calm weather, and the distance to be flown was 3,300 miles. They did not take the almost constant headwinds into account, however, although British officials at the field had word that over the ocean these winds were blowing eastward at 10 miles an hour.

The Most Reverend Francis Mostyn, Roman Catholic Archbishop of Cardiff, blessed the plane and sprinkled holy water on the wings. And despite the reported adverse winds, the *St. Raphael* started down the runway. She struggled into the air at 7:32. Around noon she was sighted over southern Ireland, doing about 70 miles an hour. This was 30 miles less than the scheduled cruising speed, for the adverse winds proved to be much stronger than expected. Nevertheless, the plane moved out over the Atlantic. She had no radio, so no word from the fliers could be expected until they landed.

In Ottawa, officials assigned troopers of the Royal Canadian

Mounted Police to report at their new Lindbergh Field the next day to be ready to handle a great crowd. And in an Ottawa hotel Mrs. Leslie Hamilton told reporters she had come up from New York to give her husband a hearty welcome. The story got around somehow that she was separated from Hamilton and hoped to effect a reconciliation. And it seemed for a time that he would come in on schedule: the Standard Oil tanker *Josiah Macy* reported at 9:44 in the evening after takeoff that she had sighted the lights of a plane in mid-Atlantic.

After that there was no further news of the *St. Raphael*. For a while Mrs. Hamilton expressed confidence that the occupants would be saved. "Leslie has been in so many tight corners in his time and has come out of each with flying colors that I feel absolutely sure that he will be found. He and Colonel Minchin are an ideal team. Leslie is dashing and never worried, while the colonel is calm and cautious."

But nothing was ever heard again of either the two airmen or the Flying Princess, as the press had dubbed the first woman to defy the Atlantic in a plane. And Mrs. Hamilton took pains to deny the romantic tale that a successful flight would have meant a joyful reconciliation. She had never been separated from her husband, she said.

The loss of the Flying Princess and her shipmates did not deter other entrants in the Atlantic air derby. On September 2 the Farman *Blue Bird* lumbered into the air at Le Bourget and headed toward the New World. The plane, which Maurice Drouhin had been all set to fly before Levine appeared in the role of siren, now looked like a formidable contender for westward flight honors. A sturdy biplane, she was fitted with two 500-horsepower water-cooled engines in tandem nacelles built into the upper wing. To keep the big Hispano-Suizas going for forty hours or so, she carried 2,600 gallons of gas. Her loaded weight approximated 25,000 pounds.

Leon Givon and Pierre Corbu raised the heavy machine off the runway but couldn't coax her higher than 1,000 feet. And about ninety miles west of Paris they roared into a thick fog. They flew through it for a while but finally decided to turn around. In four hours they were back at Le Bourget, the flight a failure but nobody drowned.

The next day Captain Frank Courtney started from Plymouth in his Dornier-Wal with F. H. Downer as co-pilot. He planned to fly to New York after refueling stops in Ireland and Newfoundland. Courtney had a paying passenger, one L. L. Hosmer, a Montreal banker. This gentleman had reportedly pungled up $7,500 for the ride, which was $2,500 less than Levine had offered Courtney in mid-July, and $17,500 less than Mabel Boll had offered Levine. But this flight, too, was a fiasco. The flying boat, which had carried Roald Amundsen within 160 miles of the North Pole, encountered head-winds soon after starting. Courtney revved up the two 450-horse-power Napier-Lion engines with which she was now fitted, but the plane's normal speed of 100 miles an hour dropped to 60 and he finally brought her down near La Coruña on the northwest coast of Spain. Again nobody was drowned or even bruised.

The prevailing westerly winds were the determining factor for most pilots still intent on flying the Atlantic. And in North America six more planes were being groomed for glory. They were the new Sikorsky of René Fonck, who had enlisted two U. S. Navy airmen in his project; an amphibious Sikorsky built for Mrs. Frances Grayson, a Long Island real estate agent; a Stinson-Detroiter sponsored by Florida and West Virginia businessmen; another Stinson sponsored by Windsor (Ontario) business interests; still another Stinson financed by the Carling brewery in England; and a single-engined Fokker owned by William Randolph Hearst.

The Fokker flight—aimed at Rome—was intended to give needed promotion to the New York *Daily Mirror,* which was engaged in a losing battle with its fellow morning tabloid, the New York

Daily News. Its chief publicist was Philip Payne, the *Mirror's* managing editor. As was not unusual with Hearst enterprises, the project flaunted the gaudy garb of patriotism. The plane was named the *Old Glory,* the national emblem was painted on the wing and the *Mirror* waxed lyrical about how the flight would advance aviation, with appropriate emphasis on the splendor of the U.S.A.

The airmen chosen for the trip were Lloyd Bertaud, who had gone back temporarily to air-mail flying after his break with Levine, and a fellow air-mail flier, James Hill, who would do most of the piloting. Hill was said to be able to find his way through any kind of thick weather and was sometimes called the "father of fog flying." Bertaud planned to do some flying himself, but to spend most of his time navigating the plane and operating the radio with which she would be equipped. The Fokker, specially built, was fitted with a 450-horsepower Bristol-Jupiter like the one that had powered the ill-fated *St. Raphael.*

The quarrels that transatlantic flights often gave rise to began as soon as the monoplane was delivered. Payne announced that he was going along on the flight. The two airmen didn't want him. Unable to fly, navigate or operate the radio, he would be merely dead weight, whose equivalent in gasoline could fuel the big engine for more than 100 miles.

Payne declared that the machine, when delivered, was already over its specified weight and that a few pounds more wouldn't make much difference. The weight was supposed to total 4,150 pounds empty but the plane actually weighed 4,690, he said. R. B. C. Norduyn, general manager of the Fokker plant at Hasbrouck Heights, retorted that the extra poundage was due to special equipment which had been ordered by the airmen while the plane was being built. The dispute was finally resolved by Bertaud, who reduced the fuel load by 100 gallons (about 600 pounds) and changed the starting point to Old Orchard Beach, Maine, instead of Roosevelt Field, thus shortening the distance to be flown by 275 miles.

Even with only 1,000 gallons in the tanks and with Payne as a passenger, the *Old Glory* was overloaded. For days the airmen waited for an up-beach wind which would help the machine rise from the hard-packed sand. Meanwhile the *St. Raphael* was lost, and William Randolph Hearst, whose San Francisco *Examiner* had backed the *Golden Eagle* in the disastrous Dole Derby, began to worry about the *Old Glory*.

"I do not think *Old Glory* should start except under the auspices and with the full approval of the government," he telegraphed Payne from California. "In view of the recent disasters I will not assume responsibility but will proceed only if the government will assume authority and responsibility. The flight is not undertaken for promotion purposes [!] but to advance aviation, and it is doubtful whether, in the light of recent events, these flights do advance aviation. These numerous disasters may retard it. Therefore I await the sanction of the government."

Hearst undoubtedly knew that the government would not sanction or assume responsibility for any such project. And Payne must have known that the actions he now reported did not constitute such sanction. "Secretary of Aviation Trubee Davison and Department of Commerce pronounced Old Glory the finest ship to attempt the transatlantic flight," he wired back (with considerable exaggeration). "In addition, Mr. Coolidge has sponsored flight by putting letter on *Old Glory* to the King, while Secretary of State Kellogg has sent message to Mussolini. No plane has had such official sponsoring as *Old Glory* with two pilots. Would rather give up all money in the world than forgo their flight. Most assured they will succeed. Best regards from Phil Payne."

These lofty sentiments were later aired in the Hearst papers. So were the following telegrams between Hearst and his editor:

"Dear Phil: Please think of my situation. Have had one airplane lost and two fine men drowned. If another such disaster occurred, effect would be terrible, not only on my peace of mind but on public opinion. I telegraphed you all this and tried to have you get pilots to accept prize and give up dangerous adventure."

"Dear Chief: The pilots appreciate your magnanimous offer, but insist they be allowed to fulfill their contracts to fly. Weather ideal today and further delay ruinous in morale of pilots. Every possible precaution taken. Army and State inspectors went over *Old Glory* this morning and gave written approval to flight [?]. I honor and love you and I know you will forgive me any mistakes I have made. Affectionately, Phil Payne."

Payne gave this last telegram to a friend at Old Orchard on September 6, to be forwarded to Hearst. Father James Mullen of St. Margaret's Church in Old Orchard blessed the silver-and-yellow aircraft, and while the wives and Bertaud's mother watched, the three men got into the machine. Bertaud's mother was crying, but Mrs. Bertaud and Mrs. Payne tried to assure her—and themselves—that the Fokker would reach the Eternal City.

Without either government sanction or her owner's publicly expressed permission, the *Old Glory* rolled a mile down the beach against a slight wind before she slanted up into the air. She sped quickly out of sight along the great-circle route that led to the metropolis of Mussolini and the Pope. Halfway across the Atlantic the airmen would drop a wreath with the inscription. NUNGESSER AND COLI: YOU SHOWED THE WAY. WE FOLLOWED. BERTAUD AND PAYNE AND HILL.

The *Old Glory* had roared off the beach at 12:31 P.M. Bertaud flashed his first message at 4:20: "Ship is tail heavy. Will send later. Love to all. We are making over 100 mph."

At 6:30 the liner *George Washington* reported that the *Old Glory* had flown past when the ship was 800 miles east of Ambrose Channel Lightship, off New York harbor. The vessel's operator heard the plane's radio but couldn't raise her. Still, she appeared to be flying well. And at 10:23 that night Bertaud radioed: "All O.K. Making good time. Please forward this. Best regards."

After that there was silence until 12:41 A.M., when the liner *California* reported that the plane had passed overhead and seemed to be all right. Three more hours passed. Then, at 4:17, nearly sixteen hours after takeoff, ships' radio operators heard the letters "WRHP [William Randolph Hearst Plane] S O S WRHP S O S." They listened avidly for more but not until six minutes later did they hear from the plane again. Then: "Five hours out of Newfoundland east."

Several ships radioed frantically for the *Old Glory* to give a more precise position. But nothing came out of the darkness. Three ships, the *Transylvania*, the *Carmania* and the *Lapland*, altered course and steamed at full speed toward the area where the monoplane might have hit the ocean.

The Anchor Line's *Transylvania* was nearest the probable splash-down site—perhaps sixty-five miles away—and her master, Captain David Bone, searched the area for half an hour. Since there was no moon, the first part of the search was conducted in total darkness. Moreover, a fresh wind roughened the sea.

Finding nothing in the area where Bone believed the plane had come down, the *Transylvania* proceeded on a zigzag course toward the point where the plane had been reported by the *California*. By this time, news of the S O S was making headlines all over the world. The Pope prayed that the Americans would be saved. Their wives said they were sure some ship would find them. And even before Captain Bone had completed his search, he began to receive messages from rival news services and producers offering fat sums for exclusive rights to still and motion pictures of successful rescue efforts.

Hearst came up with another offer—this one $25,000—to anyone who saved the downed airmen. He also chartered the *Kyle*, a Canadian vessel, to search for them. And five days later the *Kyle* came across evidence of the disaster—a thirty-foot section of the plane's wooden wing, with the American flag painted on it. The wing still contained partially filled gas tanks, with feed pipes and glass fuel gauges attached. Also attached was part of the landing gear. Apparently the *Old Glory* had hit the water with such force that the wing had been ripped from the fuselage, which, weighted with the engine, had sunk. There was no trace of the three men or of the rubber boat the plane had carried.

To most people the wreckage seemed to prove that Bertaud, Hill and Payne were dead. But to their wives, waiting in dread, it gave new hope. "I am terribly happy," said Mrs. Bertaud when she heard about the floating wing section. "Everything tells me that the condition of the parts found indicate that they were able to keep afloat until they were picked up by some vessel. I am absolutely certain they are safe. Lloyd has been in many tight squeezes before and he has always come through safely. An awful load has been lifted from my mind since I heard about the finding of the wreckage. It indicates—doesn't it?—that the ship weathered the rough sea and kept afloat after alighting."

By this time two additional wives of ocean fliers were waiting—and pathetically hoping—too.

Of the three Stinson-Detroiters recently built for transatlantic flights, two were to jump off from Harbour Grace. One of these was the *Royal Windsor,* scheduled to fly from Windsor, Ontario, to Windsor, England. The other was the *Sir John Carling,* which was to fly from London, Ontario, to the British capital.

The Windsor (Ontario) businessmen had engaged C. A. ("Duke") Schiller, a well-known Canadian bush pilot, and Phil Wood, brother of Gar Wood, American motorboat racer, to take their plane across the water. The Carling brewery, which was offering a $25,000 prize for a successful London-to-London journey, had chosen among many applicants two pilots of the Provisional Flying Corps of Canada. They were Captain Terrence Tully and Lieutenant James Medcalf.

There was considerable rivalry between the two teams. Each wanted to get away first, with Harbour Grace the last fueling stop. The *Royal Windsor* was also to carry a magnolia wreath to drop in the Atlantic in honor of that much memorialized pair, Nungesser and Coli.

The brewery plane reached Harbour Grace first. Tully and Medcalf took on a big load of gas and were ready to roll down the runway at 7:25 A.M.—about nineteen hours after the *Old Glory* had left Old Orchard. The *Sir John Carling* had no radio and neither of her occupants knew that a few hours earlier the American plane had sent out an S O S. Authorities at Harbour Grace wondered whether to tell them. They decided that such depressing news might jeopardize the takeoff. Still, the two Canadian fliers ought to know about the *Old Glory*. So an official wrote a brief memorandum and inserted it in the pilots' map case, where they would be sure to find it when they opened the case to scan the charts.

The *Sir John Carling* mounted into the air and headed east. Soon the plane was over the Atlantic. And that was the last that was heard of her. Four days later officials of the brewery announced that the fliers' widows would divide the $25,000 prize, and that in addition each would receive about $8,500 from Lloyd's.

After the brewery plane was lost, the backers of the *Royal Windsor* ordered Schiller and Wood to call off their flight. It was an action which probably averted another tragedy.

On September 14 two events thousands of miles apart called up memories of the fliers who had lost their lives in flights over the world's greatest oceans. Off Old Orchard Beach, Phil Wood dropped the Nungesser-Coli wreath from the *Royal Windsor*. It was dedicated to all those who had died "for the development of aviation." And some 600 miles off San Francisco the Hawaii-bound Matson liner

Maui paused to cast thousands of flowers onto the waters. The floral pieces came from many parts of the country. One of them, given by former pupils of Miss Doran, was fashioned in the form of a Bible. It had a cork base and was designed to float for weeks on the surface of the deep, which, in three days, had swallowed up six men and a woman.

13

THE SEXY AMERICAN GIRL

The August and September disasters had one good result. They restored some additional sanity, even among potential sponsors, to the popular attitude toward ocean flying. Twenty-three men and two women had now died in efforts or preparations to fly the North Atlantic and Pacific, and these gambles for ephemeral fame began to look ridiculous.

The backers of the Windsor-to-Windsor project had been the first to take action by calling off that flight. Then the Navy canceled the leaves of Lieutenant Lawrence Curtin and Ensign Steve Edwards, who were to have flown with Fonck. Thereafter the Philadelphia *Evening Bulletin* withdrew its $25,000 prize for a flight from Europe to the City of Brotherly Love. The Boston and Cleveland chambers of commerce withdrew similar awards for flights to their cities.

Newspapers all over the world declaimed that stunt flying ought to be discouraged. Lord Thomson, Secretary of State for Air in the Labour government, said "I think the extraordinary passion for flying the Atlantic is very like the charge at Balaklava—it is magnificent but not aviation. No one can fail to appreciate the splendid courage being shown, but I am afraid it is going to do harm to aviation. I am particularly opposed to carrying passengers on such flights. Nobody on a trip of this kind should go as waste weight."

Australia announced that no aircraft except seaplanes, flying boats or amphibians would thereafter be permitted to make over-water flights of more than fifty miles. T. Douglas Robinson, U. S. Navy Secretary, called for legislation to prevent improperly qualified aviators or planes from embarking on ocean flights. He was obliged, however, to turn down a request from a spokesman for a hundred relatives and friends of Schlee and Brock asking that the airmen not be permitted to fly from Tokyo to Midway. Legislation to curb dangerous flights had not been enacted.

Captain Bone of the *Transylvania*, along with other master mariners, also joined the chorus against reckless over-water flights. Bone pointed out that surface ships were not allowed to go to sea without competent navigators, yet airplanes could take off for ocean journeys without anyone capable of calculating their positions. If the precise position of the *Old Glory* had been given before she plunged into the sea, he said, some vessel might have arrived in time to save three lives.

Failing to persuade the Navy to forbid Schlee and Brock from braving the Pacific, the spokesman for the airmen's relatives next asked that warships be stationed along the line of flight. The Navy declined. Then he asked that a fast cruiser be assigned to bring the two men home so they would not be tempted to make the air journey. This brought another negative reaction. In the end the two airmen bowed to the concern of their relatives and loaded their plane on the *Korea Maru* for a prosaic sea voyage to San Francisco.

Not all officials favored the kind of legislation Mr. Robinson advocated. President Coolidge said it might throttle the development of aviation. So despite all the furor, no law was enacted to prevent further aerial escapades either by Americans or by Europeans.

Only four days after the *Kyle* had picked up the broken wing of the *Old Glory*, another Fokker started across the Atlantic. This one was headed westward from Baldonnel, Ireland. It was a machine much like the Hearst plane and powered with the same kind of engine. It was named *Princess Xenia*, in honor of the Russian-born wife of an American millionaire and sportsman, William B. Leeds, who helped finance the flight. And it was piloted by Captain Robert MacIntosh, a Scotsman who was an Imperial Airways cross-Channel pilot, and Commandant James Fitzmaurice, of the Irish Free State Air Force.

The fliers hoped to win the $25,000 prize for a flight from Europe to Philadelphia, apparently being unaware that the award had just been withdrawn. A few minutes before they started, a black cat walked across MacIntosh's path near the hangar. He picked up the animal and said it was an omen of good luck. But two hours later the plane ran into turbulent headwinds which cut her speed to 60 miles an hour. After another hour, in which the airmen came down to within 30 feet of the water in a vain effort to escape the invisible aerial blows, they dumped some of their gas and flew back to Ireland, landing safely at Beale Strand, near the small seaside resort of Ballybunion, Kerry.

It was getting late in the year for flying the North Atlantic, especially from the Old World to the New. Courtney in Spain and Givon and Corbu in France decided to postpone their projects. Dieudonné Costes and Joseph Le Brix, whose Hispano-powered Breguet biplane had been poised at Le Bourget for months, turned their gaze to a less stormy region and mapped a four-lap flight across the South Atlantic. And in mid-October they safely completed the over-water part of it, flying a distance of 2,125 miles—from St. Louis in Senegal, to Port Natal, Brazil—in 21 hours and 15 minutes.

Of the six American airplanes which a month earlier were being readied for eastward crossings, two were now lost and a third—the *Royal Windsor*—had bowed out. Soon René Fonck also quit. Deprived of his U. S. Navy crewmen and unable to get substitutes familiar with the Sikorsky, he returned to his native land by steamer.

After Fonck's withdrawal the only plane that seemed anywhere near ready to attempt an ocean passage was the Sikorsky amphibian of Mrs. Grayson, the Long Island realtor. Mrs. Grayson was an interesting if not glamorous figure. A rather formidable female in her mid-thirties, she was an ardent feminist and believed to the point of fanaticism that it was possible—with the planes of the day—to fly the Atlantic at any time of the year.

After graduating from high school in Muncie, Indiana, she studied piano for a time at the Chicago Musical College so she could accompany her brother, who had a talent for singing. But when her brother died, she took a course in recitation and dramatic arts at Swarthmore, where she met John Brady Grayson, twenty years her senior. They were married in 1914, and amicably divorced nine years later.

For a while Mrs. Grayson worked for a newspaper syndicate and then went into the real estate business on Long Island. She made a small fortune and became interested in flying. On Saturday afternoons she often visited Curtiss Field to watch the planes. She also took a few lessons and learned to fly small craft—with a pilot beside her.

When Lindbergh rocketed to fame she decided that a feminist ought to fly the ocean too. What man can do, woman can do also, she used to say, not quite accurately. She visited the factory of Igor Sikorsky, who showed her an amphibian he was building for a South American concern. This craft—a sesquiplane with a long upper and a stubby lower wing—had a boat hull, and wheels that could be lowered for airport landings. It could come down on and take off from land, ice or water, provided these surfaces weren't too rough. And it could fly for a while on either of the two Whirlwind engines.

To Mrs. Grayson, the amphibian seemed to be the answer to transatlantic flying. She got in touch with another feminist—Mrs. Aage Ancker, wealthy daughter of a Pittsburgh steel manufacturer, who had a summer home in Aiken, North Carolina. Mrs. Ancker, who had married a Dane and lived in Copenhagen, agreed to help buy the plane and defray other expenses of a flight which would end in the Danish capital. The whole enterprise would cost about $50,000.

Mrs. Grayson had never soloed, nor had she flown a two-engined plane, so she didn't feel competent to pilot the Sikorsky. She also lacked the ability to navigate or operate a radio. She looked around for women who had these skills, but when she couldn't find a female team, she was forced to fall back on men. As pilot she hired Wilmer Stultz, a well-known ex-Navy flier. And as navigator and radioman she chose Brice Goldsborough. The compass expert, who was on leave from the Pioneer Instrument Company, was adept in both fields. He was also a capable aviator.

It seemed like an excellent team, even if it had to be male. And when the plane was completed in September, Stultz and Goldsborough began the load, fuel-consumption and other tests incidental to transatlantic flights. The plan was to take off from Old Orchard, Maine, but the tests were made at Curtiss Field. They didn't attract much interest. Mrs. Grayson, like most other feminists, lacked the quality which in those days was called "It." And the latest aeronautical disasters had soured the public on ocean flying. The North Atlantic air derby no longer gripped mankind's attention. It needed an infusion of something potent to regain its old fascination.

It got what it needed on September 14, when a brilliant-orange Stinson-Detroiter landed at Roosevelt Field after a flight from Wheeling, West Virginia. Both of its occupants were natives of Lakeland, Florida. One was a modest young man named George Haldeman, who was one of the best fliers in the country. The other was a stunning young woman with a diminutive, curvaceous figure, hazel eyes and a husky contralto voice. She was clad in fawn-colored knickers, white skirt, checked sweater and stockings, and wore a gay bandeau around her bobbed brown hair. She told reporters she was Miss Ruth Elder. The plane which had brought her to Roosevelt was named the *American Girl*.

Miss Elder was not only very pretty, she could actually fly a plane. Back in Lakeland she had been a stenographer and later a dentist's assistant. She had become interested in planes and had learned how to manage them. And she had become acquainted with Haldeman, an experienced aviator.

Impressed by the fame which Lindbergh had so quickly achieved she had interested T. H. McArdle, a retired Florida realtor, and Edward Cornell, a grapefruit grower, in a transatlantic project of her own. They, in turn, had interested some businessmen and bankers in Wheeling. Together the various promoters had raised $35,000 to buy a plane and defray Miss Elder's and Haldeman's expenses until they could take off. Unlike some backers of ocean flights, these men didn't insist on a cut of the take. They merely wanted to help two young fliers. And after the Stinson had been built, they tried to persuade the pair to postpone their flight until spring, when there would be reasonable assurance of better weather. But the two wanted to go right away.

Miss Elder, who was twenty-three, was the most photogenic woman flier the newsmen on Long Island had ever seen. And she didn't say a thing about "advancing aeronautical science" or "strengthening the bonds of friendship between great nations." She admitted frankly that she wanted to be the first woman to fly the Atlantic, that she didn't think women were strong enough to make such a flight alone, and that she therefore needed the help of George Haldeman. She was always ready to pose smilingly and charmingly for pictures and she exuded physiological allure. Moreover, an intriguing mystery soon materialized to heighten popular—or at least male—interest in her. Was she married or wasn't she?

News dispatches from Lakeland said she was the wife of Lyle Womack, a young salesman of electrical signs who was then in the

Canal Zone. But the petite aviatrix declared this wasn't true. She knew a Lyle Womack, she said, but he was just a "very dear friend."

"Why can't they just let me fly my plane?" she asked with an enchanting pout. "I've said over and over again that I'm not married and never have been married and that I did not sign my name 'Mrs.' Ruth Elder before I left Wheeling, as some have said." She also denied emphatically that she was providing advance publicity for a forthcoming motion picture called *The American Girl.*

Two days later, after a hurried exchange of telephone calls and telegrams between newspapers in Lakeland and New York, the attractive newcomer admitted that she was Mrs. Womack. "Well, yes, I'm married. I've been married two years." She continued, "I never denied I was married. I misunderstood the reporters and they misunderstood me. They asked me if I was married to a man in Oklahoma or Arizona and I said 'No' because I'm not. I'm always known as Miss Elder when I fly. Why does everybody butt into my affairs?"

It seemed for a while that one of those to butt most vigorously into her affairs would be Mr. J. J. Lannin, owner of the Garden City Hotel and Roosevelt Field. Mr. Lannin was one of many Americans who were concerned about ill-qualified ocean fliers and planes. Though no machine which had flown directly from Roosevelt had come down in mid-Atlantic, Lannin had worked out a new set of rules for the field: Any plane taking off for a projected ocean flight must have more than one engine. It must also be able to alight on and take off from the water. It must have a flight radio and an emergency radio capable of sending distress signals on water or land. It must carry a competent navigator. And it must pass rigid safety tests given by experts.

The *American Girl* met none of these requirements. But one of her pilots had a lot of pulchritudinous persuasiveness. In fact, she had so much that after Mr. Lannin met her he forgot all about his new rules. He granted permission for the *American Girl* to use

Roosevelt Field any time Miss Elder, or Mrs. Womack, found it convenient to do so.

For nearly a month bad weather prevented either the Stinson-Detroiter or the Sikorsky from starting. During this period of enforced idleness Miss Elder was much in evidence around Curtiss and Roosevelt and posed repeatedly for pictures. Indeed, she became almost as big an attraction as Lindbergh had been before he flew to Paris. Sizable crowds came to see her. Many of her worshipers were little girls who wore multicolored bandeaux around their hair. These were the "Ruth ribbons" the flier had temporarily made famous.

While waiting for a good word from Dr. Kimball, Miss Elder took Frank Jardone, Department of Commerce inspector, up in a small biplane, and won her official pilot's license by proving herself a capable airwoman. She also denied more rumors that she was advertising a new cigarette and that she would fly only to Newfoundland and then return to publicize the movie with which her name had already been linked.

Mrs. Grayson kept a watchful eye on her glamorous rival as well as on her own crew. Most of the tests were now finished, but the bad weather was not. On October 4, painters colored the Danish flag on the Sikorsky's tail surfaces. And six days later the plane started for Old Orchard, where the plan was to take off from the beach.

Aboard, beside Mrs. Grayson, were Stultz, Goldsborough, Doc Kinkaid and Boris Libinsky, a Sikorsky mechanic. En route, on behalf of the realtor, Goldsborough tapped out a message to the *New York Times*. Preceded by the request that it be forwarded to all news agencies, it caused some earthlings to wonder if fame was going to the flying feminist's head:

> The plane took off beautifully. Pilot Stultz began to lift our graceful Sikorsky ship when 2,000 feet from the starting line. We were off the ground in twenty-five seconds flat and headed out over the Sound. Weather fine for the first leg of our transatlantic flight.

After further tests with ship, weather permitting, will carry the progressive American woman's greetings to my splendid associate, Mrs. Ancker, in Denmark. Goldsborough navigating and radioing. "Doc" Kimball timed the takeoff and is listening to motors. Chief Engineer Libinsky getting much-needed sleep. I am enjoying the trip.

FRANCES GRAYSON

Another ocean race appeared to be in the making, this one with a feminine twist. But the newspapers didn't have much time to build it up. Perhaps alarmed by Mrs. Grayson's latest move, Haldeman and Miss Elder filled their plane with 520 gallons of gas and at five-forty the next afternoon started down the Roosevelt runway.

It was the most exciting takeoff since Lindbergh's. A big crowd had assembled, and the Nassau County cops had a difficult time keeping people and cars back. Haldeman had planned to start toward the west, using the ramp which had been built for the Byrd plane. But the wind wasn't right and at the last moment he taxied to the west end of the field, turned the plane around and headed east. There was time only to clear a narrow lane before he started.

The little Stinson-Detroiter was carrying 70 gallons of gas more than the *Spirit of St. Louis*, and she had two people aboard instead of one. But Haldeman showed superb skill in keeping her in the middle of the lane, and she ran only 3,000 feet before she got off the ground. She barely cleared the telephone wires at the end of the field. But she did clear them and quickly flew out of sight.

Haldeman had decided on a southern course where they would meet more ships and probably get better weather than on the northern great-circle route. But within a few hours they ran into a storm that belted the plane into sickening plunges and leaps. For eight hours the *American Girl* fought forces which seemed determined to destroy her. But the little monoplane, expertly handled by Haldeman, stood up under the buffeting and the Whirlwind kept going.

The storm finally blew itself out and Miss Elder was able to spell her companion at the controls. They flew on all next day and all next night. No ships appeared in the circle of sea below them. They were unreported for twenty-eight hours. People back home wondered if another ocean tragedy had taken place.

On the morning of the thirteenth the oil pressure began to drop. Either the gauge was out of whack or one of the lines was leaking. Haldeman throttled back the Whirlwind. The plane's speed dropped to 70 miles an hour. He nursed the engine along. It was still going five hours later when he sighted a tanker a few miles ahead.

He circled over the ship. Miss Elder leaned out and dropped a message. It fell into the sea and was lost. Haldeman circled again. His companion dropped another message. This one hit the tanker's deck. "How far are we from land and which way?"

Sailors on the 3,700-ton Dutch tanker *Barendrecht* painted the answer on the deck: "TRUE 40 360 MILES TERCEIRA, AZORES." The *American Girl* circled the ship several times more while Haldeman and his co-pilot considered what to do. They had 130 gallons of gas left, enough to reach the islands. But the engine was now knocking badly. The oil pressure was down to 5 pounds.

Haldeman decided to ditch. He stalled the plane down on the crest of a long swell so gently that the machine floated like a gull. They had been in the air for thirty-six hours and had flown 2,632 miles from Roosevelt Field.

Miss Elder climbed to the top of the cabin and began to put on her inflatable safety suit. After a while Haldeman pulled himself up too. A lifeboat from the tanker headed toward them. The crew tossed a line to the fliers. "Take George first. He hasn't got a safety suit," Miss Elder said. So Haldeman came aboard first, followed by the first woman to be rescued from a plane in mid-Atlantic.

Then the lifeboat crew bent lines to the plane and the *Barendrecht* moved alongside to take the tired machine aboard. A winch was about to lower a cable when a swell smashed the plane against the ship. Suddenly there was an underwater blast. Flaming gasoline swirled to the surface. Haldeman theorized later that the engine had

196

been driven back into the gas tank and caused it to explode. Another theory was that the carbide drift flares had blown up when sea water poured in on them. Whatever the cause, the tanker hurriedly backed off and the *American Girl* disappeared forever beneath the waves.

Anton Meder, wireless operator of the tanker, was one of the first of many Europeans to salivate at the sight of the luscious little morsel from Lakeland. In a message reporting the rescue, he said: "Miss Elder, though fatigued, was immediately ready to send telegrams to her folks at home. We all thought of her as one of the littlest, prettiest and most courageous of girls. A real American girl." He added that Haldeman was a "brave and real man," but it was easy to see where the crew's main interest lay.

One of the messages sent from the *Barendrecht* was to Lyle Womack in Balboa. LANDED BY STEAMSHIP BARENDRECHT. BOTH SAFE, UNINJURED. WIRE LATER. LOVE RUTH. Womack replied: WORLDS OF LOVE FOR THE BRAVEST GIRL IN THE WORLD. ANXIOUSLY AWAITING YOUR RETURN. LYLE.

Reporters asked Womack how he felt about the flight. "I'm sorry she didn't succeed, but I'm so glad she's safe I couldn't have cared if she had landed at Sandy Hook," he said. "Since she took off, sleep has only been a matter of minutes with me. I have lived at the cable office."

The transatlantic air derby was back on the front pages. But not all the comments on its latest manifestation were enthusiastic, especially those by members of Miss Elder's sex. Dr. Katherine Davis, a leading sociologist, called the flight "a mistaken thing for a young girl to do." Winifred Sackville Stoner, founder of the League for Fostering Genius, said, "A good typist is of much more service to humanity." And Mrs. Franklin D. Roosevelt, wife of the former unsuccessful vice-presidential candidate, observed, "My personal feeling is that it is very foolish to risk one's life as well as that of a pilot in the face of contrary advice from almost everyone who knew anything about aviation. All the experts told Miss Elder that she should not try it but she was determined to go ahead. Of course there is no denying that she exhibited marvelous courage, and for that we must pay her tribute. Nevertheless, it seems to me unquestionably foolish for a young woman to fly alone with only a pilot over such a long distance."

Even less kind appraisals came from several European sources, including the *Zwölf Uhr Blatt* in Berlin, which described the flight as "mere foolhardiness" and "crazy sensationalism." Miss Elder's purpose "was not to advance the science of aviation but to pose as the pluckiest girl in the world. She has done her share," the paper concluded sarcastically, "to confirm her countrymen in the idea— if that is possible—that the American girl is the supreme effort of creation."

But critical comments, whether thoughtful or malicious, were drowned in the tumult of hysterical adulation for the first female flier to brave the ocean airways and live to talk about it. In the Azores, people crowded around Miss Elder as if she were an angel, and newspaper correspondents flashed details of everything she did, including what she ate at various meals and her promises to try again in 1928. Haldeman, a good-natured, understanding man, kept pretty much in the background.

In the Portuguese islands Miss Elder met another pretty girl who was trying for aeronautical fame but was not getting it. Lilli Dillenz was an Austrian actress who had traveled as a passenger aboard a Junkers three-engined seaplane from Germany to the Azores. The project was financed by the Hamburg American Line, but Lilli's backers were a group of Austrian businessmen who had put up $12,500 for her transatlantic fare. In return they were to receive 50 percent of the money she made as the first woman to complete an air journey across the Atlantic.

Many offers of money were now coming in but they were addressed to Miss Elder and not to the cuddlesome *Fräulein*. One $50,000 proposal called for Miss Elder to appear as Queen Guenevere and Haldeman as King Arthur for a ten-day Florida performance advertising indoor greyhound racing. Another suggestion was that the petite aviatrix appear—at $12,000 a week—at a chain of tea-rooms. Other bids, for $5,000 each, sought her endorsement of cold cream and hair nets. And a movie company sent along an invitation to star in a picture for a fee of $75,000.

Lilli got a little publicity by offering her rival a place in the Junkers when it took off for America. But the American girl wanted to see Paris. As it turned out, the German plane never got much farther westward. Its male crew tried several times to coax it into the air with Lilli and a big load of gasoline aboard, but their efforts culminated in a crash which wrecked the plane and severely jolted the occupants.

Miss Elder and Haldeman sailed for Madeira and Lisbon in the small Portuguese mail steamer *Lima,* whose captain sent out daily news reports of their doings. The girl from Lakeland had lost her flying helmet when the Stinson sank, but Captain Goos of the *Barendrecht* had given her his white cap, which she wore cocked jauntily on one side of her head. It topped off a fetching picture.

While the *Lima* wallowed and shuddered in the seas sweeping westward from Africa, Portuguese officials and hostesses twittered about the reception to be accorded the Americans. Some of the Portuguese felt that neither flier rated a big celebration. Others thought that an impressive welcome would curry favor with that rich and sometimes liberal America.

Miss Elder's marital status occasioned much discussion. Could she stay with propriety in a hotel when unchaperoned by her lawful husband? Where *was* her husband, anyway? And what was his name? It was a difficult situation. But Mrs. Fred Morris Dearing, wife of the American minister, came to the rescue by inviting Miss

Elder and Mr. Haldeman to stay at the new and attractive legation in Lisbon. It went without saying that they would occupy separate rooms.

There was also the matter of girlish modesty. Some members of Portuguese high society had gained the curious impression that Miss Elder would be pained by publicity. She would shrink, they thought, from being stared at and pointed at. But how shield her from the vulgar gaze? How protect her delicate sensibilities? After all, she couldn't be made to vanish.

In the end, the couple received quite a good welcome in the Portuguese capital. Airplanes filled with newspapermen and photographers circled over the *Lima* as she steamed up the Tagus, and two machines came low and dropped flowers on the deck. Mr. Dearing was on hand to greet them. He took them to the office of General Antonio Carmona, the dictator, who chatted with them for fifteen minutes. Then the American minister took them to the legation, and later they lunched at the Portuguese Aero Club, which awarded both fliers its medal.

The Portuguese gave the Americans free passage on the airline from Lisbon to Madrid but didn't lose by the operation. The airline charged other passengers on the Junkers the equivalent of $150 apiece, twenty-three times the usual rate, to be shipmates with Miss Elder and Haldeman. And the plane was booked solid. An additional thrill was provided all hands by the port engine, which broke down in flight with a sound like tin cans cascading from a dump truck. But the plane reached Madrid intact and the fliers were greeted there by Ogden Hammond, United States ambassador to Spain.

They stayed in Madrid only a few hours. General Miguel Primo de Rivera, the local dictator, did not appear at first at the embassy reception. But Miss Elder telephoned him and said she wanted to meet him—and he came. At eleven o'clock the Americans took a train to Bayonne, where the French placed a plane at their disposal.

Haldeman gunned it into Paris in record time, to win the admiration of French aviators.

The French were busy entertaining Costes and Le Brix, who had returned from their South Atlantic hop, and had no official welcome for the American pair. Perhaps the U. S. ambassador also was getting tired of greeting American aviators, for he didn't show up at Le Bourget when Miss Elder and Haldeman came in. Several thousand other people—both French and American—were on hand, however, and the pair rode through crowded streets to the Hotel Lotti. There were no big doings in their honor at the embassy, but a Baron Pichon threw a midnight party for them, an affair which brought together the leaders of French Army and Navy aviation. And in the next few days Miss Elder laid a wreath on the tomb of the Unknown Soldier and paid the inevitable visit to Mme. Nungesser, who kissed her and said she still hoped her son would be found alive.

Miss Elder also did a bit of shopping. Among her acquisitions were a mink coat, two evening gowns, several sports outfits—including an all-white ensemble with a red-and-white sweater—and a number of hats, shoes, bags and other items. Isaac Liberman, president of Arnold Constable & Co., which financed these transactions, said that the total came to 30,000 francs, at that time about $1,100.

While Miss Elder was shopping, the *Barendrecht* lumbered into Baytown, Texas. There an Associated Press reporter handed Captain Goos three checks, for $400, $100 and $500, representing money raised by citizens of Wheeling. At Miss Elder's cabled suggestion it was so divided that the first check went to Captain Goos, the second to the sailor who had commanded the lifeboat which took the pair off the plane, and the third was cashed and the proceeds distributed among other members of the crew.

"It is a strange experience for us to be rewarded for saving human life," said Captain Goos. "But nevertheless we cannot be anything but grateful to the people of Wheeling and to the Associated Press for handling this token, for token I must consider it, and not reward. Hence, as I now see it, accepting it will not tend to commercialize that rule of the sea by which we are all bound— 'Save human lives at any cost.' " He added that he would donate his share of the token to a fund for the relief of Dutch seamen's widows and orphans.

Before boarding the *Aquitania* for home, Miss Elder posed in the studio of Ludovico Auteri Marrazzan, an Italian sculptor, to have her features immortalized in bronze. She also addressed the French public over the radio.

She and Haldeman came home on November 11—just a month after they had taken off from Roosevelt Field—to be met down the bay by Grover Whalen, ride up Broadway under ribbons of ticker tape and meet Mayor Walker at City Hall. The mayor, who had an eye for pretty women, posed for a picture in which Miss Elder looked her best. "Pulchritude," he informed the citizenry of the nation's largest metropolis, "is no bar to courage."

Almost forgotten in the city welcome was Lyle Womack, who had come up from the Canal Zone to welcome his wife and who was on the *Macom* when she came off the liner. A reporter said that Womack hugged Miss Elder and lifted her off her feet, but their reunion did not appear to be overly effusive. In fact, Womack got little attention. He said rather plaintively that he had played football and been middleweight boxing champion in college, but nobody seemed greatly interested. He also said he was tired of being called Miss Elder's husband. But that didn't grip anybody either.

For a few days he hung around New York, attending banquets, letting in newsmen, and when interviews were in progress, answering telephone calls. For his wife was now a busy woman. Contracts totaling $200,000 had to be considered, and people were constantly coming in to see her.

One contract—which she signed—called for $100,000 for one

hundred days of vaudeville appearance in cities throughout the country. There would be movies of her takeoff and of the receptions in the Azores and Europe, and she would talk for a few minutes at each showing.

She had already made $17,000 for newspaper and news-syndicate stories and photographs, and there was talk of a role in the *Ziegfeld Follies*. All in all, she was doing considerably better than Haldeman, whose best offer was $10,000 for a lecture tour. Indeed, she was doing so well that Womack didn't see much use in hanging around. And presently he left for Balboa where his father had a hat factory. He said hopefully that Ruth would join him there later. It is doubtful that he believed it.

The following March Mrs. Womack signed a contract with Paramount to play the title role in a movie called *Glorifying the American Girl*, to be produced by Florenz Ziegfeld. Reporters wondered if there had been something, after all, in those early rumors about a motion picture.

In September 1928, Womack filed suit in Balboa. He asked for a divorce on the grounds of cruelty. The petition said his weight had dropped, his efficiency for work lessened and his health and reason been endangered. Womack also declared that his wife had subjected him to many sleepless nights by her transatlantic project and had caused him much embarrassment in New York when she failed to kiss him on the *Macom*. During the last fourteen months of their marriage, his wife had paid little attention to him, apparently more interested in flying across the Atlantic than in their life together. Referring to the incident on the *Macom* when he lifted her up, he added: "I embraced her and attempted to kiss her, whereupon she said: 'Don't be a damned fool.'" Since her return, Womack added in his petition, she had treated him with scorn and indifference, assuming a superior attitude and showing him no affection. The suit was uncontested and in December the petition was granted. In Los Angeles, where Miss Elder was appearing in vaudeville, she said the news hurt her "a great deal" and that she didn't want a divorce and still loved Lyle. After the divorce action Womack sailed for the Antarctic with the Byrd expedition. His father told reporters that the main reason for his son's decision to go to the bleak bottom of the world was his unhappiness over his broken marriage.

In 1929 Miss Elder married Walter Camp, Jr., son of the former Yale football coach who used to select the All-American teams (on which Old Eli was usually well represented) and author of the *Daily Dozen* calisthenic exercises. Young Camp, who had played for Yale, was then president of Inspiration Pictures. The marriage proved unsuccessful. For Miss Elder, so did four more that followed.

Despite earlier promises, the one-time American girl did not attempt to fly the Atlantic again.

14

"AM I A LITTLE NOBODY?"

To some reporters it seemed that the October 11 takeoff of the *American Girl* had caught Mrs. Frances Grayson flatfooted. But the feminist denied she was engaged in a transatlantic contest. Minimizing the role of men in the cast, she told newsmen at Old Orchard, "There is plenty of room over the Atlantic for two women, and plenty of glory for all. We believe that we have an entirely different purpose from Miss Elder's and will go ahead with our program. We began planning more than five months ago and we shall certainly make no change in our plans. The work will not be hurried and there will be no semblance of a race. If we complete our work and the weather conditions are propitious we will take off tomorrow."

By now both Sikorsky and Wright officials were advising Mrs. Grayson to postpone her flight until spring. As the cold sharpened, the danger of icing increased. Dr. Kimball had officially suspended his special service for transatlantic projects. The time for ocean flying was over for the year, he said, and the Weather Bureau was low in funds. Still, he continued on his own to provide data when fliers asked for it.

To the counsel from plane, engine and weather experts was now added a plea from an unexpected quarter—Mrs. Ralph O. Brewster, wife of the governor of Maine. The Sikorsky had not yet been formally christened, and Mrs. Grayson had arranged for Mrs.

Brewster to do the honors with a bottle of Poland spring water, one of the proud products of the Pine Tree State.

Mrs. Brewster swung the bottle and broke it over the blue boat hull's nose with one blow, a feat seldom seen in plane christenings. Later she handed Mrs. Grayson—and reporters—a typewritten statement. It was the most unusual statement made at any plane christening in the Lindbergh era.

> Prayers of women everywhere will go up for your success if you shall decide that it is wise for you to start. The hazard of the enterprise, however, and the question as to its fruits lead me to express what I believe to be the earnest entreaty of Maine women that you may decide to wait. I come here for this christening not only to indicate the cordial good will and hospitality of the citizens of Maine and their appreciation of the courage of the pioneer, but also with the hope that some words of mine on behalf of your sisters may dissuade you for this year from undertaking such a flight. Governor Brewster joins me in the confidence that you will reach a right decision with a due regard for all concerned.

Mrs. Grayson expressed surprise at these words and presently countered with a statement of her own:

> While I deeply appreciate the plea of the women of your great state, as expressed by Mrs. Brewster, to postpone what they regard as a hazardous undertaking, I wish to send this message to the women of the United States. That we fully realize the seriousness of our expedition and have fully prepared for the so-called hazards of this glorious month of October. In urging me not to go, I feel that you have assumed as great a responsibility as if you had advised me to go. The *Dawn* will waken American women to greater efforts and bind together the women of two continents.
>
> FRANCES GRAYSON

The Grayson statement also was given to the waiting reporters. Mrs. Brewster said she had no comment to make on it.

While the women were disseminating, discussing or refusing to discuss statements, the male members of the Sikorsky's crew began getting the newly christened *Dawn* ready for a dawn takeoff, continuing to work far into the night. But before morning a 60-mile gale whipped up the waves and made a start impossible. The next day the gale, plus a high tide, nearly wrecked the plane. Stultz, Goldsborough and some local fishermen battled wind and waves for hours until they hauled the amphibian farther up the beach and secured its yellow wings with lines and anchors. This was the day on which a young woman from Portland presented Mrs. Grayson with the left hind foot of a rabbit which she said had been shot ten years before by a one-eyed Negro in a graveyard at midnight in the dark of the moon. The donor added that since she had acquired it she had always had good luck. Mrs. Grayson accepted it laughing and stowed it in her pocket.

The *Dawn* crew and a dozen reporters and photographers were staying at the Brunswick, a summer hotel which had reopened at Mrs. Grayson's request a month after the normal season ended. The only heat in the building, aside from the kitchen stoves, came from a fireplace in the lobby. But local waitresses and chambermaids had stayed on and the cook had obligingly agreed to postpone his annual deer hunt to accommodate the visitors.

On October 14, while still waiting for better weather, Mrs. Grayson gave a dinner for the newsmen. Here she revealed that she would carry other good-luck talismans besides the rabbit's foot: a Bible; a picture of her mother; a Persian coin dating from the seventh century and unearthed on the Sikorsky estate near Kiev; a letter to a little girl in Denmark written by her mother in America; another letter to a little girl in America written by her mother in Denmark; and a picture of Francis Scott Key, which was to be taken along at the request of her godmother, Mrs. Anna Key Palmer, a great-great-grandniece of the "Star-Spangled Banner" man.

At this dinner, which was held a day after the Elder-Haldeman rescue, Mrs. Grayson told her guests that her plane was the most suitable one in existence for an ocean voyage. "The theory about there being a season for transatlantic flying is wrong and I will prove it is wrong," she added. "I am going to be the first woman to fly across the Atlantic and mine will be the only ship since Lindbergh's to reach its destination. I will prove that woman can compete with man in his own undertakings."

She revealed that she had received a cablegram from Mrs. Ancker, in Copenhagen. DENMARK AWAITING YOU, it said. DON'T BE INFLUENCED BY ANYTHING BUT YOUR OWN JUDGMENT. And her judgment was that the Sikorsky should take off early the next day. The first stop would be Valencia, Ireland, or Croydon, England, whichever seemed most feasible as the plane neared Europe.

The newsmen gave Mrs. Grayson a little pearl necklace. Their spokesman, in a graceful speech, declared that each pearl represented a separate prayer for her good fortune. But the good fortune did not come immediately. The gale hadn't blown itself out, and the next morning there was still a cross wind of 25 miles an hour, which would have made a takeoff hazardous.

Not until October 17 was the weather sufficiently favorable. Stultz got the *Dawn* airborne but found it was nose-heavy. He circled around, dumped 260 of her 921 gallons of gas and came down. He and Goldsborough decided that cans containing 50 gallons of gas had been stowed too far forward. They transferred them to the rear of the plane.

The next day there was trouble with the landing gear. Stultz couldn't make the wheels alongside the hull come up quickly enough to cope with a possible emergency descent offshore, and in a down position they would have impaired the amphibian's seaworthiness. Mrs. Grayson phoned Igor Sikorsky and demanded that he appear in person. He did, and fixed the gear. The designer also computed the weight of the craft and found that it totaled 11,558 pounds, 500 more than had been estimated.

October 22 dawned cloudy but clear—good enough for a takeoff. Stultz coaxed the amphibian up but couldn't gain altitude. The

Dawn sank down again. Stultz got the wheels up, dumped gas once more and came down safely on the water. At least the landing gear was working.

Stultz and Goldsborough began figuring how much of the gas load they would have to discard. Mrs. Grayson went to her room in the cold hotel. She looked out the window awhile, and then took paper and pen and began to set down her thoughts.

> Waiting.
> Who am I?
> Sometimes I wonder.
> Am I a little nobody? Or am I a great dynamic force—powerful—in that I have a God-given birthright and have all the power there is if only I will understand and use it?
> Sometimes I am torn between the knowing I have a great, living, breathing power of understanding by heritage and again I take cognizance of wordly values. Then I become a little nobody.
> This morning, as I sit here at a window and look out over a turbulent gray ocean—gray fog, gray clouds, all is gray—and the lashing of the waves, the rain, the wind remind me that it is almost November and the world says "Impossible to fly any more this season."
> The Weather Bureau folded their maps and said "Impossible weather. No more flying this season." And then I take account of the many discouraging delays. The weeks and months of delays—shall I listen to the warnings of an unbelieving public or shall I listen only to that "voice within"?
> Truly it is a day overcast with drab gray.
> The winds are against us. They have been all day. They have been against us for weeks. In struggling with myself, shall I give the command to turn back?
> Quit?
> Shall I let wise wordly heads, wise aeronautical sages influence me? Shall I?
> Are they right? Can it be that I am wrong? Wrong after all these many months of hard preparations, these many months of listening to that still, small voice?
> I cannot—I will not—believe I am wrong.

The day may be gray, the world may give me advice, but I will stand here in Old Orchard, Me., where the beauty of this gray scene thrills me, and I will wait until the sun shines through. For the sun is ever shining and it will shine here again. The winds will blow westward [they needed a wind blowing eastward].

I have but to maintain faith and courage and know I am right—that I am wisdom because I am of Him who is all wisdom.

Things do not just happen. I did not meet Mrs. Ancker by chance and for nothing. I did not select my amphibian plane at random or by chance. Before contracting for this ship which is to carry three lives I listened to that still, small voice.

Things have moved forward, step by step, unfolding day by day. Each delay has taught its lesson.

We thought we were ready Oct. 18 [actually October 17]. We took off, yet within me I knew things were not quite ready. So we had to come back. The time was not opportune. The weather looks as though it might continue adverse for many long months.

Yet life has taught me that these are but seeming and passing conditions. It is now time for me to show my strength, keep my faith and prove myself.

I am who or what I really am, a little nobody or a living, forceful power to carry out part of His great plan.

I will win.

I must not quit too soon.

Success is just ahead and the clouds between must disappear.

I will wait.

She gave the statement to a *New York Times* correspondent, saying he could send it in "if something happens."

The next morning, October 23, the weather was again favorable. There was even a following wind to help the plane along. The *Dawn*, with 350 pounds less fuel than she had carried on the last attempt, ran a mile down the hard beach and lurched into the air at six-twelve. She quickly flew out of sight. John Hutchinson, proprietor of the Brunswick, dismissed the help and prepared to close down the hostelry for the winter.

It soon became apparent that the weight-and-balance problem

in the *Dawn* had not been completely solved. In a turbulent area over
the ocean the Sikorsky nosed over and headed for the water. Goldsborough heaved out five 5-gallon cans of gas (totaling 150 pounds)
which had been stored in the cabin. Stultz leveled the plane off when
she was only ten feet above the waves. Everybody relaxed.

Mrs. Grayson asked Goldsborough to send out some messages.
The first, to her father in Muncie, told of the successful takeoff and
sent her love to all the people back in Indiana. The second, addressed to Mrs. Stultz and Mrs. Goldsborough back in Old Orchard,
said that their husbands were hard at work.

The third message was addressed to Mrs. Coolidge:

> I greet the first lady of the country first from the *Dawn.* I am
> off after six months' preparation, confident in the success of my
> two-fold purpose: to prove the amphibian plane the logical one for
> transatlantic commerce and to prove that woman has her place in
> the advancement of the science of aviation.
>
> FRANCES GRAYSON

The fourth message was sent with the request that it be relayed
to the proper party—Her Majesty the Queen of Denmark.

> The *Dawn* is winging her way toward Denmark. Your Majesty
> knows ere this that one of the women of your great land, Mrs.
> Ancker, helped make this expedition possible. Confident of success
> we salute you beneath the glorious October sun. Four hundred thirty-
> seven years ago Columbus sailed westward in his wooden ships [it
> should have read "435 years ago"]. Today we are sailing eastward in
> an all-metal ship of the air. Columbus discovered America. We hope
> to discover a new method of transatlantic commerce—the amphibious
> plane.
>
> FRANCES GRAYSON

The fifth and final message was addressed to Governor and
Mrs. Ralph O. Brewster at Augusta, Maine.

> The commander and crew of the *Dawn* appreciate the hospitality
> extended to them by you and your people. All is well on board.
>
> FRANCES GRAYSON

The commander of the *Dawn* was wrong again. All wasn't well on board. Though the plane was now 450 miles out and the fuel load was less, Stultz couldn't gain much altitude. And with the weather worsening he wanted to be well above the sea. In an effort to gain height he turned the plane around and headed westward into the wind, a useless maneuver. He made the decision to turn without consulting anybody. Goldsborough, in the radio nook forward, didn't know the plane was heading westward until Stultz told him. Mrs. Grayson didn't know about it until she felt the machine bank and glanced at the compass in the cabin.

At about this time white puffs of smoke shot out of the top exhaust pipes of the port engine. One cylinder began to misfire. After the vibrations knocked out the tachometer, there was no way of telling how fast the wheezing Whirlwind was turning over.

The plane began to sink. By valving 1,500 pounds of gas, Stultz was able to hold an altitude of 300 feet. The port engine was still turning slowly, throwing oil over the blue-and-yellow ship, but doing practically nothing to pull it along.

Then Stultz sighted the *Coahoma County* of the American Diamond Line. Goldsborough informed the freighter's radio operator that they might have to come down. The ship's operator suggested they come down to leeward of the vessel. It was raining but the sea was smooth. Stultz, Goldsborough and Mrs. Grayson talked it over and decided to try to reach Old Orchard. They informed the freighter of this and flew on.

Now they were bucking a headwind with only one good engine. They had been four hours going out. It took them six to come back. They made it, however, and Mrs. Grayson promptly telephoned to Doc Kinkaid in Paterson. He took the first train for Old Orchard.

Hutchinson reopened the hotel. He re-engaged the chambermaids and waitresses but had to hire a new cook. The old one said he couldn't put off his deer hunt any longer.

Kinkaid examined the ailing engine and ordered a replacement.

He said a valve had broken in the head of a cylinder and had fallen on the piston head. The upstroke of the piston had brought the broken part to its original position, where it fortunately stuck. Had it not done so, Doc said, the engine probably would have exploded, driving chunks of metal into the other engine and wrecking the plane. The disabled Whirlwind had only two gallons of oil left. It had spewed thirteen gallons into the air and over the plane.

A coolness had developed between Mrs. Grayson and Stultz. The pilot told reporters he'd be delighted if the realtor would let him cancel his contract with her. It was getting pretty late in the season for ocean flying, he added. And after the new engine had been installed, Mrs. Grayson indicated that she might let him withdraw from the enterprise. She announced that the plane would return to New York instead of taking off for Europe. She also came up with another statement which she handed to the newspapermen.

The purpose of the flight to New York, it said, was to confer with Mr. Sikorsky. She wished to find out why Stultz had found it necessary to turn around just before the port engine failed. "After careful analysis," she concluded, "I have decided that expert opinions and further tests are advisable before attempting another takeoff. I believe I am exercising common sense and good judgment."

Back in New York, Mrs. Grayson conferred with Bernt Balchen and said later that he had agreed to pilot the plane in place of Stultz. She also said Clarence Chamberlin might be a member of the crew. Balchen told reporters he wouldn't pilot any ship he hadn't tested thoroughly. Privately he felt that the Sikorsky didn't have enough range for a transatlantic flight and that it was too late in the season, anyway. Chamberlin said that if he was engaged by Mrs. Grayson he would insist on running the expedition himself.

In the midst of this male refractoriness it became known that Thea Rasche, a German stunt flier then in New York, might be available for the pilot's seat. But Mrs. Grayson denied any intention of taking on the shapely *Fräulein*. Reporters got the impression that while there might be room for two women over the Atlantic, there wasn't room for them in the same plane.

On November 4 Mrs. Grayson sailed for Europe on the *Majestic* to confer with Mrs. Ancker. When she arrived in Berlin she revealed that during the voyage she had studied winds and ocean currents which might prove useful in a transatlantic effort. In Paris she visited Le Bourget, where Major Renvoise, commandant of the airport, took her on a tour of hangars and machine shops and arranged for a flight over the French capital.

She returned home on the *Leviathan,* came out to Curtiss Field where mechanics had tuned up the Sikorsky again, and announced on December 7 that the plane would start for Old Orchard three days later. It was to be the first leg of still another ocean-flight attempt. Nobody could say Mrs. Grayson wasn't persistent.

Brice Goldsborough was still to be navigator and radioman, but the *Dawn* was to have a new pilot. Oscar Omdahl had been with Amundsen on the Dornier-Wal and *Norge* flights, and had come to America to join the Byrd expedition to the Antarctic. Balchen, an old friend, had tried to talk him out of the Grayson project. But Omdahl thought his big chance had come. A handsome young man, he knew a lot about cold-weather flying. He was convinced that icing could be prevented, or at least delayed, by liberally dosing the Sikorsky's wings and struts with glycerin.

Omdahl hadn't had much time to familiarize himself with the amphibian. On December 11 he brought the plane down from a test flight at a velocity that caused veteran pilots to gasp. It sped across Curtiss Field toward a hangar at 60 miles an hour and everybody thought it was going to be wrecked. But at the last second Omdahl threw it into a ground loop and brought it to a standstill and safety.

Bad weather and additional tests kept the plane at Curtiss for nearly two weeks more. Meanwhile her crew members decided to start the main leg of their ocean flight from Harbour Grace. The Newfoundland airport is about 900 miles nearer Europe along the great-circle route than Old Orchard is. And, thanks partly to Schlee, it now had an excellent runway. Gas and oil were dispatched there to await the *Dawn's* arrival.

On December 23 the amphibian was ready to take off, although the weather beyond Cape Cod was reported to be cold and windy. The start was set for late afternoon so that the 1,200-mile flight to Harbour Grace would be completed in daylight. A reporter noticed Mrs. Grayson putting a small automatic pistol into her purse and asked if it was a badge of authority for the commander of the expedition. She said it was not. Then she spoke of the six men of the submarine S-4 who had been trapped a few days earlier in the forward battery room of the sunken vessel while Navy divers tried vainly to save them. She saw no sense, she indicated, in suffering as those men had for more than twenty-four hours, with no real hope of rescue.

Fred Koehler, a Wright motor expert, made a fourth member of the crew when the *Dawn*, after a 2,500-foot run, rose from Roosevelt Field that Friday evening shortly after five o'clock. Koehler planned to go only to Harbour Grace. The Sikorsky's wings, struts, hull and tail had been heavily coated with glycerin, and Omdahl said he expected no trouble from icing.

Goldsborough had said he would work the radio frequently once the plane was in the air. But no identifiable messages came from the *Dawn*. At seven-ten that evening, employees of the French cable station at Orleans, on Cape Cod, thought they heard a plane pass over. It sounded like a two-engined craft but they couldn't see it.

At nine forty-five the Canadian government wireless station on Sable Island, southeast of Nova Scotia, picked up a message that might have come from the amphibian. The operator thought he made out the plane's call letters, WMU, and the words "something wrong," but he said storm interference prevented his recognizing anything more. He called the Sikorsky repeatedly but was unable to obtain an answer.

Later reports trickled in from Newfoundland. Several residents of St. John's said they heard an airplane Saturday night, twelve hours after the *Dawn* should have arrived in the area. And an operator at the Anglo-American cable station at Heart's Content, north of Harbour Grace, reported that on Sunday he heard on his home set a message that might have come from the plane. It said: "Where are we? Can you locate us?"

There were also rumors that people on Sable Island had heard an aircraft Friday or Saturday night or had picked up its call letters on their home sets. Not since the flight of the *White Bird* had so many reports about a missing plane been broadcast.

Goldsborough had left an envelope for his wife marked "Not to be opened before Christmas." Now she found it contained a check for $500. Friends of her husband's and of Mrs. Grayson's were trying to raise funds for a sea and air hunt. Mrs. Goldsborough turned her Christmas check over to them.

Unlike so many wives of lost fliers, she didn't voice confidence that her husband would be found. In a conversation with an Associated Press reporter she said, "Please tell me the truth. Do you think my husband is dead? Is there any hope? Why haven't there been any messages from the plane?"

The AP man was unable to tell her. And Mrs. Goldsborough's last words to him recalled those of Mrs. Erwin, wife of the Dallas flier lost in the Pacific. Weeping, she exclaimed, "Oh, I wish I could be with my husband now, even if he is dead."

On Christmas Day Bill Winston and Steve Parkinson, both friends of Goldsborough's, took a Curtiss Flying Service amphibian over coastal waters to and beyond Cape Cod but found no trace of the missing plane. They saw an ocean covered with whitecaps, and swells up to fifteen feet high, big enough to swamp a disabled boat-hulled plane.

The next day the Coast Guard destroyers *Monaghen* and *Shaw*, the Navy destroyers *Mahan* and *Sturtevant*, and the Navy dirigible

Los Angeles took up the hunt. The surface ships, steaming fifteen miles apart, scouted as far north as Sable Island and stopped at night lest they run past the *Dawn* or her wreckage. The airship searched as far as Emerald Bank, southwest of Sable.

Dr. Kimball and several other experts attributed the loss of the plane to ice. "When Mrs. Grayson headed out from Cape Cod and started the 240-mile water jump to Nova Scotia," the weatherman said, "she was flying through freezing weather. There may have been some rain, too. Formation of ice on the plane would have been quite possible despite the glycerin coating given the *Dawn* to prevent this danger. We use glycerin on some of our exposed instruments. It is an emergency method of some value but it is by no means a sure preventative of icing."

The meteorologist, who was well acquainted with the merits and faults of the 1927 planes, also declared that the amphibian was "a greatly overrated machine. It's all right for fairly calm weather," he said. "But there is evidence that the ocean is anything but calm now. And high seas would make short work of any plane."

Wilmer Stultz attributed the disaster to overload, poor judgment, adverse weather and the "unseaworthiness of the craft" in rough water. "To my way of thinking, though I may be wrong, it was very poor judgment to attempt the flight at this time of year. Ships are coming in from Europe two or three days late because of the storms encountered, and with their superstructures all broken to the devil by the waves. What chance would the *Dawn* have in that kind of weather?"

Nothing more was heard from the plane. Investigation cast doubt on the authenticity of the messages reported by the operators at Sable Island and Heart's Content. Still to be heard from were the ghouls who haunt widely publicized disasters. But they were not long in making their continued existence known.

Within the next few months several messages in bottles, purporting to have come from the *Dawn,* were picked up along the coast.

One, found in January near Salem, said: "1928. We are freezing. Gas leaked and we are drifting off Grand Banks. Grayson." Another, found in July, said: "We are between Labrador and Greenly Island. Come! Quick! Our radio is broken."

A year later the occupants of the plane were officially declared dead. It was discovered that Mrs. Grayson was not as wealthy as had been supposed. Perhaps she had invested most of her money in the *Dawn*, for the fortune she left amounted to less than $12,000.

15

HOW THE WIND SOCK BLEW
FOR FLOYD BENNETT

The *Dawn* tragedy rounded out aviation's most spectacular year. Never again would there be such a frenzy about ocean flying. But there were still two main successes to be scored in the Atlantic— the first westward flight and the first crossing by a woman. There were still vast areas to be explored in the Arctic and Antarctic. And the Pacific had been crossed only as far as Hawaii.

Mabel Boll still hoped to combine the first westward with the first female ocean flight. After Hinchliffe and Levine had crash-landed the Bellanca in Italy, she persuaded Levine to lend her the plane and promised the British pilot $25,000 if he would fly her westward in it when repairs were made. But Hinchliffe had other plans, and so did another lady. He had received an offer from the Honourable Elsie Mackay, beautiful daughter of Lord Inchcape, a British shipowner, of $50,000 to fly her to America. They took off from Cramwell, England, in a Whirlwind-powered Stinson-Detroiter in March 1928. They were never heard of again.

The first successful westward flight—when it came—was something of a disappointment. It was made in April by the same *Bremen* team that had failed to complete it six months earlier. The fliers were two Germans—Herman Köhl and Baron Guenther von Huenefeld—and the Irish flier James Fitzmaurice. Taking off from Baldonnel, the all-metal Junkers was forced down on Greenly Island, off Labrador.

When news of the *Bremen*'s landing reached the New York *World* its aviation editor, C. B. Allen, had what he thought was a bright idea. Balchen and Bennett had been testing the Ford tri-motor plane which Byrd expected to use in the Antarctic. It was big enough to bring all the fliers and a reporter or two to New York. So Allen suggested to Herbert Bayard Swope, the *World*'s executive editor, that the plane be used for this purpose. Swope jumped at the proposal and assured Byrd that the use of the plane in such a mission of supposed mercy—actually the *Bremen* fliers were living in comfortable quarters—would help publicize and raise funds for the coming expedition. Byrd agreed. Thereupon Swope assigned not Allen but Charlie Murphy to the rescue project.

Both Bennett and Balchen were weak from influenza when they and Murphy flew to Detroit to get the Ford. Bennett was in worse shape than his friend, for he had not fully recovered from the Teterboro crack-up. When they reached Detroit, Edsel Ford looked them over and ordered them both into the company hospital. They were still sick men when they took off for Canada two days later.

When they arrived at St. Agnes, a hundred miles above Quebec, Bennett was very ill. They put him to bed in a farmhouse, where a doctor found he had pneumonia. Before going on to Greenly Island, Balchen went in to see him. Bennett was in an old-fashioned double bed, his face the color of the white pillow. He did not open his eyes but ran his tongue over his dry lips and murmured, "Have a good trip."

"I'll see you when I get back, Floyd."

Bennett grinned feebly at his flying companion. "That depends on how the wind sock blows." He opened his eyes a crack. "One thing I want you to promise me, Bernt. No matter what happens, you fly to the South Pole with Byrd." Balchen went out. They moved Bennett to a hospital in Quebec. A few days later he died. He was thirty-seven years old. His name lives on in the Floyd Bennett Airport in Brooklyn, New York.

Balchen flew on to Greenly Island. Bad weather delayed his flight to New York with the downed foreigners. And more bad weather prevented him from reaching Washington in time for Bennett's funeral. But he met Mrs. Bennett as soon as she came back. The Byrd Antarctic expedition was shaping up then, and both Bennett and Balchen had been scheduled to accompany the commander south.

Had Bennett ever told anybody but Balchen about the flight with Byrd from Spitsbergen? Perhaps there is a hint in an angry exclamation by his wife. "I remember that meeting with her very well," Balchen said recently. "I met her at the Hotel Biltmore. She had just come back from Arlington National Cemetery. We were all very sad.

"I said, 'Cora, I'm terribly sorry. I'm going to miss Floyd terribly. And we're going to miss him on the antarctic expedition. I know he will be a great loss to the commander.'

"She turned on me with eyes blazing. 'Bernt, how can you say a thing like that?' she cried. 'This is the luckiest thing that ever happened to Byrd!'

"She didn't say any more. And I didn't know what to say. So I didn't say anything."

While Balchen was picking up the *Bremen* fliers, the Arctic again became the scene of big aviation news. Banner headlines acclaimed two daring airmen who had battled fierce storms and hard luck there for two years.

George Hubert Wilkins was a shy, modest Australian who had herded sheep, filmed Aussie troops as their official war historian and won a captain's commission and an award for exceptional bravery under fire. He learned to fly and navigate and went on two Arctic expeditions with Vilhjalmur Stefansson, the noted explorer. On one of these, Wilkins and five companions lived for a week on a floe after ice caved in the hull of their ship. Since 1926 he had been trying to determine if there was land in hitherto unexplored areas of the Arctic Ocean.

His companion in this effort was Ben Eielson, an American of Norwegian descent, who had been an Army airman and a mail flier in Alaska. Eielson was famous in that cold, mountainous territory as one of its most skillful and experienced bush pilots.

With funds from American newspaper interests and Detroit millionaires, supplemented with $15,000 he had earned, Wilkins had bought a three-engined Fokker like the *Josephine Ford* and a smaller single-engined aircraft of the same make. To prepare for their flights he and Eielson had to ferry hundreds of gallons of gasoline from Fairbanks to Point Barrow, their jump-off site.

Their bad luck started in March 1926, at the dedication of their first two planes. A reporter for the Detroit *News* stepped backward into one of the whirling propellers of the big Fokker and was decapitated. A few days later the smaller plane stalled in a trial takeoff, smashing its landing gear. Thereafter, engine failure caused a smash-up of the trimotor. Then, on a ferrying trip, the two men missed Point Barrow and flew 100 miles or more out over the sea ice, finally coming back and landing in the midst of a blizzard. It was a close call. After that, Wilkins broke his right arm working on the plane. He didn't give up even then; but soon, after trouble with a warped propeller, the plane's right wing splintered in an abortive takeoff. Finally, fog blanketed Barrow and kept the other plane on the ground until the Arctic flying season was over. And that was the end of their effort of 1926.

The following year the two men took off on March 29 in a single-engined Stinson to search for land near the Pole. Two hours after they started, the engine began to miss. Eielson brought the ski-equipped plane down on the sea ice. They took a sounding and found an ocean depth of 16,400 feet.

For two hours, in a temperature of 20 below, they worked on the

222

engine. Four attempts to take off from the rough ice failed. On the fifth try they lurched into the air. But the failing engine forced them down once more. Eielson worked on it again, getting four fingertips frozen in the process. After an hour they succeeded in rising from the ice again. They headed back toward Point Barrow.

It was now nine o'clock. They had gas for three more hours. Then the engine quit for the third time. They came down in darkness, and invisible ice badly damaged the plane. They figured they were sixty-five miles from Barrow. Weak and exhausted, they curled up in the cabin and tried to sleep. A blizzard howled around them for two days, piling snow around the wrecked Stinson. With gas drained from the tank they fueled an improvised stove, using slats torn from the cabin roof as wicks.

On April 3 they started to mush toward Barrow, dragging food and equipment on sleds they had made from parts of the plane, and scooping holes in the snow for their sleeping bags and themselves when night fell. Twelve days later they reached shore and safety. They had proved there was no land in the area. They had also proved that they had plenty of guts. But the scientific results were not spectacular and they were too tired for further exploration that year.

In April 1928 they were back at Point Barrow again. This time they had a speedy little Lockheed-Vega with a Whirlwind engine. Wilkins had bought the machine after selling the Fokker and one of the Stinsons. (The plane abandoned the previous year was never found.) After Eskimos had shoveled a runway through the snow on the bay ice, the two men took off on April 15 and flew southeast at 100 miles an hour. This time their destination was Spitsbergen. Their route would enable them to determine if there was land in a large area which had not previously been explored.

With Wilkins navigating, they flew for thirteen hours, sighting Grant Land, at the north end of Ellesmere Island, on their right. Five hours later they ran into an Arctic storm. Violent winds tossed the plane about. The windshield started to ice over and fuel was almost exhausted. They decided to come down and wait it out. Through the swirling flakes Eielson saw an expanse seemingly smooth enough to land on. Suddenly a mountain wall loomed ahead of them. The bush pilot banked sharply and landed safely on the snowfield.

Quickly they drained the engine of oil before it could harden, and piled snow around the skis lest the wind hurl the plane over and wreck it. Then they climbed back into the cabin. Wilkins figured they were close to Spitsbergen. But they had to live in the frigid cabin for four days and five nights.

Their radio had failed, so the outside world got no news of their plight. At last the storm blew itself out. For six hours the men worked, shoveling snow to clear a runway, freeing their craft from her white shroud, heating the engine oil. They had twenty gallons of gasoline left.

Eielson revved up the engine. The plane didn't budge. Wilkins jumped out and pushed against the tail. The plane crept forward, gaining speed. Wilkins ran up to the open door and pushed, tried to climb in and slipped. Eielson took off alone, saw that his partner wasn't with him, circled and landed again. This time they fastened a rope to the cabin door for Wilkins to hang on to.

He pushed at the door again and grabbed the rope to pull himself aboard. But his numbed hands couldn't hold it. He clamped the end of the rope in his teeth and again tried to pull himself into the plane as it bounced over the rough ice. Again he fell. The tail of the plane hit him and hurled him into a snowbank. He lay there a while, half buried and half stunned. When he recovered he found that all his front teeth were loose.

Again Eielson came down. They had been trying to get airborne for more than an hour and most of their fuel was now gone. They had only one more chance. If that attempt failed, Eielson would drop a rifle, ammunition, food, sleeping bag and other equipment and come back when he could in a boat.

Now Wilkins braced one leg against the cabin door frame and pushed down desperately against the ice with the other. Despite the freezing weather, he was bathed in sweat. For some seconds the plane strained and trembled as she tried to free herself from the ice that gripped her skis. Then she lunged forward. Wilkins tumbled into the cabin. The Lockheed gained speed and swept into the air.

Soon they sighted the two radio masts of Green Harbor, West Spitsbergen. They came down with practically empty tanks on smooth ice near the shore. They had flown 2,200 miles and had seen no new land. Now they could tell the world where they were. Wilkins sent out his first message: REACHED SPITSBERGEN AFTER 20½ HOURS FLYING. ONE STOP ACCOUNT BAD WEATHER.

Messages of congratulations poured in from all over the world. The *New York Times* called their flight "The greatest feat of all aviation." It printed tributes from Ellsworth, Byrd and Stefansson. Amundsen, the grandest old explorer of them all, said, "No flight has been made anywhere, at any time, which could be compared with it."

Comfortably warm in the wooden house of the radio-station manager, the two fliers learned with amusement that they had spent their four blizzard-bound days on Dead Man's Island. They said they were satisfied that no land existed between Grant Land and the Pole. "Whatever else we may have accomplished through our efforts," Wilkins added, "we will learn only as time goes on. Eielson and I have learned, at all events, the sincerity of friendship."

It was a tremendous and well-deserved triumph after two years of bad luck. And there were further rewards to come, including the highest award the American Geographical Society could offer, and money for lecture tours and articles by both men.

King George V knighted Wilkins, who chose to be called by his

middle name—Sir Hubert—because the monarch was named
George. By this time he wore a handsome dark beard which seemed
to befit a title. Soon he married a pretty actress, Suzanne Bennett,
who had come to New York to follow a stage career. Like her husband, she was a native of Australia.

16

DISASTER ON THE ICE

Fifteen days after Wilkins and Eielson reached Green Harbor, Nobile's new airship—the *Italia*—arrived at Kings Bay a few miles away. The dirigible was a sister ship of the *Norge,* with a few modifications. Layers of strong rubberized fabric now protected areas of the bag at which propellers might sling ice. Hoods covered gas-escape valves which ice might clog. And rubberized fabric covered the top of the bag as a hopeful deterrent to icing.

Nobile planned several flights out of Spitsbergen in different directions. One was scheduled for Franz Josef Land and Severnaya Zemlya (North Land), frozen island groups to the northeast. Another was to the Pole, where men would be lowered by winch and cable, Nobile to plant an oaken cross given him by the Pope, and scientists to take soundings and other measurements. There were three scientists on the flight: Finn Malmgren, who had been on the *Norge* voyage; Dr. Aldo Pontremoli, professor of physics at the University of Milan; and Dr. Francis Behounek, director of the Prague Wireless Institute, who wanted to make more atmospheric-electricity studies.

The five mechanics who had been on the *Norge* flight—Arduino, Caratti, Pomella, Alessandrini and Cecioni—also were on hand, together with a sixth, Calisto Ciocca. So were four Navy officers—Adalberto Mariano, Filippo Zappi, Alfredo Viglieri and Felice Trojani. In addition, there were Ettori Pedretti and Giuseppe Biagi, radio operators; Ugo Lago, a journalist representing Mussolini's *Il Popolo d'Italia;* and Francesco Tomaselli, another journalist and captain of a detachment of Italian mountain troops which had been brought to Spitsbergen by the expedition's support ship, the *Città di Milano.* Finally, there was Nobile's dog, Titina.

The *Italia* expedition was sponsored by the Italian Royal Geographical Society. A fund for its support had been raised by popular subscription in Milan. Mussolini's government had given no help except the loan of the dirigible, and had stipulated that the Milan committee must reimburse it for the expenses of operating the airship and paying the crew. General Italo Balbo was now Undersecretary for Air and this brash Fascist was a heavier-than-air man. He was opposed to dirigibles of any kind, was jealous of Nobile and was doing all he could to belittle the designer's activities. But Nobile had widespread popular support as a result of the *Norge* flight; and Mussolini, who wanted to glorify Italy and his regime, had a feeling that Nobile might do it for him. So he let Balbo undercut Nobile while letting Nobile go ahead with his plans.

On May 15 the airship took off from Kings Bay and started for Severnaya Zemlya, about 1,000 miles to the northeast. This Soviet-owned island group was then only partially mapped. The dirigible ran into winds and later into thick fog. In the cabin, drinking water, food and coffee froze solid. The three 250-horsepower engines burned more gas than Nobile had expected. Somewhat short of her objective, the *Italia* turned back toward Kings Bay, arriving there after a flight of sixty-nine hours. Nobile's preliminary report said that Severnaya Zemlya probably didn't exist. In Norway, Amundsen contradicted him. "I was there myself," he declared.

After a five-day rest the men were ready for the trip to the Pole. Around four o'clock in the brilliant Arctic morning of May 23, crew members eased the *Italia* out of her hangar again. Two of the men who had flown up from Italy—Tomaselli and Pedretti—were not going on this flight, which left a total of sixteen. It was a young crew;

Nobile, at forty-three, was the oldest. Most of the rest were in their early thirties, with two men at twenty-eight. And all of them, with the possible exception of their commander, were good at their jobs.

With the *Italia* floating gently a few feet above the ground, the expedition's chaplain intoned a prayer for success. The crew climbed into the ship, Nobile saluted, the cabin door closed. Lines were released. Men on the ground waved and shouted. The airship rose above the island. In the bright sunlight she looked like a big silvery whale. The engines clattered. At four twenty-eight the *Italia* droned away to the northwest.

For two hours she flew over blue water. Then ice hid the cold sea. After that, mist hid the ice. The airship droned on at a height of 800 feet. On the gray blanket below, which was lit by the rays of a weak sun, her shadow moved with her. Finally at three in the afternoon they sighted the snowbanked coast of Greenland.

Nobile now changed his course and headed straight for the Pole. At the chart table Mariano and Zappi traced the route. Viglieri held the steering wheel. Trojani and Cecioni took turns at the vertical controls. Drs. Behounek and Pontremoli watched their instruments, jotting down scientific data.

Arduino, who had been promoted to chief engineer after the *Norge* flight, moved carefully over the narrow gangways from the V-shaped catwalk enclosure to the side-engine gondolas and down a ladder to the rear one to get reports on oil pressure, gas consumption, engine temperature. Ciocca had charge of the starboard gondola, Caratti was watching its port twin, Pomella was in the rear car. The hours passed slowly. Tea froze in thermos bottles and was swallowed in lumps. Meat had to be warmed in pockets before it could be eaten.

The rising wind worried Nobile. It was behind them now and helping them along. But what would happen when they turned to come back? Perhaps they should go on to Alaska or Novaya Zemlya. "What do you think, Finn?" he asked. The Swedish meteorologist looked at his weather chart on which he had been recording predictions from Tromsö, in Norway. "This wind will not last long," he replied. "It will turn and when we fly back to Kings Bay we will have it with us."

At twenty minutes past midnight they reached the North Pole. The *Italia* slowed and came down in a long spiral. Men slapped each other's backs and cheered. A dense fog hid the ice below, making it impossible to lower anybody. But they threw the papal cross and some flags from the open cabin door, and the various items disappeared in the swirling gray moisture.

The airship circled the Pole at a height of 450 feet and a tiny phonograph played a popular Italian song. Biagi sent off radio dispatches to the Pope, the King, the Duce. Dr. Pontremoli announced that he had measured what he called "the vertical component of the earth's magnetism." Nobile passed around some eggnog prepared for the occasion by his wife.

Continuing to circle the Pole, the *Italia* waited for the wind to subside and change direction. Instead of subsiding, it blew more strongly from the way they had come. At two-thirty in the morning Nobile turned the *Italia*'s nose into it and started back toward Spitsbergen. Soon ice began to form on the ship and the whirling propellers slung jagged pieces against the bag.

It had taken nineteen hours to reach the Pole from Kings Bay, following the roundabout route along Greenland's east coast. The direct route home was shorter. But now wind slowed the *Italia*. For twenty-four hours the dirigible fought headwinds. At that point she was only halfway home, and the bucking and plunging was straining girders and struts throughout the ship. Worse, the props were now bombarding the bag harder. Alessandrini and two other crew members kept patching holes in the bag. But new ones appeared before they could cover the old.

Malmgren asked for more speed to get out of the area. Nobile ordered Arduino to increase engine revolutions from 1,200 to 1,300 a minute. This raised the ship's speed by only 7 miles an hour but almost doubled the amount of fuel being consumed. Reluctantly, Nobile ordered the throttles retarded.

By four-thirty, erratic winds were blowing the *Italia* from one side to the other. Nobile had to order full speed on all engines again just to keep the ship fairly maneuverable. But it didn't do much good. "Hold her on course!" yelled Mariano, who was acting as First Officer, to Commander Zappi. "Impossible!" Zappi retorted. "Every time I fight her onto proper course, a blast slews her tail around." Dr. Behounek, who had been keeping tabs on the course, showed Mariano his figures. The airship was often as much as 30 degrees off.

Cecioni was having similar trouble at the vertical rudder wheel as he tried to ease the jumping and diving of the ship. "One minute we get spanked from above," he told Mariano. "The next an updraft kicks her bottom. She handles like a seesaw."

At seven-thirty that morning Nobile estimated his position as 250 miles north of Moffen Island, a bearing point just above Kings Bay. He realized he might be a hundred miles off. He was. The *Italia* was 350 miles from Moffen, and far to the east.

Two hours later, at a height of 1,000 feet, the vertical controls jammed. The airship slanted down toward the pack. Nobile stopped the engines. At the last minute Vigheri took over, hit the wheel a sharp blow and freed the elevator controls. The ship began to rise. Nobile decided to go above the clouds and get a sun shot.

At 3,000 feet they burst into brilliant sunlight. As Mariano peered through his sextant, pressure in the gas cells began to rise. The pressure at the stern was higher than anywhere else. "Valve a little gas there," Nobile ordered. The pressure continued to rise. Nobile leveled off at 1,000 feet. From there he could get occasional glimpses of the pack ice.

The wind diminished a bit, as Malmgren had predicted it would. But it didn't let up nearly enough. For half an hour the ship cruised on, making 30 miles an hour on two engines. Then, at ten twenty-five, the *Italia* suddenly became stern-heavy.

They were now cruising at 900 feet. The instruments showed they were falling two feet a second. "All engines! Emergency!" Nobile yelled. "Ahead at full!" But the increased speed had no effect on the elevators. The stern sank lower until it was 19 degrees below the bow. Perhaps ice from the props had finally punctured some gas cells. Or perhaps an escape valve had been forced open by frozen moisture. "Alessandrini! Run aloft and check the stern valves!" The frightened rigger sped up the ladder to the catwalk along the ship's keel and raced toward the stern.

Now the ice pack was close below them. The only thing to do was to get ready for a crash. "Stop all engines! Shut off ignitions!" Nobile bawled. At least with that done there would be less danger of fire. Then he ordered Cecioni to heave out the ballast chain, which was weighted with small round balls. But Cecioni couldn't get it loose from its lashings.

Nobile saw the port propeller was still turning at full speed, pushing the ship into a sharp bank. He leaned out an open porthole and yelled to Caratti, who apparently had not heard his order. Then he saw that the stern gondola was about to hit the ice. Inside the car Pomella threw up his hands to protect his face.

The ice below was hard and jagged, without snow cover to soften the impact. There was a terrifying crash as the rear gondola struck. An instant later the cabin near the front of the bag smashed down and split open, spilling men like fish from a net. Most of them lay stunned or dazed. Viglieri opened his eyes in time to see the *Italia* pass a few feet above him. Through the jagged hole where the cabin had been he saw the faces of Lago and Dr. Pontremoli, who had been sleeping along the catwalk. Near them Alessandrini clung to a broken girder. All three men were staring down in horror at the men and wreckage on the ice, too shocked to utter a sound. But quick-thinking Arduino, apparently sensing that the torn gas bag would never return to this spot, began tossing out food, equipment, fuel— any stores he could find along the catwalk—to help his friends below.

Then the bag, relieved of the cabin's weight and the men in it, rose into the fog and disappeared to the east, carrying Caratti and Ciocca as well as the other four. After a while the men on the ice saw smoke rising from the direction the bag had taken. Did the smudge mark the grave of the *Italia*?

Left on the ice that morning on May 25 were ten men and Titina. Nobile and Cecioni had broken legs, and the general also had a broken right arm. But Cecioni's injury was the most severe—an ugly and painful compound fracture. Malmgren had a damaged shoulder and Biagi a dull pain in his stomach. Presently they found Pomella, who had been in the smashed rear gondola. He was seated on a block of ice. When Biagi shook him slightly to bring him out of a seeming daze, the mechanic toppled over. He was dead.

Mariano, Viglieri, Trojani and Dr. Behounek tested their limbs and found they were uninjured. And now Biagi discovered why his stomach hurt—and smiled with joy. He had instinctively grabbed the small emergency radio set and hugged it to him when he fell out. It had dug into him painfully, but now there was hope. Within a few hours he had the transmitter properly tuned, and over an improvised aerial, was sending out calls: "S O S *Italia*. S O S *Italia*. S O S *Italia*."

Wreckage, food and equipment littered the ice, some of it thrown down by the thoughtful Arduino. One of the items was a large canvas sack holding survival equipment. It contained food, a small silk tent and a sleeping bag. Mariano and Zappi bandaged the two injured men and eased them both into the bag.

Finn Malmgren stood moodily apart from the others. He considered himself largely responsible for the disaster because he had wrongly predicted that the wind would change. Shortly after the crash he had thanked Nobile for the trip and said he was going to drown himself. The general had forbidden it. Later Malmgren tried to slip away with a revolver found in the survival sack. This time Mariano discovered and frustrated his purpose after convincing him that his Arctic experience was needed by the others.

233

The next day a break in the clouds enabled Mariano to take a sun shot. He estimated their position at about thirty miles northeast of Northeast Land, the second largest island of the Spitsbergen group. A roundup of the scatter on the ice showed that there were 284 pounds of food, including pemmican, chocolate, malted milk, butter and sugar—enough for forty-five days—plus a little gasoline, splintered wood and canvas that could be used for fuel. The tent—eight feet by eight and designed for four men—now had to accommodate nine. Cold was the biggest problem. None of the men were adequately clad for ice-pack existence. There was only one blanket. Those who slept next to Dr. Behounek, a large roly-poly man, considered themselves lucky. He was soft and radiated a pleasant warmth.

They dyed the tent red to make it more conspicuous, using the liquid in the glass balls that were to have been dropped on the ice from the airship to facilitate altitude reckonings. And after a couple of days the castaways settled into a routine. Each took or was assigned a sleeping place in the tent. One man was always on watch for ships or planes.

Biagi sent out his S O S signals for five minutes before every hour, according to a prearranged plan. But he got no replies to his message. The main reason for this was the almost incredible inaction of Captain Giuseppe Romagna-Manoja, commander of the *Città di Milano*, which was 220 miles away but within easy range of the relatively weak emergency-set transmitter.

Romagna was both timid and stupid. He was afraid to make a move without authorization from Rome and had refused earlier to proceed from Tromsö to Kings Bay until curtly ordered to do so by Nobile. He was afraid that the *Città di Milano* would become stuck in the ice, although the small Norwegian steamship *Hobby* had just been there. He had received radio dispatches from Biagi that the *Italia* was fighting headwinds on the return trip but made no effort to keep in contact with the dirigible. As a result, he didn't know it had crashed.

Even after everybody else in Kings Bay surmised that the *Italia* had met with disaster, Romagna allowed the ship's radio to be used to send out numerous personal messages from the crew to friends and relatives at home. Nobody listened for messages from the *Italia*. Guglielmo Marconi himself, aboard his experimental ship in the Mediterranean, was astounded at what he heard from the *Città*. Practically every message from her announced that some crew member was in good health or that another sent his regards to somebody. "No wonder," fumed the inventor of the wireless, "that on the *Città di Milano* the *Italia*'s S O S could not be caught. They simply were not paying attention to her signals." Later Romagna came up with one of the lamest excuses of the century. "I did not think the survivors would have any radio, so we did not bother to post listeners," he said.

Not only did Romagna not bother to listen, he did not bother to move the ship to a place where she might be helpful. Day after day the vessel lay at anchor in Kings Bay, doing absolutely nothing of any consequence. Unable to take action himself, Romagna finally asked for orders from Rome. There, bureaucrats shifted responsibility from office to office, killing any chance of quick action. There was animus, too. Nobile had enemies now in Balbo and other ambitious Fascists who were delighted that the airship's voyage had ended in disaster. Balbo had refused Nobile's request that two Italian seaplanes be sent to Kings Bay for just such rescue operations as were needed after the crash. And when relatives of the lost ones made the same request, Balbo declared that no one knew where the airship was. Sending planes, he asserted, would be a waste of energy.

In other capitals there was far more concern. A dinner to honor Wilkins and Eielson in Oslo was interrupted by news from Spitsbergen that the airship was overdue. Both men volunteered for a rescue attempt. So did another dinner guest who earlier had announced his retirement from exploration and who had no cause to love Nobile. Roald Amundsen turned to his old Antarctic and Arctic companion, Oscar Wisting, and said, "Tell them I am ready to start on a search for the *Italia* at once."

Norway's prime minister telegraphed Mussolini offering to send out rescue teams. The Duce delayed answering him for a week, then had an undersecretary send out a routine reply inferring that Italy needed no help. The Norwegian prime minister knew better. Ignoring the rebuff, he started to organize rescue efforts headed by Riiser-Larsen. He felt that Amundsen, who had denounced Mussolini during the row over the *Norge*'s flight, was not the man to lead a government-sponsored search. Amundsen, incensed at what he felt was a slap in the face, determined to organize his own rescue team.

Among the party left on the ice, morale was low. Though Biagi kept sending out his calls, he got no replies. And this failure became more depressing every day. The only message he received from the base ship was the same maddening series of lies and false promises, transmitted every two hours. "We have not heard your radio. We are listening for you on the 900-meter band and on short wave. We imagine you are near the north coast of Spitsbergen between the 15th and 20th meridians [far from the actual position]. Trust in us. We are organizing help."

Aggravating their depression was the uncertainty of command. Nobile was not a natural-born leader. He didn't see the need for having one man in charge. He felt that because he was injured he should let everybody have a say in decisions. Hence, many arguments took place and different men had different ideas of what should be done.

Three days after the crash Mariano took another sun shot. The ice had drifted twenty-eight miles to the southeast. Now they could see a small island off Northeast Land. Their own ice island was slipping into the Barents Sea, whose warmer waters sooner or later would melt it. Mariano asked Malmgren how he felt about an effort to walk to the land. Malmgren looked at Nobile and Cecioni and said it was impossible. But he began to think about it.

Later Mariano and Zappi talked to Nobile about such a march. Nobile, unable to make up his mind, stalled for time. Then Malmgren came to the naval officers' support. A small party could go, leaving the injured men on the ice and directing rescuers to them. Nobile still would not approve the scheme.

Shortly after midnight the next morning Zappi spotted a bear weighing about five hundred pounds. Malmgren took the revolver and started quietly toward the animal, Zappi and Mariano following with the only other weapons in the party, an ax and a knife. Nobile grabbed the fox terrier and held her so she couldn't bark. Malmgren got to within twenty feet of the bear, crouched behind an ice hummock and fired three times. The bear turned, ran a few feet and died. Now they had fresh meat and another covering for the night hours.

That day the big floe was within seven miles of another island. Zappi renewed the argument for a march. Finally Nobile gave in. The following day Zappi, Mariano and Malmgren, the *Italia's* only expert on Arctic survival, started over the ice toward land. Biagi, who wanted to go, was persuaded to stay and work the radio. The three wayfarers took with them 120 pounds of pemmican, chocolate and condensed milk. Malmgren thought they could make ten miles a day and perhaps reach Kings Bay in three weeks. Promising to send help, the three men began their trek, stumbling and sliding over hillocks of ice. They remained visible, through field glasses, for two days, for they advanced only five miles in that time instead of the twenty Malmgren had predicted.

The six men they left still had no authoritative leader. Nobile believed that all of them were equal on the ice and that each had a right to make his own decisions. Nobody should command, he thought, but God.

Viglieri took up the task of charting the floe's position when the weather was clear enough for sights, and preserving and distributing the food. He cut up the bear in large chunks and hung them up. The meat was tough and greasy. He noted how much food there was and how fast it was being eaten. He packed what was left in waterproof canvas and tied packets along the rope so it could be saved if it slipped into a crevasse during a sudden break in the ice. It was a smart move. Before they left the floe they had to move suddenly several times when cracks threatened to widen and engulf them.

The floe drifted nearer to land and then farther away from it. Biagi continued to send out his calls. He had to use the transmitter sparingly to avoid exhausting the batteries. But he could listen for several hours a day without using too much current.

On June 1 he heard from the Rome radio that rescue efforts were under way. Lieutenant Finn Lützow-Holm, a classmate of Riiser-Larsen's, was aboard the *Hobby* with a naval plane, bound for Spitsbergen, whence he would search the surrounding area. Riiser-Larsen and another plane were aboard the *Ingefire*, also bound for Spitsbergen. Some skiers were searching for *Italia* survivors along Spitsbergen's north coast.

The radio didn't say so, but the rescue effort was much wider than this. Six nations were now in, or joining, the undertaking. In addition to Norway they were Sweden, the Soviet Union, Finland, France and Italy, and the total effort would engage eighteen ships— including two icebreakers—fifteen hundred men, twenty-two planes and nineteen sled dogs.

Italy's Fascist government had finally been forced into reluctant action: first, by an Italian friend of Nobile who threatened to finance a rescue attempt himself; second, by world opinion. Mussolini had ordered a big Savoia-Marchetti seaplane to be readied for a trip north. However, her pilot, Major Umberto Maddalena, was in Spain and it wasn't known when he could come back.

At Kings Bay, Captain Gennaro Sora, commander of the Italian mountain troops, vainly sought permission from Romagna to search for the *Italia*'s crew. Finally he told the asinine commander that he was going without it. He boarded the small Norwegian ship *Braganza* and started for Cape North at the top of Northeast Land. On the ship were two other men who volunteered to accompany him on the search, Ludwig Varming, a Danish engineer, and Joseph Van Dongen, a Dutch explorer. They had two dog teams. After the vessel had left, Romagna reported Sora for "serious insubordination."

On the evening of June 6 Biagi was again listening to the Rome radio. Suddenly he yelled, "They have heard us! They have heard us!" With trembling fingers he wrote down the news for which they had been waiting for twelve days. "The Soviet government has notified the Italian government that an S O S from the *Italia* has been picked up by a young Soviet farmer, Nicholas Schmidt, at Archangel on the evening of June 3."

Two days later Biagi got through to the *Città di Milano* and gave their position. But Romagna made no effort to move toward them. However, Biagi transmitted the floe's position, and the next day there was an exchange of messages between floe and base ship. Nobile asked for shoes, sleds, guns and boats. Romagna told of Swedish planes enlisted in the rescue effort, Riiser-Larsen's presence near Moffen Island and Soviet preparations to send a big icebreaker. It was the first time he had been of any use at all. The men on the ice prepared a smudge from oily rags, bear grease and gasoline, which they could light instantly, and readied a Very pistol salvaged from the wreckage.

Several Arctic explorers, including the renowned Fridtjof Nansen, had recommended the use of icebreakers as the best possible rescue tools. The Soviet government agreed. The Communists also saw an opportunity to show up Mussolini's Fascist regime, which was still dragging its feet in the rescue undertaking.

On the night of June 12 the icebreaker *Malygin* left Archangel with two planes, bound for the scene of disaster. Three nights later the icebreaker *Krassin* left Leningrad. Aboard the eleven-year-old *Krassin*, a 10,600-ton English-built craft and the largest icebreaker in Europe, was Professor Rudolf Samoilovich, a famous Arctic explorer and friend of Nobile's. The Russians had manned, equipped, provisioned, tested and started the ship with her crew of 136 in 112 hours. Mussolini had taken a week to think about a rescue mission and nine days more to prepare a plan. And five days later his pilot, Major Maddalena, hadn't reached Spitsbergen.

On June 17 the survivors on the floe felt a sudden surge of optimism. The air was clear, the sun warm, the sky blue. It was ideal flying weather, and in the afternoon they heard a drone which increased in volume. Anxiously they scanned the horizon. Suddenly Biagi yelled, "Planes! Planes! There!"

Approaching from the south, the machines headed straight for the tent. "Start the fire, start the signals," someone shouted. But when still two or three miles away the planes wheeled and flew south again. Riiser-Larsen and Lützow-Holm had made a four-hour search for the red tent but hadn't found it. Nobile sent a message to the *Città di Milano:* "Take advantage of favorable weather and have planes return today. Notify us of time of departure so we can be ready to make signals." But the day ended, night came and no planes returned. Perhaps the base ship had not been listening again.

The next day Riiser-Larsen and Lützow-Holm twice flew toward the red tent. Twice they flew away without having sighted it. Neither plane had a radio to help guide her in. The only available maps were inaccurate. And shadows and reflections made it almost impossible to spot a small tent on an ice floe.

That same day Major Luigi Penzo, flying a Dornier-Wal, arrived in Tromsö. The second Italian pilot assigned to the rescue mission, he found in the Norwegian harbor two three-engined machines—one from Sweden, and one from Finland—ready for a final hop to Spitsbergen.

There was also another machine—a seaplane which Commander René Gilbaud had intended to use for a transatlantic flight. The French government had turned the plane and her crew over to Amundsen. The White Eagle of Norway, as numerous admirers called him, was now nearly fifty-six, but he had been using his considerable influence to get a rescue plane.

The French crew consisted of Commander Gilbaud; Lieutenant Albert de Cuverville, co-pilot; Emile Valette, radio operator; and Gilbert Brazy, mechanic. In addition to Amundsen there was Leif Dietrichson, who had been one of Amundsen's party in 1925 when they spent twenty-four days on the ice.

The silvery blue French Latham machine was not well equipped for Arctic work. Her radio could send signals hardly more than a hundred miles, and then only when the little generator propeller turned at highest speed. With six men aboard she was dangerously overloaded. And Amundsen, impatient to be off, had spent little time in preparing it for a flight to Spitsbergen or in arranging to keep in touch with other rescue expeditions.

World-famous, but impoverished by his many polar expeditions, he climbed into the machine. Commander Gilbaud revved up the engine. Amundsen nodded his white-thatched head. The plane roared across the harbor, climbed into the air and disappeared into the gray skies to the west.

On June 19, at two-thirty in the morning, Major Maddalena reached Kings Bay in his twin-hulled Savoia-Marchetti. It had taken him eleven days from Rome, but at last he was there. The same morning, Riiser-Larsen and Lützow-Holm tried again to locate the tent. Again they failed, though the men at the tent saw them.

Still later that morning Maddalena and his crew of two tried to find the tent. They failed and came back to Kings Bay. Later in the day the two Norwegians tried again—and failed again. But the men on the ice were now hopeful. Two Soviet icebreakers were steaming toward them, Finnish and Swedish planes were en route to Kings Bay aboard ships, and Amundsen was flying toward them

in the Latham, whose radio operator had sent out a routine message
the day before. But nothing had been heard from him since. Where
was Amundsen anyway? He should have made the 600-mile flight
from Tromsö in seven hours.

On June 20 Maddalena tried once more. This time, with better
radio communication between ice floe and base ship, sensible preparations had been made. At Riiser-Larsen's suggestion, the castaways
used improvised mirrors, made of tin and aluminum, to reflect the
sun's rays at oncoming planes. Maddalena's machine had a radio,
and the base ship's supply officer had worked out a code whereby
Biagi, transmitting single letters, should be able to guide a pilot in
as soon as radio contact between floe and plane was established.
At eight o'clock that morning the men on the floe were excited and
confident. Viglieri sat on a hummock, ready with hand signals to
show Biagi the plane's course. Dr. Behounek, on another hummock,
held one of the makeshift mirrors. Trojani had a pile of oily rags
to set afire as soon as the plane was sighted.

Soon there was radio contact between floe and plane. The
machine droned into sight. Biagi signaled: "DDDD [*dextra*] 70"—
(Turn 70 degrees to the right). The plane turned. Next he signaled:
"SSSS [*sinistra*] 90"—(90 degrees to the left). The plane obeyed.
Then: "VVVV [*via*] 6"—(Straight ahead for 6 kilometers). The plane
roared straight toward them and got bigger and bigger. The men
waved and yelled. Biagi tossed his hat joyously into the air. The
plane roared right over them and flew on into the distance. The noise
of her engines faded to a murmur. Radio contact was lost. The
thing seemed unbelievable.

It took thirty minutes to re-establish radio contact as the plane
circled in the distance. Biagi kept on sending out "RRRR" (*ritorno*),
and when the plane approached, "TTTT" (*tenda*) to indicate she
was near the tent. And this time the rescuers saw them. Packages
parachuted down. Maddalena circled the camp eleven times, dropping 650 pounds of supplies. All the stuff he dropped was badly

packaged. Much of it broke and much dropped into the water. But the six men recovered two rubber rafts, six pairs of shoes and some sleeping bags.

Two days later both Maddalena and Penzo dropped more food and equipment to the castaways. The same day Swedish planes parachuted supplies, including Scotch whiskey. And the following day Swedish Lieutenant Einar Lundborg appeared in a single-engined Fokker, escorted by a seaplane in case he crashed. After making three passes at the floe he landed his ski-equipped machine safely. He told Nobile he had come to take him out.

Nobile wanted the more badly injured Cecioni to leave first. But Lundborg thought that the big mechanic was too heavy. The small plane couldn't lift both Cecioni and Lundborg's co-pilot. The Swede added that he had orders to bring Nobile out first because the base ship needed his advice about searching for the six men lost with the bag. He promised to come back for Cecioni and everybody else on the floe that evening.

Nobile consulted the others. All felt—or said they felt—that he should leave first. Finally he agreed to go. Helped by the others, he limped to the plane. In the cockpit he found his dog. One of the Swedes had put the animal in.

Lundborg flew his passengers to Murchison Bay, where the Swedes had set up an advance base. From there, again escorted by the seaplane, he started back to the floe. Several hours passed. Then the escort plane returned. The pilot said Lundborg had again landed on the floe but overturned. Another Swede flew Nobile to Kings Bay and the *Città di Milano,* where he discussed plans for rescuing his companions with Swedish fliers. He also sent the men on the floe a cheering message, saying that they soon would receive needed stores and that light planes, suitable for landing on the floe, had been ordered from England. Romagna, who had been invited to the conference but had not appeared, now turned up. Nobile started to tell him about the rescue plans but Romagna did not seem in-

243

terested. "People might criticize you for coming first, General," he said coldly. "It would be advisable to make an explanation."

The general was astounded. Lundborg had orders, he explained, to bring him out first so he could direct rescue operations. "We gave Lundborg no such orders," Romagna replied. Again he insisted that Nobile send "explanations" to Rome. In the end Nobile weakly gave in.

From then on Romagna, who evidently had instructions from Balbo, took charge. He refused to carry out Nobile's orders. He censored all the messages Nobile sent to his men. He declined Nobile's request that the ship's radio operator listen more diligently for messages from the floe. Finally he said he had orders from Rome that Nobile should not be allowed to take part in any rescue operations. If he tried to, Romagna added, he would post guards at his cabin door. Had Nobile been stronger he would have defied Romagna. It is hard to believe that any guards would have shot him.

The first communiqué about the rescue from Stefani, Italy's official news agency, said that the reasons for Nobile's return were unknown. It emphasized that future rescue operations would continue to be supervised by Romagna. And within a few hours, radio commentators and newspapers around the world had noted that a general of Mussolini's Fascist regime had permitted himself to be rescued, along with his dog, leaving his companions on an ice floe.

While the general's enemies tried to discredit him, the two Soviet icebreakers were fighting their way toward the marooned men. The *Malygin*, which had started from Archangel, soon ran into heavy floes. Near Hope Island, some 300 miles south of her objective, she got stuck and was carried in a fog close to the rocky coast. The same fog forced Michael Babushkin and his aircrew to come down on the ice. They did not get back to the *Malygin* for five days.

The *Krassin*, heading northward from Bergen, plowed blue water at 11 knots for several days. Then she encountered heavy seas and loose ice, which reduced her speed by half. Presently she was banging into floes that were eight feet thick, and despite the 10,500 horsepower of her three engines, was making little more than a mile every hour. In one twelve-hour period the white barrier stopped her three times.

In addition to forcing her bow up on the ice and backing off to try again, she had to pump 700 tons of water alternately into tanks on each side occasionally to crush the ice along her flanks. The hard chunks hit the steel hull with a hollow thunder that continued without letup like the sound of artillery while the two tall stacks of the old ship belched black smoke over the white scene.

By July 3 the *Krassin* was only sixty-five miles from the group on the floe. But it was heavy going for her. That evening she lunged up on the ice—to break it with her weight—and backed off fifteen times in one hour. Finally she got stuck too. A blade had been torn off one of her three propellers, and the braces to the rudder were twisted. Presently a storm howled over her. Caught in thick ice and burdened with three feet of snow, the gallant ship started to drift away from her goal.

On July 6 a Swedish pilot flew a small English Moth plane to the floe, made a skillful landing and took off Lundborg. Since the ice was softening, fliers felt that no more floe landings could be made. Several planes and ships in the scattered rescue fleet joined the widespread hunt for Amundsen which was now under way.

On July 10, the storm having subsided, Boris Chukhnovsky, the *Krassin*'s airplane pilot, took off with a crew of three in a trimotor Junkers to make another search. He didn't find the floe but radioed that he had seen the "Malmgren group" and gave its position. Thereafter he was forced to make an emergency landing in the fog and hit an ice hummock which damaged the undercarriage and smashed two propellers.

The next day Chukhnovsky radioed more details. Two of the

men in the "Malmgren group" waved to him, he said. A third was lying on the ground. He had been unable to drop supplies to the men because the floe on which they were drifting was too small.

By this time the *Krassin* had worked her way back to within fifteen miles of the position Chukhnovsky had given. Smoke burst from her stacks anew, she trembled and lunged forward again. Pounding against ice which for two hours kept her from moving more than a couple of hundred yards, she kept banging ahead. On the morning of July 12 a lookout spotted a man on the ice.

The *Krassin* battered her way through the ice until she came alongside the floe. Three men scrambled down a ladder and moved toward the stranger. "Malmgren?" they asked. "No. Commander Zappi." They saw another man lying in the watery snow. On a neighboring floe, strips of clothes spelled out a message: HELP—FOOD—MARIANO—ZAPPI.

The man in the snow was Mariano. He was obviously weak and sick. "What about Malmgren?" the Russians persisted. Zappi pointed downward, as if Malmgren were somewhere in the water under the ice. *"That* was a man," he said. "He died a month ago." There was no trace of the third man Chukhnovsky had described. One report said the pilot had mistaken a sleeping bag for a prostrate figure.

Mariano had a high fever, was badly frostbitten and near starvation. Like Zappi, his face was heavily bearded and his hands and clothes were filthy. Professor Samoilovich noticed that he wore fewer clothes than Zappi. Indeed, some of his clothes were on his companion.

Both Italians were taken to the sick bay and given enemas. Zappi had said he had had no food for thirteen days. The examination seemed to indicate that he had had some five days earlier but that Mariano had been without food considerably longer. There were no facilities aboard the icebreaker for chemical analysis, so there could be no scientific answer to some questions that were later raised—about the kind of food that Zappi had last eaten.

Zappi said that after leaving the group on the floe, he and Mariano and Malmgren had plodded in the direction of shore for fourteen days. But the ice kept drifting away from their goal and nullified their efforts. Malmgren, already depressed about his erroneous weather prediction, grew more dejected every day. He also became weaker. Finally he could hardly walk at all. He urged the Italians to leave him and go on. They did move on a hundred yards and rested, hoping he would rejoin them. After twenty-four hours he insisted that they proceed. They did so, taking with them— at his request—all his food. They never saw him again.

A newspaper correspondent aboard the *Krassin* sent a skeptical report of Zappi's account. The two Italians, he said, had abandoned Malmgren on a desolate floe. It didn't matter, he indicated, whether the Swede had offered them his rations or whether he had asked them to leave him. They had left him, and that was enough.

Many of those aboard the *Krassin* looked with suspicion on Zappi. He appeared to be well nourished, while Mariano was emaciated. The sole of Mariano's right foot was frozen and gangrene had already set in. The ship's doctor said the foot should be amputated. Later it was.

The *Krassin* resumed her heaving, clanging course toward the five men on the floe. That evening she reached it and took them off. Thereafter she picked up Chukhnovsky and his crew, plus five Italian Alpinists and a Norwegian guide who had set out to rescue the Russian fliers when they heard of Chukhnovsky's accident. Swedish planes brought back Sora and Van Dongen, and the *Braganza* took aboard Varming and other would-be rescuers.

Later the *Krassin* and Chukhnovsky searched the sea north and northeast of Spitsbergen in an effort to find the six men carried away by the *Italia*'s bag. Five other ships also searched areas where the bag might have come down. No trace of the men has been found from that day to this. And it is probable that none ever will. But the Arctic is a big and lonely place. Two years after the *Italia* disaster,

Norwegian scientists—still on the lookout for lost Italians—found the remains of the crew of another balloon.

The bodies of Andrée and his two companions were on White Island, about fifty miles northeast of Spitsbergen, whither they had drifted on ice after their balloon came down at about latitude 83 degrees north. Well-preserved records were found and films, which were successfully developed after thirty-three years. (The men's deaths were variously attributed to carbon monoxide poisoning from a Primus stove or to trichinosis, an ailment that sometimes afflicts polar bears. Bear meat infested with trichinae was found near the bodies.)

The search for Amundsen and his companions proved as fruitless as that for the Italians. But in September the sea gave up a clue to the manner of his death. Off the rocky Fuglöy, an island near Tromsö, the small Norwegian steamer *Brood* picked up a float from a seaplane which was identified as one from Amundsen's overloaded machine. It seemed to have been torn from the plane as if by the impact of a plunge into the water.

Before he left on his quest, Amundsen had spoken of his beloved Arctic. "If you only knew how splendid it is up there! That's where I want to die. And I only hope death will come to me chivalrously, that it will overtake me in the fulfillment of a high mission, quickly, without suffering."

It would seem that the White Eagle of Norway got his wish.

Penzo and two companions were forced low by a storm while returning to Italy and hit a high-tension wire. All in the Dornier-Wal were killed. The final human score of the *Italia* expedition was thus eight rescued, seventeen dead. Long before it was totaled, an international row was raging over the conduct of the survivors. The press of many lands belabored several unanswered questions. Why had Finn Malmgren, the most experienced Arctic expert of them all, died so soon? Why had he been abandoned? Why had Zappi been well clothed, while Mariano lay cold in a damp puddle? And why was Zappi so healthy if he hadn't eaten for thirteen days?

Swedes and Norwegians, bitter over Malmgren's fate, accused the two Italian officers of deserting him. Germans, soon to have a Fascist regime of their own, referred to the lost men as "victims of mad Fascist ambition." A Soviet paper said sarcastically: "Malmgren died of exposure on June 14. Nobile is better. His dog Titina feels fine."

But it remained for the French, angered at the loss of the sea-plane's crew, to charge Zappi with cannibalism. "I can prove," wrote a French journalist, "that Zappi was wearing Malmgren's clothing as well as his own, and that while Mariano was 'in absolute starvation,' Zappi must have eaten within five or six days of his rescue." This scribbler, who had never been near the scene of disaster, also declared that when the semiconscious Mariano was brought aboard the *Krassin* he moaned distinctly, "You can eat me but not until after I die." The inference as to whom Zappi had already eaten was pretty clear.

There was never any proof of cannibalism. And on the way home Zappi called on Malmgren's mother in Stockholm. At the end of the interview she indicated she was satisfied with his explanation. But the various charges were repeated, including the one that Nobile —a Fascist general—was a coward. In trying to discredit him, the Fascists hadn't done their regime any good.

In Italy a commission composed of Nobile's enemies inquired into his conduct. Balbo supplied it with reams of what he called "evidence." Not surprisingly the commission blamed the general for the *Italia* disaster and criticized him for leaving the floe first. It also declared Zappi and Mariano innocent of any misconduct.

Although promised a good pension if he would quietly retire from active service, Nobile declined to do so and resigned. The treatment he had received won him considerable sympathy abroad and generated more denunciation of Mussolini's regime.

17

FEMININE RIVALS

As the *Italia* tragedy unfolded, Mabel Boll again became the star of one of those little comedies of frustration in which a malicious fate delighted to cast her. After returning to the United States she teamed up again with Levine and persuaded him to renew his offer to lend her the *Columbia*. She also made her standard $25,000 transatlantic taxi offer to Wilmer Stultz. When the old plane was in airworthy condition she flew with Stultz and Levine from New York to Cuba and thought her hopes were about to be realized. The plane was in good shape again. Stultz seemed willing and spring was in the air. Everything seemed favorable for a little trip from Harbour Grace to Paris.

At this time Stultz was testing a three-engined Fokker which Byrd had acquired for his coming Antarctic expedition. The machine was in Boston and Stultz was there so much of the time that Miss Boll engaged Captain Oliver Le Boutillier as a stand-in to test the reconditioned Bellanca for the scheduled ocean hop. At the time, she had no idea that she had any feminine rivals.

There was another woman, however, who also hungered for transatlantic fame and had the money to go after it. She was Mrs. Frederick Guest, the American wife of a British Secretary for Air. Mrs. Guest had quietly bought the Fokker from Byrd because he no longer needed it for his Antarctic expedition—Henry and Edsel Ford had given him one of their trimotor machines. Equally quietly,

Mrs. Guest had retained Stultz to ferry her across the ocean. She named her new toy the *Friendship* and had it fitted with pontoons so it could land on water. During the resulting tests everybody had maintained the fiction that Stultz was still working for Byrd.

Mrs. Guest's family viewed the project with something less than enthusiasm. They pointed out that three woman passengers already had died in Atlantic ocean flights, and that another had perished in the Pacific. Mrs. Guest finally relented and agreed that some younger woman should make the trip. The task of finding such a girl was entrusted to George Palmer Putnam, a book publisher who already had brought out Lindbergh's first book *We* and Byrd's *Skyward*. The search turned up Amelia Earhart, a young settlement-house worker, then in Boston. Miss Earhart owned a plane, had logged 500 hours, and looked enough like Lindbergh to be his sister. No doubt scenting another book, Putnam persuaded her, without much difficulty, to make the flight. Later he brought out *Twenty Hours, Forty Minutes*, an account of her voyage, which she made without being invited to take the controls. And still later he and Miss Earhart were married.

On June 3—long before these last two happy events took place —Stultz, Louis "Slim" Gordon and Miss Earhart took off from Boston, landed at Halifax and went on the next day to Trepassey, Newfoundland. Miss Boll was dumfounded. She called the *New York Times* in the hope that the report of the Halifax flight would prove false. But the *Times* could only confirm the bad news.

"I can't understand it!" the Rochester heiress wailed. "Wilmer was down here only a few days ago and I asked him when he was coming back to fly the *Columbia*. He said in just a few days and that he would be here today sure." Her voice broke. "And now he has gone and taken off with this other woman and I was sure he would fly with me. I depended on him! And the very day he was to come back he flies from Boston! I don't understand it. I am so upset." By this time she was crying bitterly.

But she didn't give up even then. A few days later the *Columbia* left for Newfoundland with Le Boutillier, pilot; Captain Arthur Argles, navigator; and Mabel Boll, passenger. They encountered fog, however, and had to return to Long Island. But on June 12 the trio took off again and this time they arrived safely at Harbour Grace, which is about sixty miles north of Trepassey. Again it seemed that Miss Boll had a good chance to win the renown she craved. The *Friendship*, burdened by its floats, was having trouble getting off the water and hadn't yet started for Europe.

But bad weather at Harbour Grace kept the *Columbia* on the ground. And before dawn on June 17, after three unsuccessful runs, the *Friendship* lumbered into the air and flew to Wales, Miss Earhart going along—as she herself said—as baggage. Still, although she hadn't had a chance in the pilot's seat, which had been half promised her, she was the first woman to cross the Atlantic by air in either direction. Miss Boll had lost out again. She cabled congratulations to her rival and talked for a few hours about flying to Rome. But in the end the *Columbia* flew back to Curtiss Field.

The luckless lady told reporters that Harbour Grace was a wilderness. There was nothing to eat up there, she said, but boiled potatoes and codfish. She also accused Dr. Kimball of giving her crew weather reports which were different from those sent to her rival. Her own crew scoffed at this charge, declaring that the weather service had been excellent. And Dr. Kimball showed reporters copies of Atlantic weather forecasts which had been sent out over the critical period and which proved that there had been no favoritism.

Now Miss Boll took a boat for Europe, where she planned to make arrangements which would project her into fame as the first woman on a *successful* east-to-west flight. Levine was still talking about such a project too, and had again teamed up with Bert Acosta. By this time the first Atlantic air passenger had acquired a pilot's license. One day he took the *Columbia* up to show he was now an accomplished aviator. He seemed to be all right while he was in the air, but his descent was reminiscent of the one he had made a year earlier at Croydon. After three passes at Curtiss Field he ran into a fence, smashing the plane's propeller, landing gear and parts of her wings.

With the Bellanca again out of the running for a while, Levine and Acosta sailed for France to buy a plane in which to fly back. There was some discrepancy in the reports that Miss Boll would accompany them on their homeward journey. Levine said she'd be a passenger, but Acosta told reporters she'd never be in any plane which he had been engaged to fly.

The lady was waiting for the two men, however, when they reached Deauville, and she went around with them to airplane factories to look for a transatlantic machine. The Breguet plant couldn't deliver one in time, but they finally bought a single-engined German Junkers, and Miss Boll announced that she intended to be the first woman to circle the globe by air.

Everybody seemed agreed now that she would at least be a passenger on the Atlantic flight and Levine named the new machine the *Queen of the Air*, presumably in her honor. Acosta took the Junkers up for some tests and on one flight the single engine went bad. There was no time to get a new one before the Atlantic storm season arrived, so the project was abandoned. Miss Boll blamed Acosta for abusing the engine, but later retracted. She explained she had been "terribly upset and disappointed over another failure."

After that she apparently gave up, for the newspapers carried no further stories about her aerial exploits or attempted exploits.

18

OVER THE SOUTH POLE

In the fall of 1928 the most important scene of aerial exploration shifted from the top of the world to the bottom. Two expeditions headed for Antarctica to unlock, with the help of aircraft, some of the secrets of that frozen and mysterious continent.

The first group to get under way was a small one. With the financial backing of William Randolph Hearst, Sir Hubert Wilkins took with him Ben Eielson and another famous Alaska bush pilot, Joe Crosson, and two Lockheed-Vega planes. One of these was the machine in which Wilkins and Eielson had flown from Point Barrow to Spitsbergen. The other was new. The three airmen went south on the annual cruise of the Norwegian whaling fleet from Montevideo and made their base on Deception Island in the South Shetlands off Graham Land (also known as Palmer Peninsula), a prong of icy wasteland that curves up from Antarctica to within about 700 miles of Cape Horn.

On December 20—almost exactly eight months after they had completed their great flight in the Arctic—Wilkins and Eielson soared over Graham Land and its snow-topped mountain peaks. They looked down on a series of channels which showed that the inaccurately mapped area was not a peninsula but an archipelago. Six hundred miles out, with half their fuel gone, they also looked at a series of storm clouds coming up behind them. They turned around and arrived at their base an hour before the storm reached a violence that would have wrecked them had they been in the air.

The second Antarctic expedition to get started in 1928 was that of Commander Byrd. Much more ambitious than that of Wilkins, it comprised two supply ships—the *City of New York* and the *Eleanor Bolling*—and employed two Norwegian whaling ships to carry additional men and equipment. Fifty men were to remain in Antarctica for a year or more. To make their stay easier, they had several hundred tons of coal, food, clothing, prefabricated dwellings, scientific instruments and other supplies; ninety-four husky dogs for sledge trips over the snow; and three planes. These machines were the Ford—now named the *Floyd Bennett*—powered with a 525-horsepower Wright Cyclone in the nose and two Whirlwind 220's under the wings; a Fairchild, with a 525-horsepower Wasp; and a Fokker, also powered with a Wasp. The pilots were Dean Smith, a former mail flier; Alton Parker, who had accompanied Byrd to Spitsbergen but done little flying there; Harold June, who doubled as radio operator; and Balchen, who headed the air team.

After Bennett's revelations and Byrd's performance on the transatlantic flight, Balchen had ideas about the commander that didn't accord with his public image. He learned more about America's current number-two hero on this first Byrd Antarctic expedition. On the way south, Byrd was so cold to him that Balchen wondered why he had been asked to head the flying group, or indeed been brought along at all.

The Norwegian was on leave from the Fokker organization, but he was still its chief test pilot and performance engineer. He therefore brought with him tables of figures on the performance of Fokker planes. These machines included the *Josephine Ford*, on whose tour of the country he had a detailed record. One day at the new base, Little America, he started to compare the tour figures with the mathematics of the plane's northward flight from Spitsbergen, a subject that still fascinated him. He spread out his data and went happily to work. Byrd saw him figuring away and asked what he was doing. When Balchen told him, the commander blew up.

"God damn you, who asked you to go into that? You're not going to do anything of the kind! Just cut that out. It's none of your damned business. Lay off the whole thing or you're going to find yourself in trouble."

Balchen laid off but he continued to think. And presently Byrd gave him other things to think about.

In April 1929, two planes took off on a scouting trip. One of them—the Fokker—contained Balchen as pilot; Lloyd Berkner, a radio operator; and Byrd. The other—the Fairchild—held Parker, with June as radio man.

The two planes flew to the northeast of Little America. About 150 miles out, near the Rockefeller Mountains, they ran into thick weather. Byrd ordered Balchen to turn the Fokker back. The Fairchild followed.

Recalling this flight, Balchen said, "When we came to the neighborhood of Little America I asked Byrd where he wanted to go. He told me to go home to base. I pointed out to the right and told him Little America was down there. He said No, it was directly ahead of us. He looked out the window and apparently couldn't see anything. I asked him, 'Do you want to go to Little America?' He said he did. I turned in and we landed. He hadn't known where we were."

A few hours later Smith, Berkner and Ashley McKinley, the aerial photographer, flew out in the Fairchild to take some pictures. They headed in the same direction the two planes had taken in the morning but went about 100 miles farther. At the outermost point of their trip they spied a mountain that looked like a small Matterhorn. McKinley photographed it several times from a distance and then they headed home, for their fuel was running low. Smith tells the rest of the story in his book *By the Seat of My Pants:*

We landed after a flight of over seven hours. Lloyd had been transmitting during our return and we were greeted with handshakes and backslaps as we made our way in to report. Meetings of this nature were held in a rectangular room adjacent to Byrd's quarters: measuring about fifteen by twelve feet, it served as library, staff room, game room, and office. We pulled off our furs, spread our maps on the center table, and, excited as children, told of our flight and our discovery.

"This Matterhorn peak, how far would you say it was from the eastern end of the Rockefellers?" asked Byrd.

"We flew on for at least forty-five minutes and were still not more than halfway. I'd say it was at least a hundred and fifty miles."

"How precisely can you spot it on your map?" Byrd now asked.

McKinley and I compared notes and conferred at some length.

"From our longitude here I'd say it lies pretty close to northeast by east, call it sixty degrees. I'd put it somewhere in here," and I drew a circle about thirty miles in diameter on the map.

Byrd spoke very seriously. "This is most important. I congratulate you gentlemen on confirming my discovery. You have located this new land in almost exactly the place where I saw it this morning."

"You saw it this morning!" exclaimed McKinley. "But you didn't say anything about it after the flight."

"No. I wanted to be sure before I announced it. But I did mark it on my map. Wait, I will show you."

Byrd went into his room, closing the door behind him. We all sat mute. I caught Balchen's eye. He shrugged and rolled his eyes to the ceiling. [Russell] Owen [the *New York Times* correspondent] kept shaking his head gently. [Laurence] Gould [geologist and second-in-command of the expedition] looked amused.

After about five minutes Commander Byrd returned, spreading a map on the table.

"Here is the course of our flight this morning," he said, pointing to a penciled line. "And over here is where I marked the new peak." He showed us a heavy cross, drawn with a softer pencil than the course of the flight itself. Sure enough, if transposed to my map his cross would fall close to the center of my circle.

"Now that you have seen this mountain, I feel justified in announcing the discovery. I have decided to call the area Marie A.

Byrd Land in honor of my wife. Russ, you are authorized to report this to the *Times*. Please let me check your story before you send it."

The Commander shook hands with Mac, Lloyd and me. "Congratulations again on a splendid flight. This is a historic day."

McKinley and I walked together to the mess hall. "It takes keen vision to be a great explorer," he cracked. "You and I will never be great explorers."

Byrd's remarks to Owen recall the censorship he imposed on the stories sent out by the *Times* man, who was the only correspondent in Little America. Although the newspaper was paying $175,000 for the exclusive rights to expedition coverage, Byrd insisted on blue-penciling dispatches, rewriting them and including new material in them to suit his program, which seemed to be one of systematically building himself up as a heroic figure.

Owen, Smith reports, was at first so shocked at Byrd's way with the news that he was sick in bed for several days. Many American newspapermen heard about this censorship and Balchen recently confirmed Smith's report of it. He also confirmed other details of his fellow pilot's story, including the affair of the mountain which his own keen eyes had been unable to discern in the thick weather but which Byrd had seen through a cloud, darkly.

Most of the men at Little America were drawn to each other by the cold, the darkness, the homesickness. But Byrd remained aloof and unapproachable. He also stirred dissension in the ice-bound settlement by setting one man against another. Arthur Walden, veteran dog-team trainer and driver, showed his resentment openly. He had been hired to manage all the dog-team transportation. But he soon learned that Byrd had told the other drivers that each was in charge of his own team. It hardly made for harmony.

Hearing an argument among the mechanics, Balchen discovered that Byrd had told each man that he alone had the commander's confidence. Each man should watch all the others, Byrd had said, and report to him any signs of disloyalty. The Norwegian let the mechanics know in emphatic terms that this state of affairs would end at once. As long as he was in charge of the planes, the only reporting had better be to him.

Similar strange confidences, Balchen learned, had also been made to the other pilots. To each of them the commander had hinted that he would be the chief pilot on the South Pole trip. As it turned out, Balchen was behind the wheel only because his superior knowledge of engines and flying forced Byrd to choose him.

The feat involved a trip of 875 miles from Little America to the Pole and the same distance back. But the *Floyd Bennett*, with a total of 965 horsepower, drank gas so greedily that she couldn't fly the 1,750 miles on what her tanks would hold. It was therefore necessary to cache 350 gallons before the flight at a spot 450 miles south of Little America so that the big plane could come down after the Pole flight and refuel from 5-gallon cans before resuming her journey to Little America.

The *Floyd Bennett* took off for the bottom of the world on the afternoon of November 28, 1929, with Balchen as pilot, June as radioman and co-pilot, McKinley photographer and Byrd in the role of navigator. They had Amundsen's old charts, with their various landmarks, to guide them, and Balchen had studied them intensively. And for part of the way they also had the dog-sled trail of Larry Gould and a party of scientists who had gone ahead to explore the frozen continent, set up emergency caches, relay late weather information to the Pole fliers and act as a rescue crew in the event of trouble.

While piloting the plane, Balchen kept the kind of flight log Byrd might have been expected to keep on his trip northward from Spitsbergen. Every half-hour the Norwegian would note down items such as outside temperature, plane speed, altitude and landmarks. Three hours and forty-five minutes out, for example, he reported that they had sighted Gould's party and had dropped chocolate, cigarettes and some radio messages that had come in for them after they left Little America.

Later they approached the Liv Glacier, named by Amundsen for the daughter of Dr. Fridtjof Nansen, the Norwegian scientist, explorer and statesman. They were then flying at 8,200 feet. It was the maximum altitude which the Ford, with its still-heavy load of gas, was able to attain. But it was 1,300 feet short of the glacier's height.

Balchen waved frantically to June to kick out a 150-pound sack of emergency food—food they would need if they were forced down. The plane rose a little but not enough. The Norwegian waved again. June kicked out a second sack. But now a torrent of air, pouring down from the glacier, kept the laboring Ford from climbing. The plane was like a salmon trying to scale a waterfall that kept beating it down with every leap.

There was one thing left to try. Perhaps inside the downdraft there would be an upward current of air, a vertical back eddy that would carry them up and over the white barrier. Balchen eased the Ford up to the side of the cliff, the plane's right wing almost scraping the ice. Suddenly the machine shot upward and soared over the summit with 200 feet to spare.

Byrd, in the navigator's compartment, had a mariner's sextant with a natural horizon to which was fastened a carpenter's level bubble that was reflected in the sextant's horizon mirror. The bubble, unlike those in standard bubble sextants, was completely undampened and kept moving from one side of the tube to the other. It seemed to Balchen that the instrument must be useless for taking observations. And indeed, Byrd gave him no positions on the flight, either to or from the Pole.

They flew on toward the south, and after nine hours Balchen took out the pocket slide rule he usually carried with him. He jotted down and added up some more figures on elapsed time and plane speed, and estimated their position at latitude 89 degrees, 40 minutes south, about twenty miles from the Pole. He wrote a note to Byrd and fixed it to the harness of a little wheel that ran on a wire leading back through the cabin to the navigator's compartment. "According to my dead reckoning," it said, "we should be over the Pole in 14 minutes."

Presently a note came back from Byrd over the trolley wire: "That checks with my figures too."

Fourteen minutes after Balchen's message, at one-fourteen in the morning, South Pole time, Byrd handed an announcement to June for transmission to the world. "Aboard Airplane *Floyd Bennett* in flight, 1:55 P.M. Greenwich time, Friday, November 29. My calculations indicate that we have reached the vicinity of the South Pole, flying high for a survey. The airplane is in good shape, crew all well. Will soon turn north. We can see an almost limitless polar plateau."

The message flashed out through the clear Antarctic air, sped north with the fleetness of light and crackled in the receivers of the *New York Times*. And the great newspaper announced it to the world, which soon began sending its congratulations to the gallant commander. Typical of the many laudatory messages he received was one from the President:

> I know I speak for the American people when I express their universal pleasure at your successful flight over the South Pole. We are proud of your courage and your leadership. We are glad of proof that the spirit of great adventure still lives.
>
> Our thoughts of appreciation also include your companions in the flight and your colleagues, whose careful and devoted preparations have contributed to your great success.
>
> HERBERT HOOVER

On the flight northward from the Pole, Byrd came into the cockpit several times. Balchen noticed that his breath was redolent of cognac. The commander had in his flight bag several pints of this stimulant, which he said he needed to treat a heart ailment. Now he was applying himself to the remedy with a diligence that seemed to bespeak an intention to cure himself in the shortest possible period. And by the time Balchen brought the plane down at the refueling cache Byrd was, if not cured, at least feeling no pain. In fact, the man whose leadership was being praised around the world was barely able to stand.

Balchen recalls that the commander staggered around in the snow shouting, "We made it! We made it!" while the others lifted, carried and poured seventy 5-gallon cans of gas. June asked the Norwegian if there was any more heart medicine aboard. "If there is," added the radioman and co-pilot, "we'll have to take it away from him."

But apparently Byrd had disposed of the whole supply. It took the plane four and a half hours to reach Little America from the gas cache, and when it arrived the commander was again in possession of all his faculties. A stranger meeting him there would not have suspected that he differed in any way from the world's conception of a great navigator who had guided three lesser men to and from the bottommost point of the globe.

Such a stranger might have gained a different impression had he met Byrd after the flight to the east on December 5. This time Alton Parker was pilot and his shipmates were June, McKinley and Byrd, in their usual roles. They flew out about 300 miles over previously unexplored territory and returned some seven hours later.

When the door of the Ford was opened, in the presence of the entire population of Little America, June and McKinley were seen to be sitting on their leader, who was stretched out flat on the floor. The commander—soon to be elevated to rear admiral by President Hoover—was struggling and loudly cursing. He seemed to be raving mad. Suddenly he became limp and silent. Two more men helped his shipmates carry him to his bunk. After a refreshing sleep he recovered his usual dignified mien.

The trip to the South Pole and back was the last flight Balchen ever made for Byrd. After that he was sent out on sledge trips to measure crevasses. Later he was placed in charge of the West Side Camp in nearby Floyd Bennett Bay. Byrd seemed anxious to have no more to do with him. The admiral didn't even want to see the records of the flight tests and the performance analysis Balchen had made prior to the South Pole journey. He had no use for such data, he said. Balchen could do as he wished with it.

Out on the sledge trips, Balchen had time to think of other odd things that had happened during his acquaintance with Byrd. There was that dinner at the Hotel Astor in New York after the *America*'s flight to France. Byrd and Noville received the Navy's Distinguished Flying Cross on that occasion, though neither had flown the plane and Byrd had come up with no observations. Balchen and Acosta didn't get the award. Mayor Walker wanted to know why. Navy Secretary Wilbur replied that the Navy had no power to confer medals on other than Navy men. The explanation didn't satisfy some of his hearers. The *America*'s flight had been a private venture and the regulations held that the D.F.C. should be awarded for flights made on duty with the nation's armed forces.

That D.F.C. was to haunt Balchen. After the Antarctic expedition members returned to New York in June 1930, President Hoover awarded the medal to Byrd for a second time. He also gave it to Dean Smith, who was on leave from the Air Corps Reserve; to June, on leave from the Navy; and to Parker, on leave from the Marine Corps Reserve. Even Carl Petersen, a civilian and a radioman, got it for flying with Balchen to rescue the Ford plane when it ran out of fuel after caching the gas for the South Pole flight. But there was no Distinguished Flying Cross for Balchen. Why? This time both Admiral Byrd and his personal public relations man supplied the answer. Balchen wasn't a member of the U.S. Armed Forces. Also, he wasn't a citizen.

But if he didn't get the medal, he did get a notice from the government. As he walked out of the White House where the others had received their awards, Balchen received a subpoena from the immigration authorities. He had broken his residence requirements by going to the Antarctic, and his first citizenship papers were therefore void. As a result, he was about to be deported to Norway.

The newspapermen scanned the subpoena and raced for telephones. In the afternoon dailies, the story made a sizable stir. Balchen went back to his hotel room and sat down on the bed, sick at heart. After a while the telephone rang. The high-pitched voice of Representative Fiorello LaGuardia rattled the receiver.

The congressman from New York was so angry that at first Balchen could make out only a few phrases. ". . . goddam outrage . . . talked to the President . . . introducing a bill tomorrow." The flier asked him what bill. "To make you a citizen, of course. Shipstead of Minnesota and a couple of other good Scandahoovian congressmen are here with me and we're bringing it up on the floor of the House the first thing in the morning. Just called to tell you not to worry."

With his citizenship secure, Balchen went back to the Fokker factory in Hasbrouck Heights for a while, then returned in 1934 to Antarctica, this time with Lincoln Ellsworth. The two men proposed to fly across the entire Antarctic continent in a single-engined Wasp-powered Northrop monoplane. But the daring project was frustrated twice—first when the plane was damaged by ice breaking up in the Bay of Whales, and then when a fierce storm forced Balchen to turn back.

19

FADING FAME

What seemed so important as a new decade began—the first stylish westward Atlantic crossing and the first solo crossing by a woman flier—interests few people today. Yet the yellow pages of old newspapers reflect the nationwide excitement these feats stirred up when they took place. The first came in September 1930, when Dieudonné Costes and Maurice Bellonte gave the French something more to cheer about. In their red Breguet biplane, the *Question Mark*, with its 650-horsepower Hispano-Suiza, they flew from Paris to Curtiss Field, a distance of 4,100 miles by the route they took, in 37 hours and 18 minutes. And in May 1932, Miss Earhart soloed the Atlantic in her sleek 450-horsepower Wasp-engined Lockheed-Vega, taking off from Harbour Grace and coming down at Culmore, near Londonderry, northern Ireland. In this effort she had been encouraged, coached and flown to Harbour Grace from New York by the ubiquitous and ever helpful Balchen.

Time has dimmed the memories of the heroes and heroines of the Lindbergh era. Some are dead, some completely forgotten, some recalled with derision or dislike. Lindbergh lost millons of admirers when he became an isolationist and spoke up and down the country against American moves to help the Allies resist the Nazis before the United States entered the war. The fact that he later showed American fighter pilots in the Pacific how to increase the range of their Lightning pursuit planes did not dispel the resentment his political talks had aroused.

Bellanca, perhaps the greatest aeronautical designer of his time, got financial backing from the Du Ponts, Otto Kahn and other millionaires, and for several years continued to turn out fine planes. In 1931 two Bellancas engaged in the first transatlantic race—and both completed the crossing. The Whirlwind-powered machines started from Floyd Bennett Field, New York, within seventeen minutes of each other.

The first plane carried Clyde Pangborn and Hugh Herndon, Jr. The second held Russell Boardman and John Polando. Both crews ran into fog. The first Bellanca came down in Wales. The second, after a flight of 49 hours, landed in Constantinople, setting a new nonstop distance record of 5,041 miles. Thereafter, Pangborn and Herndon flew around the top of the world and in September took off from Sabishiro Beach, north of Tokyo, dropping their landing gear to speed their journey. They flew over the Kuriles and the Aleutians and down the North American coast, to make a belly-landing at Wenatchee, Washington. Their voyage of 4,500 miles, completed in 41 hours and 13 minutes, was the first nonstop flight across the Pacific.

Despite the excellence of its planes, the Bellanca Aircraft Company couldn't make money. After several years of thumping losses— ranging up to $532,000 in 1931—the firm was tottering on the edge of bankruptcy when the designer got an unexpected financial break. A Midwestern plumbing-supply company, which had piled up a substantial profit, bought the aircraft concern so it could make use of the Bellanca tax loss and get on the New York Curb Exchange, where the aircraft firm was listed. Bellanca received about $2,000,000 for his interest in the firm and discovered he could live happily without making any more profitless planes. He died in 1960, at the age of seventy-four, beloved by all who knew him.

Clarence Chamberlin also had little success with aircraft

manufacture. In 1928 he became president of a firm which turned out small sports planes in Jersey City, N.J., but the concern failed two years later during the Depression. The flier had drawn no salary because, as he explained, the company's financial situation didn't warrant it. Later Chamberlin ran a flying school on Long Island and still later a semiweekly air passenger service to Maine. Eventually he went into the real estate business. Today he and his wife sell houses in and around Shelton, Connecticut, nine months of the year and go to Florida for the winter. There Chamberlin, now in his seventies, fishes, gathers oysters, sits under a palm tree and entertains visiting friends.

Chamberlin said recently that after the *Columbia*'s transatlantic flight Levine paid him only $10,000 of the $25,000 he had promised. But the flier collected the $15,000 which had been offered by the Brooklyn Chamber of Commerce. On the whole, he feels he did pretty well. "I was a little sore at Levine at the time, but I soon got over it," he said. "After all, I was so anxious to fly the Bellanca to Europe that I would have paid money to do it."

Levine's exploits on the downhill side of glory repeatedly made him an object of interest to the police. The first of a long series of arrests took place in November 1930 in Vienna, the city which had awarded him its Golden Cross after his transatlantic flight with Chamberlin. A communiqué from the constabulary said he was suspected of preparing counterfeit French coins. In Vienna, it seemed, they could anticipate crimes by arresting on suspicion.

The former used-car salesman had a believable explanation. He was planning a solo world flight with an automatic pilot, he said, and wanted some medallions to hand out before, during and after the flight. So he had gone to a Viennese medal designer and asked if he could make dies for small emblems showing an airplane on one side and Levine's face on the other. He had some French coins in his pocket, he added, and had shown them to the medal maker, suggesting that the medallions could be like them. The designer, who apparently did not consider Levine one of nature's noblemen, had turned the American in.

Levine was held in jail for a week, until his wife cabled the $7,150 needed to bail him out. The Viennese police had been overzealous, and the charge was dropped two weeks later for lack of evidence.

The following January the New York police sent out a general alarm for Levine after he had twice failed to keep an appointment with an assistant district attorney. The official wanted him to explain how he had obtained $22,000 worth of AT&T stock which he had pledged as collateral for a $25,000 loan from the Manufacturers Trust Company. The telephone stock had been stolen from a Nassau Street brokerage house.

It was a year before the law caught up with him. Not until February 1932 did detectives find him in a Madison Avenue sanitarium where he was recovering from a broken leg. The fact that he was registered there under the name of C. Elliott Jaffee didn't make the police search for him any easier. For a week a patrolman was stationed by his bedside. Then Levine posted $10,000 and the guard withdrew. When Levine got out he pleaded innocent to charges of forgery, larceny and receiving stolen securities. His bail was continued and he didn't go to jail.

In May of that year Levine's wife sued him for a separation. She asked $1,000 a week alimony and $25,000 counsel fees (at least, her lawyers did). Her husband, Mrs. Levine said, had abandoned her two years earlier and had failed to support her and their two girls ever since.

Mrs. Levine declared that her spouse had made $6–$7,000,000 in his metal-salvage operations after World War I and that he was currently worth $4,000,000. In happier days, she added, he used to allow her $20,000 a year for clothes and had given her $150,000 worth of jewels.

270

Levine, testifying later before Referee Jacob Marks, admitted that his salvaging projects had netted $10,000,000, but he swore he had nothing left with which to pay alimony. However, he had an option on "a wonderful machine" for making steel tubing by a cold process. He also had a financial backer.

One spicy revelation marked the hearing. When asked if he had had a companion on a trip to Europe in 1930, he said he had been accompanied "by a lady named Boll."

In the end, Referee Marks recommended that Levine be directed to pay his wife $135 a week alimony.

After several civil suits on other matters, Levine was arrested in August 1933 in Jersey City and released on $2,500 bail. This time the charge was having attempted to pass a counterfeit $100 bill to a ticket agent of the Pennsylvania Railroad. A year later he was arrested in Long Beach, Long Island, on a charge of disorderly conduct. Residents of the place said he had been in a fight. Police added that the battle started when Levine arrived in a taxi to call on a woman acquaintance and found her leaving the premises with another male friend. Levine spent the rest of the night in jail and was released in the morning on payment of a $10 fine.

In September 1934 Levine was found unconscious in the kitchen of a friend's home in Brooklyn. The doors were closed and five jets on the gas range were open. A note to his friend said: "I just can't go on. You and your family have been awfully sweet to me and I deeply appreciate your kindness. Please forgive me. C.A.L."

A doctor from Kings County Hospital revived the ex-millionaire, and he dropped out of the news until the following August. Then he obtained an uncontested divorce in Reno from the former beauty-contest winner. He promptly married a woman who said she was then living in the separation city.

Two years later Levine was indicted by a federal grand jury in New York on a charge of smuggling tungsten into the country from Canada. Named with him as defendants were a Pullman porter and two residents of Toronto. The government contended that the porter —who pleaded guilty—had brought in the powdered metal, used in tempering steel, in small packages which he hid in Pullman berths. He said he handed the packages over to Levine in New York. A jury found Levine guilty and Federal Judge Henry Goddard sentenced him to two years in the Lewisburg, Pennsylvania, penitentiary. He served eighteen months of the term.

In January 1942 Levine ran afoul of the law again. Los Angeles authorities claimed he had helped smuggle a German citizen into this country from Mexico. Of his three co-defendants, two pleaded guilty and turned state's evidence. So Levine, who denied the charge, couldn't convince the jury of his innocence. He went back to prison for five months.

After that he dropped out of the news again. The last time Chamberlin heard of him he was connected with a small record company in New York. This probably is as good a place as any in this book to say *sic transit gloria mundi.*

It also seems a good place to recall that Miss Boll married Count Henry de Parceri, described as a Polish nobleman in his early thirties, in April 1931. The event, said the news item from the City of Light, was "shrouded in mystery," although the ceremony was performed by the mayor of the Eighth Arrondissement. Two years later another dispatch from Paris said she had divorced Parceri. The decree was granted, it added, "in recognition of reciprocal faults of both parties." The item also said that although Parceri had described himself as a Polish count at the time of their union he was saying now that he was just "a plain American citizen." He had acquired this status, he explained, in 1926, the year before Miss Boll first took to the air.

In 1940 Miss Boll married Theodore Cella, harpist and assistant conductor of the New York Philharmonic. She died nine years later, at the age of fifty-four.

.   .   .

Acosta's later history was more tragic than that of Miss Boll. In 1929 the spectacular stunt flier lost his Department of Commerce license for violating rules against low flying over airports. This deprived him of his only means of livelihood and the following year he was arrested in the home of his wife at Freeport, Long Island, charged with failing to support her and their two children. Acosta explained that he couldn't support anybody, but he was held in $2,500 bond. Levine heard about his plight and bailed him out of jail.

In 1937 Acosta went to Spain to fly for the Loyalists as a bomber pilot. But he returned a month later, saying the planes they had offered him were no good. After that came a long series of hospitalizations for various illnesses. And in September 1953 the once-dashing airman, who had taken a lovely girl away from the Prince of Wales, died in the Jewish Consumptives' Relief Society's sanitarium near Denver. He was fifty-nine years old.

Balchen had a distinguished military career after his early flying experiences. For a time during World War II he commanded a staging base on the west coast of Greenland for American bombers and fighter planes bound for Britain. In this role he made numerous rescue flights to wrecked fliers on the big snow-capped island. During one five-month effort—during which marooned men were kept alive by air drops—Balchen made three belly-landings on the ice in a heavy PBY flying boat, a feat never before attempted. For this the Air Force recommended him for the Medal of Honor. He didn't receive it.

Later he commanded an American Liberator squadron based in Scotland which dropped hundreds of tons of supplies to underground troops in occupied Norway and flew out thousands of Allied personnel who had been interned in Sweden. After the war he undertook a special project at the request of General Carl ("Tooey") Spaatz, commander of the U.S. Strategic Air Force. Spaatz told him in the presence of Generals James Doolittle and Ira Eaker that if he com-

273

pleted this supersecret task and stayed alive he would be promoted
from colonel to major general. He did so and retained his health.
But he remained a colonel.

Still later he commanded the Tenth Rescue Squadron in Alaska.
It consisted of a thousand men and forty planes ranging from heli-
copters to four-engined transports. The squadron averaged a rescue
every 2½ days—over 1,300 in all. Again the Air Force tried to
promote him to the rank of general. Again the move failed to win
approval. A high Air Force official told Balchen later that his superiors had recommended his promotion to general seven separate
times. And each time, this official said, Senator Harry Byrd—a
member of the powerful Senate Armed Services Committee—killed
the project because of what he listed as "personal and special reasons." He added that the admiral's brother also had vetoed the
recommendation for the Medal of Honor.

Today Balchen is a consultant in engineering, planning and
programing for General Dynamics Corporation. He also does jobs
for the Air Force, for he is on active-retired status which means he
is available when needed. His hair has turned from blond to pure
white but at the age of seventy-one he still has 20/20 vision in his
blue eyes. He was asked recently when he planned to retire. He
looked at the questioner somewhat sharply and said, "Never."

Of the explorers, Nobile worked for several years in the Soviet Union
after the *Italia* disaster. In 1931 the German rigid dirigible *Graf
Zeppelin* flew into the Arctic with several scientists and explorers
aboard, among them Professor Samoilovich and Lincoln Ellsworth.
At Franz Josef Land it came down to meet the *Malygin*, for which it
had a bag of mail. A boat put out from the old icebreaker and in it
was Nobile, his once glossy black hair now gray at the temples.

"I had to look twice to recognize him," Ellsworth wrote later.
"He had aged visibly. The *Italia* disaster had made a different man
of him. As he left in the bobbing boat of the *Malygin*, which was still

looking for *Italia* survivors—waving goodbye as he stood unsteadily in the stern—the scene held an element of pathos that I can never forget."

Nobile tried unsuccessfully to set up a dirigible-construction program in the Soviet Union. Later, through the influence of Pope Pius XI, he got a post on the engineering faculty of a Catholic school of aeronautics in Chicago. With the defeat of the Fascist powers in World War II he found Italian officials ready to welcome him again and resumed a position he had held years earlier—professor of aeronautics at the University of Naples.

Wilkins went back to Antarctica in 1929 and made a series of short flights over Graham Land which filled in many empty spaces on the map. While he was there he learned that Ben Eielson, who had started Alaskan Airways with Joe Crosson, was missing on a flight to rescue the passengers and cargo of an ice-bound American ship off Cape North, Siberia. Nearly every airman in Alaska and some Soviet fliers searched for the famous bush pilot and his mechanic, but they had been killed in a crash on the Siberian coast.

In 1931, with some financial support from William Randolph Hearst and Lincoln Ellsworth, Wilkins tried to reach the North Pole in a reconditioned submarine. The ship was an old craft which was about to be scrapped under the London Naval Treaty, and it proved itself thoroughly inadequate to the task of crossing the Atlantic and running under ice which, from under water, often looks like an upside-down mountain range. After a series of irritating failures, which cost far more than the dollar for which the vessel was sold to Wilkins, the venture had to be abandoned.

After that Wilkins gave up exploring on his own account. From 1933 to 1936 he was manager of Ellsworth's four Antarctic expeditions. He died in Massachusetts in 1958.

Ellsworth, so often financial angel for other men's exploration projects, finally won world acclaim in 1935 for an achievement almost wholly his own. After three failures in Antarctica, he and

Herbert Hollick-Kenyon, a Canadian Airways pilot, took off in a single-engined Northrop monoplane from Dundee Island, off the tip of Graham Land, for a 2,100-mile flight across the frozen continent to Little America, which was then unoccupied. The two men started on November 23 and made five stops en route. On the first hop their radio failed. After another they were held down for a week by a blizzard. Finally their fuel ran out twenty-five miles short of their goal. They walked into Little America and found food and whiskey. When they were picked up in January 1936, they had not been heard from for nearly two months. The great flight seemed to satisfy Ellsworth's hunger for dangerous adventure. After that he lived quietly until his death in New York City in 1951.

Byrd went to the Antarctic four more times. On the second trip he spent more than four months in a hut 123 miles south of Little America to make weather observations inland and was nearly overcome, it was reported, by carbon monoxide fumes from a generator engine. Later, with June as pilot, he flew over Marie Byrd Land and confirmed that the mountains of Antarctica are a continuation of the Andes.

Although he was nominal leader of the third, fourth and fifth expeditions, these enterprises were run by the Navy. One of Byrd's biographers complains that the admiral was not accorded due deference by fellow officers. By then, however, Antarctic exploration was no longer an affair involving forty or fifty men, but an enterprise employing hundreds. Byrd died in Boston in 1957.

20

OLD PLANES AND THEIR BROOD

The planes of the twenties and thirties are quiet now and most of the people who flew in them will never fly again in this world. Of the first three machines that soared over the North Atlantic, only one is still in existence. The *Spirit of St. Louis* found its final resting place in the Smithsonian Institution in Washington.

The *Columbia,* the best of the trio, became the first plane in history to fly the Atlantic twice. In 1930 Levine sold her to a wealthy Canadian who presented her to Captain J. Errol Boyd of the Royal Canadian Flying Corps. Boyd and Lieutenant Harry Connor of the U. S. Naval Reserve flew the battered old machine from Harbour Grace to Tresco, one of the Scilly Isles, where a choked fuel line forced them down. Next day they completed their journey to London.

The Bellanca factory retrieved the renowned relic and kept her in a barn near its plant at New Castle, Delaware. One day a cinder from a Pennsylvania Railroad locomotive set fire to the grass in a nearby field. The fire spread to the barn and the fine old plane went up in smoke, as some thought she had gone that evening at Roosevelt Field, years earlier.

The *America,* wrecked off Ver-sur-Mer, was never reassembled. Soon after her return piecemeal to the United States her wing and engines were sold to become parts of less famous Fokkers.

In a way, however, the *America* lives on. Hailed years ago as the precursor of future transatlantic airliners, she has been succeeded by an ocean air fleet that every day puts into the air between North America and Europe an average of 200 civilian planes carrying a total of upwards of 15,000 passengers and more than 1,200 tons of cargo and 100 tons of mail, not to mention a huge flock of military aircraft. With twice and in some cases nearly thrice the wingspread of the *America* the biggest of the modern airliners weigh more than fifty times as much and fly more than six times as fast as Uncle Tony's creation. They carry up to 490 passengers and have crews—including a dozen or more hostesses—of as many as 19 people.

In the Henry Ford Museum at Dearborn there are four other relics of the twenties. One is the *Bremen*, which came down on Greenly Island. Another is the *Pride of Detroit*, which might have circled the earth had not anxious relatives and friends intervened.

The last two machines, both fitted with skis, wait in the main hall, side by side. One, fashioned of wood, metal and fabric, is the *Josephine Ford*, named for a millionaire manufacturer's daughter. The other, made of metal, is the *Floyd Bennett*, named for a brave and skillful aviator who deferred to a commander whose rank, education and fame were superior to his own.

The two old trimotor planes are bright and well kept. Thousands of people admire them every year. The words on the cards which identify them say that each of them circled a pole of the world. And one of these legends is true.

Appendices

Appendix A

HOW TO "PLAN" A POLAR FLIGHT ON PAPER

In 1960 a polar expert who had long doubted the authenticity of Byrd's North Pole claim decided to examine it closely. Gösta H. Liljequist, professor of meteorology at the University of Uppsala, has been interested in cold regions for years. He was meteorologist of the Norwegian-British-Swedish expedition to the Antarctic in 1949–52, and organized and led the Swedish-Finnish-Swiss expedition to Northeast Land, Spitsbergen, during the 1957-58 International Geophysical Year. His knowledge of polar history and polar expeditions does not come entirely out of books.

In the May 1960 issue of *Interavia: World Review of Aviation and Aeronautics,* published in Geneva in four languages, Professor Liljequist presented a careful study of Byrd's claim (text appended). It included an analysis of the *Josephine Ford*'s tour of the United States, the weather conditions during the flight from Spitsbergen, the time the plane spent in the air and the distance that had to be covered.

He studied both American and Norwegian weather maps on the day of the flight and found that—despite Byrd's statement that he had a following wind on the way back from the Pole—there was no wind of appreciable strength that day between Spitsbergen and latitude 90 degrees north.

As we know from the report of the National Geographic Society's committee of experts, there was no regular flight log. All Byrd's

281

meager records were contained on those two charts. When the committee of experts finished with them, it gave them back to the Navy. The Navy says it gave them to National Archives. And Archives says that if the Navy did, they can't be located.

But even if they could be found today the charts wouldn't mean anything. It's a simple matter for anybody who understands navigation techniques, or who can get a capable and innocent aide to help him, to fake observations and fool experts who believe in his integrity.

Professor Liljequist said recently that as far as he knows, no committee of aeronautical and meteorological experts was ever formed to consider the Byrd-Bennett flight. As for the possibility of faking observation, he explained: "It is easy to 'plan' a polar flight on paper. Given the speed of the plane, it is an hour's job to work out the observation backwards, i.e., compute the 'observed' solar altitudes at a number of places along the route."

Concerning Byrd's claim that he had verified "in every detail" Peary's findings of 1909, Professor Liljequist noted that the whole North Pole area is covered with pack ice. "It is then very easy to 'verify' the findings," he added. "A photo of the Pole area also can be taken wherever you like from just a little north of Spitsbergen—it contains nothing but pack ice."

Dr. Frederick Albert Cook claimed that he reached the North Pole on foot in 1908, being the first man to achieve that distinction. Although some people still believe his statement, he was pretty thoroughly discredited within four months.

Byrd's claim to have been the first explorer to reach the Pole by plane is still accepted after more than forty years. His supposed exploit is described in text books, encyclopedias and scientific periodicals published all over the world.

Perhaps it was accepted originally with a little too much haste. Apparently the committee of experts never considered the speed of the plane and the distance to be flown in relation to the time Byrd spent in the air. Although at one point in their report the experts say that the *Josephine Ford* averaged 74 miles an hour (85.1 statute miles if they meant nautical miles) during the last 45 minutes of her reported approach to the Pole, even this speed would not have been sufficient—as Professor Liljequist has pointed out—for the plane to have reached the Pole and returned to Kings Bay in 15½ hours.

It seems odd that this simple calculation was not made. Possibly the most charitable explanation is that the National Geographic Society's distinguished experts were not looking for a fraud. That Byrd's claim to have reached the Pole *was* a fraud seems clear beyond any reasonable doubt. In fact, it seems to have been the biggest and most successful fraud in the history of polar exploration.

Did the "Josephine Ford" Reach the North Pole?
By G. H. Liljequist, Uppsala, Sweden

At the end of April, 1926, final preparations were being made at King's Bay, Spitsbergen, for the start of the dirigible "Norge" on her flight over the North Pole to Alaska, when a second expedition appeared on the scene. This was the American ship "Chantier" carrying the Fokker aircraft "Josephine Ford." Then on May 7th the Amundsen-Ellsworth-Nobile expedition's "Norge" arrived in Spitsbergen from Rome.

The "Josephine Ford" was the first to leave. With Commander Richard E. Byrd as leader and navigator, and with Floyd Bennett at the controls, she took off at 0037 GMT on May 9th in beautiful weather. She returned to base the same afternoon, having completed her mission: the first flight to the North Pole.

283

Two days later, on May 11th, the "Norge" started her flight across the Arctic Ocean to Alaska via the North Pole.

The flight of the "Josephine Ford" is of great interest from both a historical and a technical point of view. It still merits a thorough and objective analysis.

The "Josephine Ford" was a trimotor monoplane, built by the Fokker factories in Holland in 1925. The type was designated Fokker F-VII-3m. It is described in "Jane's All the World's Aircraft" for 1927.

The aircraft was equipped with three Wright Whirlwind J-4B engines. They were among the first in the series and had the same maximum output as the J-4A, namely 200 h.p. each at 1,800 r.p.m.

The propellers of the "Josephine Ford" were Reid-Levasseur with twisted steel blades. These fixed-pitch propellers were inferior to the Hamilton Standard Adjustable used with the J-5 engines (240 h.p. each at 1,980 r.p.m.) on the Fokker aircraft which went into production at the company's American factories in 1927. The American Fokkers had a maximum speed of 119 statute miles an hour.

"Jane's" for 1927 gives the "Josephine Ford" a cruising speed of 102.5 m.p.h. or 89 knots (165km/h). This is, however, a sales value. It is doubtful whether it could have been maintained throughout a long flight.

In studying the flight of the "Josephine Ford," one is immediately struck by the time difference between the outbound and the return flight, 8 hours 26 minutes compared with 6 hours 52 minutes. The difference could be explained by a more or less constant 10.6 knot wind from the north. This would give us the same cruising speed as published in "Jane's," 89 knots. On the other hand, the prevailing weather situation would not lead one to expect a northerly wind as an average over the whole route, even though Byrd's report contains the information that the wind freshened from the north just after the plane had left the Pole. The reports give the maximum speed of the "Josephine Ford" as 117 m.p.h., but do not mention the cruising speed.

In trying to determine the cruising speed of the plane—especially the speed that would have been used on a very long flight—I have analysed both the cruising speeds of the aircraft on actual flights and the results of a test flight.

In the fall of 1927, the "Josephine Ford" was taken on a long tour of the United States, with Floyd Bennett as pilot and Bernt Balchen as copilot. The total distance flown was 7,005 nautical miles, and total time in the air was 100 hours 55 minutes. The tour contained 45 stops.

The average length of each flight was 156 nautical miles at 1,000–1,500 feet or lower, and the average time 2 hours 14 minutes.

From the flight log I have computed the ground speed for each of the 45 flights. In 24 cases, the speed was between 66 and 80 knots, i.e. around 72.5 knots. Excluding five flights with very low speed, obviously much wind-influenced, the average speed of the remaining 40 cases is 72 knots. The mean value for all 45 flights is 70 knots.

In other words, the cruising speed of the "Josephine Ford" was around 75 knots or a little lower in the fall of 1927. Just before the tour all three engines had been overhauled at the Wright factories and were in top working condition during the entire flight.

In June 1927, another Fokker F-VII-3m flew from San Francisco to Honolulu, a distance of 2,400 statute miles, in 25 hours 43 minutes, i.e. at an average speed of 81 knots. This aircraft was equipped with more powerful Wright J-5C engines. The plane had a light to moderate tail wind all the way, and consequently its air speed must have been less than 81 knots, say 70 to 75.

During the polar flight, the "Josephine Ford" was equipped with skis instead of wheels, which must have slowed her down by a few knots, particularly as the skis had been damaged in a mishap and provisionally repaired with oars. It seems a logical conclusion that the average cruising speed of the "Josephine Ford" on the North Pole flight was about 70 knots. This is a rather different figure from the 89 knots published in "Jane's."

In order to determine whether this low cruising speed may be considered reasonable, I have made a study of the performance qualities of the Fokker F-VII-3m. My data are obtained from a verified test flight made on October 29th, 1927, at the Naval Air Station at Anacostia, D.C., with an American-built Fokker with Wright J-5C engines. The propellers were Standard Steel Adjustable, superior to those of the "Josephine Ford." This aircraft reached a maximum speed of 118 m.p.h. and consequently the maximum speed of the "Josephine Ford" must have been lower than 118 m.p.h.

This test flight was of course performed with a wheel-equipped aircraft. By substituting skis for wheels the parasite drag is increased. A technical expert has assisted me in obtaining a rough value for this increase from photos of the plane in "Jane's" and Byrd's report. The results of the calculations show that in the ski-version the speed is slowed down between three and four knots, depending on the power of the engines.

285

During a flight, only about 60 percent of maximum available power ought to be taken out for any length of time. For very long flights even this is a somewhat high value. With an output of 60 percent of available power, the speed of the ski-version of the aircraft is found to be 72 knots, as compared with 75 knots for the wheel-version.

The values obtained from the actual flights are thus verified. If we assume the cruising speed of the "Josephine Ford" to have been 75 knots, we have made no underestimate.

Let us now consider the weather conditions during the flight. At the time, meteorological observations were made from Spitsbergen, from northern Russia and from a few places along the Siberian coast and Alaska. They suffice to reconstruct a weather map with a reasonable degree of correctness.

I have studied the American Historical Weather Maps for the Northern Hemisphere, which give daily synoptic charts for 1300 GMT and also synoptic charts for 0100 GMT analyzed at the Norwegian forecasting centre at Tromsö, where at the time special attention was paid to Arctic weather conditions in view of the "Norge" flight. The two sets of charts differ in details, but are the same in all essentials.

Both show that an anticyclone covered almost all of the Arctic, with a high-pressure ridge extending via the Barents Sea to eastern Russia. This remained stationary from May 8th to May 10th and must have been situated north of Spitsbergen, where easterly to southeasterly winds prevailed.

Estimating wind directions and speeds from the two charts, we find that the Tromsö chart indicates SE-ESE winds of 10 to 20 knots at King's Bay, very light southerly winds between 80 and 88° N and poleward winds from Greenland of about 10 knots in the Pole area. The Historical Weather Maps confirm this picture, though they give the direction of the poleward winds in the Pole area as coming from eastern Alaska or western Canada. These winds refer to 2,000–4,000 feet, where the plane stayed during the flight.

The inference is that the flight may be considered as having taken place in a no-wind atmosphere. At any rate, had a wind worth mentioning arisen between the Pole and Spitsbergen, it should under no circumstances have been found south of about 85° N, since the ridge remained stationary.

On the flight north, Commander Byrd made six astronomical observations with a bubble sextant on the route between Amsterdamöya [Amsterdam Island] and the Pole, and four more at or near the Pole. None were made on the homeward flight, the sextant having been damaged.

However, in making an analysis of the flight only the speed of the plane, time and distance plus wind and/or weather conditions are of objective value.

We possess one certain fix on the northbound flight: the northern point of Amsterdamöya at 79° 47′ N. The plane left King's Bay at 78° 55′ at 0037 GMT, passed Amsterdamöya at 0122 GMT, reached the Pole at 0903 and left it again at 0915 GMT. For the homeward flight the only time notation is that Grey Hook (Gråhuken) was sighted straight ahead at 1430 GMT. The time of arrival at King's Bay is not given.

Byrd gives the flight time as "nearly sixteen hours," and Amundsen has written that the returning aircraft was sighted just after 1600 GMT, while Balchen, who was a member of the "Norge" expedition, gives the time of arrival as 1607 GMT. Accepting 15 hours 30 minutes as total flight time and subtracting the 12 minutes spent over the Pole, we arrive at an average ground speed of 87 knots (100 m.p.h.) for the total distance of 1,330 nautical miles.

With our estimated speed of 75 knots, the "Josephine Ford" could in 15½ hours have flown not more than 1,162 nautical miles, bringing it not farther north than 88° 36′ N. Allowing for delays in climbing, the time spent circling over the Pole and the detour around Amsterdamöya on the return flight, a time of 15 hours for the direct flight north and back is more probable. This would have brought the "Josephine Ford" to a point 88° 17.5′ N. To have reached the Pole, the aircraft should have returned to King's Bay between 1830 and 1900 GMT, not a few minutes past 1600 GMT.

The discussion has until now been limited to ground speed in a no-wind atmosphere, conditions which would appear to have prevailed according to the synoptic weather charts.

To have reached the Pole, the plane would have had to have a tail wind of about five knots as an average for the outward flight, and the wind would also have had to change direction and increase to about 22 knots as an average over the entire distance from the Pole to King's Bay on the homeward flight. As already mentioned, the fresh winds can have occurred only during the first half of the homeward flight, in which case they would have had to reach at least 40 to 50 knots from the north.

Such a strong northerly gale should have made itself felt at Spitsbergen soon afterwards, which it did not. The whole of the Arctic was covered by an anticyclone, and a 40–50 knots gale close to this high pressure area is highly improbable.

Commander Byrd's flight in the "Josephine Ford" gave inspiration to a generation of men interested in polar work. However, it would seem appropriate that a committee of aeronautical and meteorological experts be given access to the flight log and all available data to study the question whether in actual fact he did reach the Pole.

Appendix B

After Balchen retired from active service in 1956 a New York publisher suggested that he write his autobiography. He agreed and the publisher assigned a well-known writer to help him. Now, Balchen decided, he would tell the truth about the North Pole flight, the *America*'s transatlantic flight and the South Pole journey. He sat down at his typewriter and turned out 250,000 words.

He soon discovered that truth, crushed to earth, does not necessarily rise again. Both Richard Evelyn and Harry Flood Byrd were still alive and the publisher felt that their reactions to unpleasant disclosures would probably be vigorous.

The book firm did agree to print some passages which implied Byrd was not the peerless leader he was generally reputed to be. But the Byrd family learned about what was being prepared for publication and its reaction was far more stormy than had been expected.

Although the Admiral had died while the book was being written, lawyers representing Senator Byrd threatened author and publisher if even the watered-down version of *Come North With Me* came into general circulation. They talked of libel, slander, defamation of character. They declared that Balchen could be deported for such nefarious conduct, despite the fact that he was an American citizen by special act of Congress.

The publisher agreed to hold up the first edition—of which 4,000 copies had been printed—and bring out a second edition in

which all offending passages would be expunged. They informed
Balchen he would have to pay for the rewriting and other expenses.
He did. It was the only way, he thought, to keep his book alive.

The first change involved his account (on pages 66 and 67) of
a conversation between Bennett and himself during the *Josephine
Ford*'s nationwide tour. This recital had already been toned down,
but it still could stir doubts in thoughtful minds. It goes as follows:

> My eye runs over the instrument gauges, and automatically I note
> down the speed and fuel consumption for the last time. I start to slip
> my log book into my shirt again, but something in the back of my
> mind keeps bothering me. I run over the data I have compiled on the
> tour, and frown, and check the figures carefully on my slide rule,
> once more. There must be a mistake. "Tell me," I ask Bennett, "what
> do you get for our average cruising speed?"
>
> Bennett takes his own log out of the leg pocket of his coveralls.
> "Let's see. About seventy miles an hour."
>
> "So do I. There's something here that doesn't quite jibe," I
> ponder. "With ski landing gear on, the speed couldn't be more than
> sixty-eight, could it? Well now, my diary says you were gone fifteen
> and a half hours from Kings Bay to the Pole and back. Figuring
> roughly, 1,550 land miles round trip, that would be averaging better
> than a hundred miles an hour."
>
> "We had a tail wind, though."
>
> "But you had to buck that wind all the way back to Spitsbergen."
> I shake my head. "Our figures must be way off, because they put your
> turning point a couple of hundred miles short of the Pole."
>
> "We're both cockeyed somewhere," Bennett shrugs. "Well, it
> doesn't matter now. We won't be flying this bucket across the
> Atlantic or anywhere else. You'll be working in the Fokker factory,
> and I'll be looking for a job."

In the second edition this passage suffered what might be called
a sea-lawyer change. Whether the result is rich and strange, however, is debatable.

> My eye runs over the instrument gauges, and automatically I
> note down the speed and fuel consumption for the last time. Still
> figuring, though it looks like an academic question now, I run over

the data I have compiled on the tour. "Tell me," I ask Bennett, "what do you get for our average cruising speed?"

Bennett takes his own log book out of the leg pocket of his coveralls. "Let's see. About seventy miles an hour."

"So do I. To fly across the Atlantic from New York to, say, Paris— a distance of about 3,600 miles actual flying, or say 3,700 to be on the safe side—would require about 53 hours' flying time. That would mean breaking the world's endurance record for sustained flight.

"If the *Josephine Ford* had those bigger Wright Whirlwind engines that have just come on the market," I tell Bennett, "I believe we could do it. With those babies we'd get an extra thirty horsepower, or close to it, per engine."

"That's right, *if* she had them," Bennett shrugs. "Well, it doesn't matter now. We won't be flying this bucket across the Atlantic or anywhere else. You'll be working in the Fokker factory, and I'll be looking for a job." He tilts a wing. "What's that wind sock down there say?"

On page 112 there was another change. It involved one sentence in the report of the flight of the *America* to France.

First edition:

Though we had beautiful starlight all last night we have received no estimates of our position from Byrd, and I wonder why he hasn't taken celestial observations. At noon a penciled message from him is brought up to the cockpit: "It is impossible to navigate."

Second edition:

We hope that at the altitudes at which we have been flying we may have been getting the benefit of winds from the west to increase our speed through the clouds. At noon a penciled message from Byrd is brought up to the cockpit. "It is impossible to navigate."

Page 162, which deals with the voyage toward Antarctica in 1928, also underwent revision.

First edition:

Only Commander Byrd is nowhere in sight. Alone in his cabin on the poop deck, he is starting his new memoirs already. I do not think he has spoken to me a dozen times during the whole voyage. His feeling against me, whatever it is, has been more evident since Floyd Bennett's death, and sometimes I wonder why I have been brought along at all. I have heard rumors that this pilot or that has been assured confidentially that he will be the lucky one to fly Byrd over the South Pole, but he has never discussed the flight with me. "Dicky Byrd is very well known, but nobody knows him very well," Billy Mitchell [whose project for a separate air force Byrd opposed] said once. Well, there is an old Norwegian saying that a sailor has no secrets from his mates, and perhaps I shall know him better when we have all lived together for a year in the isolation of the polar ice.

Second edition:

As for our leader, Commander Byrd, he is not in sight at this moment, and I imagine that he is probably fully occupied at his desk, where he spends much time these days. Working alone for long hours in his cabin on the poop deck, he is starting his new reminiscences. And he must have much detailed planning to do on various aspects of the expedition. I wonder idly sometimes who will be the lucky pilot to fly him over the South Pole. He has said nothing about it to me, so I have no idea. Of course, I would like to know him better, but he is too busy to have much time to talk. Well, there is an old Norwegian saying . . .

Pages 180 and 181, which describe life in Little America, were also completely rewritten.

First edition:

We have been living together half a year now, and still I do not know Commander Byrd any better. Even in the confinement of Little America, where the rest of us are drawn to each other more closely by the darkness and the homesickness, he has managed to hold himself apart. The men do not understand his cold detachment, and they go instead to Larry Gould with their various problems. You could put it this way: that Byrd is a commander, but not a leader. Some of the men are beginning to show their resentment openly, and veteran Arthur Walden makes no bones about his feelings. He has been hired to manage all the dog-team transportation; but Byrd has told the other mushers they are in charge of their own teams, and Walden's Yankee pride is outraged. Now he mopes by himself in Blubberheim [his hut], and acknowledges Byrd only with a sour nod.

There are other signs of dissension in camp, as the winter drags on. I have noticed the mechanics scowling at each other lately, and making sarcastic remarks behind one another's backs. Their team spirit is gone. Once I come on three of them in a violent argument, each insisting that he alone is responsible for servicing the big Ford. I explain that they are assigned to the two aircraft all alike [the Fokker had been wrecked] and their job is to work together and help each other whenever they can. Then it comes out that Commander Byrd has taken them one by one for a little walk, and told each man in turn that the responsibility rests on his shoulders, and he should watch the others and report at once if anything disloyal occurs. I let them know that I am running the aviation unit; I report to Byrd and they report to me as long as I am head of the department.

Why does Commander Byrd continue to sow these little seeds of jealousy, I ask myself. Is it a perverse amusement that leads him to pit one man against another? Harold June and Dean Smith and the other pilots have all been taken on these little walks of his and Byrd has hinted confidentially to each of them that he will be the chief pilot over the Pole. Night after night I lie in my bunk, trying to understand him. There is no doubt that he is capable of rash courage, as he showed when he voluntarily risked his life in the rescue flight to the Rockefeller Mountains [where Balchen, Gould and June were marooned for a week when a storm wrecked the Fokker], when there was no real need of his coming, or the time he unhesitatingly jumped overboard to save a seaman from the icy Bay of Whales. Is it devotion to his men, and if so, how do you reconcile this with his distrust of them? Is it a desire for public acclaim, then? Or does a deep-seated inferiority require him over and over to prove himself to himself?

Sometimes I think it will be easier to solve the mystery of the South Pole than to find an answer to this man.

Second edition:

Members of all polar expeditions are inevitably subjected to environmental conditions vastly different from those they have been accustomed to enjoying in civilization. During the winter night, these unnatural conditions—the eternal cold, the darkness, the high winds, and enforced confinement in austere and fairly cramped quarters—naturally exert a certain depressing effect on the men of an expedition, and occasional tensions and unrest tend to arise among them. In such conditions, and with the general lack of privacy, each man's true self will invariably emerge and stand revealed to his companions. There is no doubt that the type of man best fitted for a wintering party in polar regions is the man who is not only physically fit, but also even-tempered, with inner intellectual resources, and not overly sensitive.

Splendidly equipped and manned as it is, our expedition is not exempt from these psychological pressures from the environment, and everything is done to offset their effects as much as possible. For this purpose, it is of the utmost importance, during such a stay, that a work schedule be set up in such a way that every member of the party has a certain amount of work to perform daily. At Little America this system is used to good effect. Larry Gould, the second in command, has the task of delegating many of the camp chores. These go to different men each day, so that no one has an undue amount of the more unpleasant work, such as dishwashing, snow shoveling, and cleaning of latrines. Our day usually starts with Larry, who bunks next to me, and myself, getting up at seven o'clock in the morning and calling the rest of the men in our barracks. Breakfast is at eight and then the camp work day begins, except for those who have been on night duty. A list has been posted the day before assigning the chores for the day. In these assignments, everyone is included; even Commander Byrd cheerfully takes his turn at washing dishes and setting tables. I might add that it is no small job to wash dishes for, or wait on, forty-odd hungry men, especially when that is not your regular trade. However, this system has the effect of helping keep all members of the expedition psychologically and physically occupied. This somewhat lessens the tensions.

In addition, of course, each of the scientists and technicians has his own specialized work to do—meteorology, physics, glaciology, radio communications, and so on. In our spare time during the winter darkness, many of us study. I have brought with me the latest literature on aerodynamics and mathematics, which I use in available hours to brush up for my eventual return to my work as test pilot in the States.

On pages 185 and 186 the revisionists dealt with the account of the second trip to the downed *Floyd Bennett* after its cache-establishing operation—a rescue for which Carl Petersen received the D.F.C. Smith says in his book that a fuel-pump leak caused the big trimotor to run out of gas about twenty miles short of Little America. Balchen and Petersen came out in the Fairchild with a hundred gallons of gas in 5-gallon cans, and left. Smith and McKinley lugged the red cans across the snow, carried them into the cabin and hoisted them up through the hatch for June to pour into the wing tanks of the Ford without help from Byrd. And after Byrd had tried to help McKinley and June crank the center engine, Smith adds, the naval officer said, "My back won't take it," and retired to his sleeping bag in a small tent he had rigged on the snow. They needed three men on the crank to get the engine started and Smith had to be in the cockpit to rev up the Cyclone if it caught.

First edition:

> Still the Ford does not show up. We wait all day, puzzled, and at night Carl Petersen and I take off again, carrying more gas and also repair tools in case there had been an accident. They are still in the same plane, unable to start the engines and so irritated by their failure that they barely speak to me when I arrive. We put on the heaters, and in less than an hour all three engines are turning smoothly. Byrd and the others pile into the Ford without a backward glance, and take off so fast that Pete, working inside the tent (enclosing the Fairchild's engine which he was then heating up), does not even hear them leave. We pick up the gear they have left lying around on the snow, jam everything into our little Fairchild, and rejoin them at Little America long after midnight.
>
> Next morning I am the one that Byrd takes for one of his little

walks. He is still brooding about last night, I can see, and he curtly demands to know why their fuel consumption was higher than expected. I reply that I cannot give the answer right now but I suspect the pilot did not lean his mixture properly. "I'll go over the whole engine installation thoroughly," I promise him, "to make sure my figures are right." I take out of my pocket my little slide rule, the same one I used in crossing the Atlantic. "I've been keeping very careful figures on mileage and fuel consumption, just as I did on the *Josephine Ford* and the *America*—"

He interrupts, his eyes full of cold fire. "Forget about that slide rule. From now on, you stick to flying. I'll do the figuring."

I do not know what I have said to make him so angry, so I do not say anything more. He keeps on walking, shaking his head moodily, complaining aloud to no one in particular. Why weren't the other pilots able to start the big Trimotor, he wants to know. Why haven't they learned how to handle engines in cold weather? They had the same trouble trying to start the Fairchild on the rescue trip to the Rockefeller Mountains. He whirls on me: "How is it you always manage to do the right thing?" he accuses. "Why do I have to come back to you?"

I have no answer, because it is hard to understand why it is wrong to do something right. What he says next is even harder to understand.

"I made up my mind a long time ago you'd never be my pilot," he says in irritation. "But now I have no choice. You will fly to the South Pole with me."

Second edition:

Still the Ford does not show up. We wait all day, puzzled, and at night Carl Petersen and I take off again, carrying more gas and also repair tools in case there has been an accident. They are still in the same place, unable to start the engines and so busy trying to get to the bottom of the trouble that they barely speak to me when I arrive. We put on the heaters, and in less than an hour all three engines are turning smoothly. Commander Byrd and the others pile into the Ford and take off so fast that Pete, who is working inside the tent, doesn't even hear them leave. We pick up the gear left on the snow, jam everything into our little Fairchild, and rejoin them at Little America long after midnight.

Next morning, with the air of someone who has important business on his mind, Byrd takes me for a walk. He is still concerned about last night, I can see, and he demands to know why their fuel consumption was higher than expected. I reply that I cannot give the answer immediately. Since the flight tests before the depot-laying trip bore out the correctness of my computations, perhaps the trouble was that the mixture was not leaned properly. I am still confident of the accuracy of our test results. However, I promise Byrd that to make doubly certain, we will again go over the *Floyd Bennett's* entire fuel system and recheck the engines completely. Obviously, if there is anything wrong it must be eliminated before undertaking the South Pole flight.

"I am going to assure both you and whomever [*sic*] is piloting that plane," I tell Byrd, "that our figures are right, before the *Floyd Bennett* takes off."

Byrd pauses and then raises another big question that is bothering him. Why, he wants to know, were the pilots not able to get the engines started last night? For that I can offer no explanations except the obvious one that the motors have to be heated properly before being cranked up.

Byrd keeps on walking, his lips firm, his expression thoughtful. Then he turns to me, and some of the strain seems to have left his face.

"All right," he says, "get started right away with those fuel and engine checkups—just to make sure." I sense the conference is over, and we turn back toward the barracks. "Oh, and by the way," he adds, "I'll want you to pilot the plane. You will fly to the South Pole with me."

The final excisions took place on pages 301–303. The following passage, which appeared in the first edition, was entirely cut out of the second, whose text is three pages shorter than that of its predecessor:

What is important, what is not? Take the strange contradiction in Commander Byrd's record of his North Pole flight. According to his own figures, the *Josephine Ford* was in flight 15 hours and 30 minutes and spent 13 minutes [sometimes Byrd put the time at a minute longer] circling the Pole, which leaves a total of 15 hours and 17 minutes to fly 1,340 nautical miles [1,542 statute miles. The distance sometimes varies a few miles in different estimates]. This means the average cruising speed would have had to be 87.2 knots [100.3 mph]. Now, I was chief test pilot for the Fokker factory which built the *Josephine Ford,* and with Floyd Bennett I flew it more than a hundred hours around the States, and we could never achieve a cruising speed better than 65 knots [74.8 mph]. From actual test data—plus my little pocket slide rule that Byrd despised —I compute that with ski installation the best cruising speed that could have been squeezed out of the plane would have been no more than 74 knots [85.1 mph]. In Byrd's stated time of 15 hours and 17 minutes he could therefore have traveled a maximum distance of only 1,131 nautical miles [1,300.7 statute miles] and the farthest North Latitude he could have reached was 88 degrees 15.5 minutes, or 104.5 nautical miles [120.2 statute miles] short of the Pole. All his life I waited for Admiral Byrd to give some explanation of the discrepancies in his log. To the best of my knowledge he never did, at least publicly.

One of the last times I saw him was on the pilgrimage of "Air Pioneers" to Kitty Hawk, North Carolina, arranged by the National Advisory Committee for Aeronautics to honor the Wright Brothers on the fiftieth anniversary of powered flight. Byrd and I had not met for a long time. I had been on duty in Alaska and Thule and I was then sent on a nation-wide lecture tour by the Air Force, to support recruiting and help promote general understanding of our new strategic problems in the Far North. At Bolling Field, where the party assembled for the flight to Kitty Hawk, I went over to pay my respects to Byrd, who questioned me as to my work.

It was a cold, windy day when we landed at Kitty Hawk near the big obelisk on the hill from which Orville and Wilbur Wright had taken off on their first flight. At the monument, Byrd came over to me and asked me to step aside from the rest of the party, as he had something to say to me. I assented gladly and we went over beside a helicopter parked by the monument. To my complete surprise, he abruptly began to berate me and complain violently about various things that left me utterly mystified. The gist of his puzzling accusations seemed to be that I was seeking publicity, that this was detracting from the public's recognition of his achievements in the Arctic, and that he did not intend to stand for such goings on. Coming out of the blue as it did, the tirade caught me completely aback. I can think of no words of mine that could possibly have occasioned it.

Someone at Kitty Hawk must have overheard this exchange, because it was mentioned soon afterward by a Washington columnist; however, the locale was given incorrectly.

Such was my last conversation of any length with this magnetic but in many ways inscrutable personality. It was a deeply saddening end to a long association. It still did not seem to me very long ago that a young Lieutenant Commander and his aides had landed at Kings Bay from the *Chantier* and walked through our camp to Amundsen's hut. As my mind went back, once again, I seemed to be sitting beside Floyd Bennett in the *Josephine Ford's* cockpit, somewhere between Detroit and Chicago, jotting air speed and fuel consumption figures in my notebook for Uncle Tony. Again I heard Commander Byrd's voice above the roar of motors in the navigator's compartment as the *America* droned toward Europe under a black sky blazing with stars. I thought of his unhesitating courage—how he instantly plunged into the icy Antarctic sea to rescue a drowning man at grave risk to his own life. And I relived that day when we had talked together near Little America . . . those other words, spoken there on the snow of the Ross Shelf: "Forget about that slide rule. From now on, you stick to flying. I'll do the figuring."

Did the saddening outburst at Kitty Hawk go back, in some way, to those adventurous years? Or did the growing public recognition of my own work somehow disturb this man whose personality seemed composed of such strangely conflicting elements? It was inconceivable to me that there would be any need for concern on this score on Byrd's part, for his position was assured for all time.

Is the difference in miles between 88 degrees 15.5 minutes North Latitude and the Pole important, after all? Even if Byrd missed the Pole by a hundred miles—which would make Amundsen the first human being in history to reach both Poles—this is not what matters. Byrd dreamed a big dream, and that he may have failed to achieve it does not make his dream less big. A great man is always a little strange, different from the rest. With some understanding of the conflicts that must have gone on in his mind, the secrets that he carried locked in his heart, he becomes more human to us, and therefore his achievements become greater still. Byrd's effort broke through the psychological barrier that existed in men's minds, and he led the way for others to fly to the Pole. His importance lies in this vision he had, the concept of tomorrow's air age, and he belongs to the great company of pioneers who helped to usher in the new era of polar flight.

That last paragraph is clearly the opinion of a magnanimous man. But even the favorable portion didn't get into the second edition.

Acknowledgments

During the late twenties and early thirties I was a reporter for the New York *Evening Post* (now the New York *Post*) and the New York *Evening World*. For weeks on end I was assigned to the Long Island airports to cover the men and women who were preparing for transatlantic flights. I talked with many of them, watched their final takeoffs and wrote for my papers about them. Within the last few years I have renewed my acquaintance with a few of them, read the stories I wrote at the time, and pored over news of transatlantic, polar and transpacific flights in the *New York Times*, New York *Morning World*, New York *Herald Tribune*, New York *Daily News*, New York *Journal*, New York *Daily Mirror*, Washington *Post* and *The Times* of London. In addition, I have read numerous magazine articles on the flights and have discussed at length the events of those days with old reporter colleagues.

In the compilation of this book I am indebted to many people. They include Bernt Balchen; Clarence Chamberlin; Mrs. Giuseppe Bellanca; C. B. Allen and Lauren D. Lyman, aviation specialists for the *Morning World* and the *New York Times,* respectively; Dorothy Stahl; Ted Olson; Reidar Lunde, chief editor of the Oslo *Aftenposten;* the Norsk Polar Institutt; Professor Gösta Liljequist of Uppsala University; Leslie R. Henry, curator of the Department of Transportation, Henry Ford Museum; Arthur G. Renstrom, head of the Aeronautics Section, Science & Technology Division, Library of Congress; and Bob Loomis, a superlative editor.

Of the authors whose books I have read as background material, the following have been especially helpful: Roald Amundsen, *The South Pole* (Murray, London, 1929), *My Life As an Explorer* (Doubleday, Page & Co., 1927), *First Crossing of the Polar Sea,* with Lincoln Ellsworth (George Doran Co., 1927); Bernt Balchen, *Come North With Me* (Dutton, 1958); Richard E. Byrd, Jr., *Skyward* (Putnam, 1929); Clarence Chamberlin, with C. B. Allen, *Record Flights* (Dorrance & Co., 1928); Wilbur Cross, *Ghost Ship of the Pole* (William Sloane Associates, 1960); Anthony H. G. Fokker, with Bruce Gould, *Flying Dutchman* (Holt, 1931); Leslie Forden, *Glory Gamblers* (Ballantine Books, 1961); Edwin P. Hoyt, *The Last Explorer* (John Day, 1968); Frederick Thomas Jane, *All the World's Aircraft, 1909–1940* (S. Low, London); Charles A. Lindbergh, *The Spirit of St. Louis* (Scribner's, 1963); C. R. Roseberry, *The Challenging Skies* (Doubleday & Co., 1966); George Simmons, *Target: Arctic* (Chilton Co., 1965); Dean Smith, *By the Seat of My Pants* (Little, Brown, 1961).

INDEX

303

About the Author

RICHARD MONTAGUE began a journalistic career between terms at college as a reporter on the old New York *Herald* in 1922. Later he worked for the New York *Herald Tribune* in London and New York, and for the New York *Evening Post* and the *Evening World*. After the *World* folded in the Great Depression he became foreign editor and later literary editor of the embryonic *Newsweek* magazine, and thereafter held a number of short-term publicity jobs for welfare and charitable agencies. Since then he has worked for the Voice of America and for *America*, the U.S. Information Agency magazine, which is distributed in the Soviet Union. He has been married twice and has three children and four grandchildren.

OCEANS, POLES AND AIRMEN

Richard Montague

The first flights over wide waters and desolate ice

The late twenties and early thirties were aviation's most romantic years. Neither before nor since has flying produced such a host of eager adventurers. They soared over—or plunged into—blue oceans. They roared above—or crashed down on—white ice. Both their nicknames and names conjure images of heroines and heroes.

Flying Schoolmarm, Flying Princess, Flyin' Fool. Amundsen, Byrd, Bennett, Nobile, Lindbergh, Balchen, Elder, Acosta, Earhart, Chamberlin, Levine, Nungesser, Fonck, Wilkins. The aircraft they flew in bore proud names too. *Columbia, Spirit of St. Louis, America, Old Glory, Golden Eagle, Pride of Detroit, St. Raphael, Dawn, American Girl.*

It was a time of frantic excitement, of delirious ticker-tape parades, of sudden fortune and fame, of sudden death. Some

(continued on back flap)